THE TENDER YEARS

CHILD WELFARE

A series in child welfare practice, policy, and research

Duncan Lindsey
General Editor

The Tender Years

*TOWARD DEVELOPMENTALLY
SENSITIVE CHILD WELFARE SERVICES
FOR VERY YOUNG CHILDREN*

Jill Duerr Berrick
Barbara Needell
Richard P. Barth
Melissa Jonson-Reid

New York   Oxford
OXFORD UNIVERSITY PRESS
1998

Oxford University Press

Oxford   New York
Athens   Auckland   Bangkok   Bogota   Bombay   Buenos Aires
Calcutta   Cape Town   Dar es Salaam   Delhi   Florence   Hong Kong
Istanbul   Karachi   Kuala Lumpur   Madras   Madrid   Melbourne
Mexico City   Nairobi   Paris   Singapore   Taipei   Tokyo   Toronto   Warsaw
and associated companies in
Berlin   Ibadan

Published by Oxford University Press, Inc.,
198 Madison Avenue, New York, New York 10016

Oxford is a registered trademark of Oxford University Press

Library of Congress Cataloging-in-Publication Data
The tender years : toward developmentally sensitive child welfare
services for very young children / Jill Duerr Berrick . . . [et al.].
p.   cm.—(Child welfare)
Includes bibliographical references and index.
ISBN 0-19-511452-3 (cloth).—ISBN 0-19-511453-1 (pbk.)
1. Social work with children—United States.   2. Preschool
children—Services for—United States.   3. Infants—Services
for—United States.   4. Foster children—United
States.   5. Child welfare—United States.   6. Child
development—United States.
I. Berrick, Jill Duerr.   II. Series: Child welfare (Oxford
University Press)
HV741.T44   1998   97-1632
362.7'0973—dc21   CIP

9 8 7 6 5 4 3 2 1

Printed in the United States of America
on acid-free paper

Contents

Preface

The United States has witnessed a record influx of infants, toddlers, and preschoolers into the foster care system in the past decade. There has not been, however, an accompanying shift in policy or practice to attend to the developmental issues these youngsters bring to child welfare. This volume presents a developmental framework for critiquing child welfare services, a description of children's experiences with child abuse and neglect and foster care, vignettes of the families whose young children have been returned to them from foster care, an insider's perspective on how child welfare workers are coping with the "infantilization of child welfare," and practice and policy responses that may arise from these experiences.

We worked together on this project for nearly four years. Our perspectives on the issues were often at odds—at least at the outset. The hazards of one approach often outweighed the benefits of another, and the implications of a developmental approach frequently took on multiple meanings. By reviewing these issues, our data, and data from other sources, we arrived at a shared perspective about the fundamental issues we raise herein. We have included discussions of many of the issues we pondered in this book and detail the framework that emerged to help guide our decisions. We believe that the process of resolving these differences makes for a stronger volume.

Time to devote to these issues was provided with support from the generous contributions of the David and Lucile Packard Foundation. The foundation's interests in safeguarding the future of children set a tone for the study from the beginning; honest and probing inquiry into the conditions of young children were the hallmark of our interactions with its staff. Conversations with Carol Larson at the Packard Foundation helped crystallize the idea for this project and sharpened our subsequent thinking.

Four directors of county child welfare agencies and their staffs were pivotal to the initial implementation of this work. Our thanks to them is immeasurable, since they opened their counties to our searching eyes and endless questions. Pat Englehard, Tom Clancy, Ivory Johnson, Rick Clark, John Oppenheim, Judy Boring, Stuart Oppenheim, and Mary Ann Tse deserve special thanks for their willingness to participate in the study. Child welfare managers and technical staff in an additional five counties were also instrumental in allowing us access to data on child maltreatment during the second phase of our work. The support we received from the California Department of Social Services was essential to gain access to data on foster care. Special thanks are extended to Marjorie Kelly, Werner Schink, and Ray Bacon for their contributions to our work.

We also appreciate the support we received from the California Social Work Education Center for a curriculum development project to improve teaching about kinship care and guardianship services that we used as a means to expand our interviewing and focus groups to ten counties and to clarify further a range of issues related to permanency planning for young children. We are indebted, of course, to the staff in several counties who assisted with this project through their participation in our focus groups. Their commitment to high-quality services for children and families was evident in their discussions about their work. We are also deeply grateful to the families who participated in focus groups and who shared their intimate experiences with us. Many of these discussions were painful for them and for us; their courage in sharing their families' journeys is a tribute to their personal strength.

We thank the Abandoned Infants Assistance Resource Center at the School of Social Welfare, University of California at Berkeley and its staff—especially, Jeanne Pietrzak and Amy Price—for sharing our awareness of a variety of issues related to child welfare services for infants and young children who are affected by alcohol, drugs, and HIV. And we benefitted greatly from the intellectual support provided by the School of Social Welfare itself.

Within our own organization, we were proud to have the assistance of many students and staff. We hope we captured all their names in the following list: Michael Armijo, Melissa Lim Brodowski, Emily Bruce, Laura Frame, Sheryl Goldberg, Susan Katzenellenbogen, Seon Lee, Brian Simmons, Rebecca Van Voorhis, and Daniel Webster. Vicky Albert was involved in this project during the first year and was helpful in laying the groundwork for our later work on the issues of reporting child abuse and neglect.

This book is the only one that specifically addresses the spectrum of child welfare services for young children. We believe that the guiding developmental framework that we provide and apply to related discussions on poverty, child maltreatment, foster care, reunification, unstable placements, kinship care, and group care will be useful for readers who are interested in any child welfare topic. Although we have streamlined the text for the nontechnical reader by moving much of our methodological material to the appendix, we also believe that the review of this material will be of interest to investigators in all areas of child welfare services.

We have tried to be comprehensive in reviewing various aspects of the child welfare system for young children. That does not, by any means, imply that this book is exhaustive. A truly comprehensive look at all services for young children was beyond the scope of our task, and few readers would have the time to digest such a volume. Still, results from our work on this important topic suggest that considerable changes are necessary in the structure of the service system to accommodate better the developmental needs of young children.

Berkeley   J.D.B.
January, 1998   B.N.
                                                                                   R.P.B.
                                                                                   M.J-R.

THE TENDER YEARS

1

Child Development and Child Welfare

Marcus has been in a foster home for one year. He is able to jump from a low stool, can walk upstairs with alternating feet, and shows emerging skills in balancing upon each foot. He has age appropriate fine motor skills and is able to build a tower of nine blocks. His pencil grasp is still immature and he is not yet able to copy horizontal and vertical lines; he clearly enjoys drawing and fills page after page with energetic scribbles.

—Excerpts from a case file of a child aged 2½

The tender years are a time of discovery and wonder, with development proceeding at a rate unparalleled in the rest of the life span. These first years of life are precarious, however, as the fragile health and well-being of children are subject to a variety of threats. In the very early years, children's inability to communicate through language and their restricted mobility give them little meaningful capacity for self-protection and therefore they must be protected by others. In the United States, few service systems have been universally designed for young children (Kamerman & Kahn, 1995), leaving infants, toddlers, and most preschool-age children outside of public view, relying principally on their families for care and protection. Yet this protection is often inadequate, as the Massachusetts colonial legislature recognized 250 years ago by passing a statute in 1735 to protect the developmental future of "children whose parents were un-

1

able or neglected to provide for the sustenance and support of their children" (cited in Folks, 1902, p. 168). Whether from their parents, the social environment, or other sources, young children continue to face a variety of possible dangers.

Just a century ago, infants' lives were regularly claimed by infection, disease, or accidental death (Zelizer, 1985). Because of the legacy of high infant mortality, families in many countries still do not celebrate the birth of an infant, but have a large public ceremony when the child reaches his or her first birthday. The first anniversary of life marks a family's good fortune to have eluded the principal hazards of infancy and brings with it the promise of a fair opportunity to raise a child. Today, the infant mortality rate has diminished considerably, but infants in the United States are more likely to die in the first year of life than they are in any other Western industrialized nation. Even when children do not die from abuse or neglect, they are still vulnerable to early death. Mortality rates for poor children are at least three times higher than they are for other children (Mare, 1982). Children who have been reported for child abuse are three times more likely to die before adulthood than are children in the general population and twenty times as likely to be victims of homicide (Sabbotta & Davis, 1992).

Many children who escape early death are compromised throughout their childhoods by poor health—a result of environmental hazards, malnutrition, poor nutrition, and inadequate health care. Women who receive no prenatal care—although less than 3 percent of all pregnant women—are more likely than other women to use drugs and smoke cigarettes and have children whose health is compromised (Shiono, 1996). Other preventive health care services, such as vaccinations, are not routinely administered to all young children. A study by the Centers for Disease Control (CDC, 1993) indicated that childhood immunization rates have plummeted in recent years. Other studies have shown that half the children under age two are not fully immunized—rates for young poor children are even worse (George, 1993). Access to basic, preventive health care services is significantly compromised for many young children (Kaiser Commission, 1995).

The lack of health care services is only one of the many perils young children face. Many young children also encounter significant environmental hazards in their everyday lives that pose serious risks to their well-being. An alarming 3 million young children may suffer the effects of lead poisoning (Needleman, Schell, Bellinger, Leviton, & Allred, 1990), which can impair their mental and physical development. Young children are also increasingly exposed to HIV and AIDS in all parts of the country. AIDS is the eighth leading cause of death among young children (Klerman & Parker, 1990) and one of the top five leading causes of death for women aged 25 to 44 (CDC, 1995). Thousands of children who will be orphaned because of their parents' debilitation or death from AIDS may enter the child welfare system for care (Groze, Haines-Simeon, & Barth, 1994).

The well-being of millions of young children is also jeopardized by poor nutrition or malnutrition, which causes anemia and sometimes retards their growth (National Center for Children in Poverty, NCCP, 1990). Substantial and, possibly, permanent reductions in learning may also occur (Brown & Pollitt, 1996).

Maternal substance abuse poses yet another significant risk for young children. Although the exact effects of drug use on the fetus and newborn have not yet been determined, evidence shows that the potential for adverse outcomes for newborns is further compounded by compromised caregiving and social environments (Robins & Mills, 1993; Shiono, 1996).

The United States is home to over 23 million children under age six, about one-quarter of whom live at or below the poverty line (NCCP, 1995). The poverty rate for young children has been increasing more rapidly than it has for any other group in recent years (General Accounting Office, 1994), so much so that children under age six are now the poorest citizens of this country (NCCP, 1995), and African American and Hispanic young children are often the poorest of the poor (U.S. Department of Health and Human Services, DHHS, 1996). Children who are raised in extreme poverty (defined as families living on incomes below 50 percent of the poverty line) face the most severe challenges. Approximately 6 percent of Caucasian children under age six lived in extreme poverty in 1993, and the rate for African American young children was 31 percent (U.S. DHHS, 1996).

If poverty was a single phenomenon, with isolated or uncertain effects, these figures would not be particular disturbing. However, the numerous effects of poverty on children's development have been well documented (Korenman, Miller, & Sjaastad, 1995). The longer young children live in poverty, the greater the deterioration in their home life and the worse their developmental outcomes (Duncan, Brooks-Gunn, & Klebanov, 1994; Garrett, Ng'andu, & Ferron, 1994; Korenman et al., 1995). The strains of raising young children on the economic margins may be great and may cause some parents to become punitive or emotionally absent from their children (McLoyd & Wilson, 1991). Poor children, in general, are more likely to live in less stimulating home environments (Brooks-Gunn, Klebanov, & Liaw, 1995). Because regular interaction and caregiver-child activity are paramount, the absence of such interaction and exposure puts young children at a significant disadvantage.

Poverty is associated with a series of deleterious outcomes for young children, including higher rates of premature birth; low birthweight; early death; significant health problems; stunted growth; learning difficulties; depression; developmental delays; lower IQs; and, what is most germane to this book, child abuse and neglect and placement in foster care (Hampton & Newberger, 1985; Huston, 1991; Sedlak & Broadhurst, 1996). In 1994, over 1,200 children died as a result of child abuse or neglect in the United States, 88 percent of whom were under age five when they died (National Committee to Prevent Child Abuse, 1995).

The challenge of ensuring that children stay alive and well amid the "social toxins" that are becoming more prevalent in American society is great. Garbarino (1995) described social toxins as a series of environmental hazards that include deteriorating neighborhoods, violent communities, reduced educational opportunities, and an increasingly "empty and nasty" cultural backdrop that challenge the abilities of the most resolute and well-meaning parents to raise their young children well.

For our society to thrive, children should progress through the early years with the capacity to learn and grow. The first few years are a critical developmental period for the optimal growth and maturation of all children. Major developmental advances start in the womb, when fetuses take shape, their brains develop, and their nervous and circulatory systems are established. In infancy, young children begin to learn about the external world, including its sights, sounds, tastes, and smells. Infants have the opportunity to develop their first relationships from the moment of birth, when they are held, spoken to, fed, and comforted. These early experiences give organization to children's development and influence children's capacity for future development (Perry, Pollard, Blakley, Baker, & Vigilante, 1995). The hallmark of the early years includes significant exploration and constant learning—testing the environment, mastering skills, and developing new strategies for communication. Throughout this period, building relationships with others—first, with parents and later, with other children—is a key feature of the early childhood experience.

The majority of children are reared by their biological parents and have the advantage of developing within an environment of constancy. The ability of their parents to provide safe, stimulating, and nurturing environments for children varies considerably, but most parents are able to provide basic care and protection for their young children. Some families, however, are overchallenged by the demands of parenthood. Raising young children can be particularly demanding when parents are faced with unstable incomes or jobs, great personal stress, depression, cognitive impairments, substance addiction, or isolation from friends (Burgess & Conger, 1977; Steinberg, Catalano, & Dooley, 1981; Wolfe, Jaffe, Wilson, & Zak, 1985; Wolock & Horowitz, 1979).

These are the families who are the most likely to maltreat their children—some by omission and others by commission—and to come to the attention of the child welfare services system. The large majority of these children will have little direct or lengthy contact with the services or supports of this system. Yet, each year as many as 50,000 young children will be separated from their parents by child welfare authorities and the juvenile court and placed in substitute care. More than 1 percent of all infants will reside in foster care at some time during their first year of life and for many, it will be every day of that year. We estimate that nearly 3 percent of all young children will experience such grave threats to their well-being that they will be placed in foster care at some point before age six. According to Perry et al. (1995, p. 286), "profound sociocultural and public policy implications arise from understanding the critical role of early experiences in determining the functional capacity of the mature adult—and therefore our society." This is especially the case for children who are exposed to child abuse and those who are placed in foster care. The need to understand the effects of maltreatment, the course of placement in foster care, and the optimal design of the child welfare delivery system for these young children is the reason for this book.

Child Development and Child Protection

The twentieth century has witnessed a growing consensus that the "public ought to protect all citizens, including children, from cruelty and improper care" (Schultz, 1922, p. 223, cited in Bremner, 1971, p. 217). The U.S. Children's Bureau, established in 1912, was the product of this recognition that the federal government had the responsibility to promote the welfare of the "whole child," including maternal and child health, dependence, delinquency, and child labor (Abbott, 1938). Most important, it symbolized the continuing emergence of a perception of children "as precious beings of special importance who needed particular protection and careful prolonged preparation for adulthood" (Kadushin & Martin, 1988, p. 55). Since 1980, intricate sets of federal and state laws have grown to codify the public interest in preventing child abuse; protecting abused children; and providing proper, planned, time-limited out-of-home care for children only when necessary.

Child welfare policies, especially policies on child abuse and foster care, are relatively new and based on the developmentally undifferentiated research and theory available in the late 1970s. The focus of much of that research was on describing children who were receiving child welfare services and, crudely, how long those services were provided (see, for example, Maas & Engler, 1959; Shyne & Schroeder, 1978).

All evidence from studies completed before the passage of the fundamental child welfare law—the Adoption Assistance and Child Welfare Act of 1980 (P.L. 96-272)—indicates that the current child welfare system clearly was not designed with young children in mind. The two National Studies of Social Services to Children, conducted in 1974 and 1994 by Westat, showed that in 1974, 12 percent of the children in foster care were younger than six, whereas in 1994, this proportion had nearly doubled to 23 percent (Maza, 1996). In 1975, the Children's Defense Fund (CDF, 1978) gathered basic information on children placed in out-of-home care in a stratified random sample of 140 counties in the United States. The CDF found that just 17 percent of the children in foster care were under age six, 32 percent were aged six to twelve, and 51 percent were aged twelve or older. Hubbell's (1981) study of the demographic characteristics of children in foster care in 1977 in three anonymous communities in the United States—state capital, a large city, and a small town—reported that in all three communities, the average child in foster care was 9.7 years old. In contrast, the first report from the Adoption and Foster Care Analysis and Reporting System (1996) estimated that the median age of such children in 1994 was less than 8.7 years and indicated that 35 percent of the children were younger than six.

Central to the development of P.L. 96-272 were research and demonstration projects conducted on foster children who were considerably older than today's typical foster child. In the 1970s, the Oregon Children's Services Division conducted what is arguably the most influential demonstration project in America's child welfare history. In many ways, this study provided the blueprint for the current child welfare system, yet only 15 percent of the children in the sample were under age six (Emlen, Lahti, Downs, McKay & Downs, 1978).

Why Children Receiving Child Welfare Services Are Younger

The 1980s and 1990s have simultaneously witnessed an echo baby boom that has increased the number of births and a growing proportion of mothers involved with the correctional system following the use of illegal drugs. Estimates of the proportion of newborns who were exposed to illicit drugs range from 4 percent (Gomby & Shiono, 1991) to 11 percent (Chasnoff, 1988), but a far higher proportion of newborns have been exposed to alcohol and cigarettes (Shiono, 1996). Whatever the prevalence of prenatal drug-exposed children in the general population, there can be little doubt that the vast majority of children entering foster care are affected either by direct exposure to drugs or by living in drug-involved families and communities.

Since 1990, there has been no apparent change in the fact that more than 20 percent of all children who enter foster care are infants, many of whom were exposed to drugs (Goerge, Wulczyn, & Harden, 1995; Needell, Webster, Barth, & Armijo, 1996). At least in Illinois, more than 40 percent of all child abuse reports are of substance-exposed infants, and about 30 percent of these substance-exposed infants are ultimately served by the child welfare system (Goerge & Harden, 1993). In 1992, more than half the children who entered foster care because they were exposed to substances entered after they were one year old; that is, they were reported as infants but entered foster care as toddlers or older.

In addition to problems of substance abuse, a small but important group of young children entering foster care are infected with HIV. Although .04 percent of all infants in the United States are HIV infected (National Center for Health Statistics, 1994), nearly 8 percent of all infants who are abandoned in hospitals are reported to be HIV infected (James Bell & Associates, 1993). When they do enter foster care, the stays of HIV-affected children are often long, partly because the problems of perinatal substance abuse and HIV are entwined. Mothers are most commonly infected with HIV through their own intravenous (IV) drug use or sexual relations with IV drug users (CDC, 1989; National Institute on Drug Abuse, 1994), and research by Edlin et al. (1994) established a strong link between HIV infection and the use of crack cocaine.

For a variety of reasons, young children are entering the foster care system in extraordinarily high numbers. The incidence rate of admissions to foster care for children from birth to age 4 is now twice what it is for children aged 5–17 (Goerge et al., 1994). As shall be discussed in greater detail later, the census of all children in care is young—at least for now—in good measure because one-fourth of young children entering foster care will not have been reunited with their biological parents or adopted after *six years* in foster care.

Although the ages of children receiving child welfare services has changed, there has been no concomitant change in policy or practice to reflect a developmental perspective; the child welfare law does not speak to the ages of children. Prior to the passage of P.L. 96-272 some attention was paid to placing foster care in a developmental framework, but these efforts were modest and had little impact on public policy. As early as 1975, Wald (p. 11) questioned the one-law-fits-all notion that allowed a child welfare law that was silent on the issue of children's ages:

> Should we have different laws dealing with six-month-old children in placement, two-year-old children in placement, five-year-old children in placement, ten-year-old children in placement? Currently the law treats all children alike, no matter what their age. *How can we build in developmental knowledge to make the laws more sophisticated and more likely to serve the best interests of children?* (italics added)

We pursue the answer to Wald's question throughout this book. We begin by presenting our understanding of what a developmental perspective involves.

Theories and Approaches to Child Development

In this discussion we consider the cognitive, affective, and physical characteristics of children and the familial and environmental circumstances under which they need to grow to be successful adults. A transactional-ecological developmental model has emerged as the most influential approach to understanding development, based on the view that children and their environments undergo regular restructuring in response to each other (Garbarino, 1990; Perry et al., 1995; Sameroff & Chandler, 1975). In this model, early traumas like child abuse or placement in foster care have enduring consequences, primarily when children continue to experience chronic negative influences. For more than two decades, we have trusted that human development usually exerts powerful "self-righting influences . . . so that protracted developmental disorders are typically found only in the presence of equally protracted distorted influences" (Sameroff & Chandler, 1975, p. 189).

The characteristics of both the child and the caretaking environment must be considered to achieve even moderately accurate predictions of future development. Both the child and environment are constantly changing, and these changes are interdependent. The combination of children's individual makeup and their social environment results in opportunities and risks for development. Risks can be either direct insults to the child's well-being (like lead poisoning or abuse) or manifestations of a lack of opportunities (such as the lack of a parent figure who interacts positively with the child). With a transactional-ecological model, apparently inconclusive research results linking developmental outcomes with single indicators of "risk" (for example, children living in poverty, abused and/or neglected children, or children in foster care) are completely understandable.

Individual and developmental differences. Developmental processes in children are complicated by individual differences. Exposed to the same event, some humans feel virtually no pain and others suffer acutely. Individual differences are also apparent in cognition, emotional responsiveness, and temperament. Even infants show dramatic differences in cognitive performance that are good predictors of their performance in later childhood (Columbo, 1993). Temperament appears to be relatively stable over time, with temperamentally "difficult" infants having such characteristics as slow adaptation to change, irregular biological patterns, and a negative mood (Korner et al., 1985; Riese, 1987). The temperament of infants can clearly contribute to "differential vulnerability to adverse circumstances among [them]" (Beckwith, 1990, p. 62). So can high and chronic states of infant arousal that some infants undergo when they experience separation from a caregiver or other perceived threats to their well-being (Perry et al., 1995).

The infant, toddler, preschooler, school-age child, and adolescent will respond quite differentially to the same event. The infant will probably not be traumatized by witnessing an armed robbery, whereas the adolescent usually will not be traumatized by being away from his or her primary caretaker for a few weeks. The seven month old will be more likely to experience distress during separation from a parent than will the seven week old or the seven year old.

Resilience and Protective Factors

Some children develop stable, healthy personalities and display considerable adaptation despite their disabilities and severely compromised environments. In studying the effects of child maltreatment, the lack of predictable negative outcomes for many subjects has left us to question why some children fare better than others. Resistance to stress is both environmental and constitutional (Werner, 1990). Resilience is a characteristic of the individual that mitigates stress. The value of resilience may be greatly exaggerated, however, when it comes to understanding how young children appear to transcend their environment. Perry, a neurobiologist, and his colleagues (Perry et al., 1995), who are interested in trauma among young children, argue that "Of course, 'children get over it'—they have no choice. Children are not resilient, they are malleable. In the process of getting over it, elements of their true emotional, behavioral, cognitive, and social potential are diminished—some percentage of capacity is lost, a piece of the child is lost forever. . . . Persistence of the destructive myth that children are resilient will prevent millions of children, and our society, from meeting their true potential" (pp. 285–286).

Whereas environmental properties may help ease the influence of stressful life events for children (Masten & Garmezy, 1985), for an infant, the primary caregiver (or caregivers) contributes the most to support the resumption of his or her adaptive responses. For young children taken as a whole, the environment has a profound influence on their cognitive and social development (Brooks-Gunn, Klebanov, & Duncan, 1996).

Individual characteristics, such as cognitive ability, attractiveness, athleticism, and educational achievement, buoy children, adolescents, and young adults against hardship, but they are almost certainly less important in infancy. Significant people in a child's life (including grandparents, siblings, friends, teachers, and foster parents) can play an enabling role when a parent is incapacitated, not by removing stress entirely but, rather, by helping the child face challenges in a measured fashion that allows the child to increase his or her competence and confidence (Anthony, 1987; Farber & Egeland, 1987; Sheehy, 1987; Werner & Smith, 1982). As long as the balance between stressful life events and protective factors is favorable, successful adaptation is possible, but even the most resilient child will have problems when stressful events greatly outweigh protective factors (Werner, 1990). Cicchetti (1989) foreshadowed Perry et al.'s (1995) concerns about the use of the term *resilient* in a similar critique of *invulnerable*, a term that he argued should not be used when describing maltreated children because it gives the impression that these children do not need help and are immune to the experiences to which they have been exposed. Cicchetti asserted that all maltreated children "will 'pay a price' for their misfortune" (p. 419). We agree that the concepts of resilience and invulnerability should not be applied to the circumstances of young children and may interfere with clear thinking about developmentally appropriate services.

A transactional model suggests that many maltreated children can go on to be well-functioning adults if they are given sufficiently intensive and lasting aid. A comprehensive developmental perspective, therefore, acknowledges that the transactional influences on development are not only familial but environmental (Bronfenbrenner, 1979; Garbarino, 1982; Masten & Garmezy, 1985). Children respond to a range of normal environments and may show quite a bit of adaptability within that range.

Environments that fall outside the range—those that are abusive or neglectful or do not provide "average expectable conditions" (Scarr & Ricciuti, 1991, p. 10)—are likely to produce abnormal physical, cognitive, and affective outcomes. The challenge in creating developmentally sensitive child welfare services is to contribute to the promotion of relationships and resources that are needed for children to achieve productive lives within our legal and resource constraints.

Environments

Poverty is the setting in which one is most likely to find children living in conditions that do not meet the standard of average expectable conditions (Coulton, Korbin, Su, & Chow, 1995). Studies that are reviewed later indicate that poor children are far more likely to be reported for abuse and to enter foster care than other children even though most poor parents do not abuse their children and few poor parents will ever have their children removed from them. Plausible explanations for this relationship between poverty and problems in parenting include greater parental stress, isolation, more drug abuse and chaotic circumstances. Biased responses by authorities may also contribute to the official record of this relationship—although confidential household surveys and data on deaths from child abuse indicate that severe and very severe violence are, indeed, far more likely to occur in poor households (Gelles, 1992; Pelton, 1978). In Gelles's study, the rate of severe violence was 62 percent higher in poverty-income families than in non-poverty-income ones, and the rate of very severe violence was 25 percent higher in poverty-income families. Among children *under* age six the rate of very severe violence was about 5 percent for children whose families' incomes were below the poverty level and 2 percent for those living above the poverty level. Adult developmental phenomena are at work here, too, since the risks of committing such violence were greatest among poor parents aged twenty-five or younger.

Violent communities also represent a consistent threat to children's growth and development. Richters and Martinez (1993) argued that children who live in violent communities are far more likely to suffer adaptational failures (such as severe behavioral problems in schools) if they are living in unstable and/or unsafe homes. In their study, they found that the odds of early adaptational failure among children from stable, safe homes were only about 6 percent, but that these odds increased 300 percent for children from homes that were either unsafe or unstable and by 1,500 percent for children from homes rated as both unstable and unsafe. Because the erosion of children's families is not an inevitable process of living in violent communities, it does not mean that all children who grow up in those communities experience such outcomes. In Cicchetti and Lynch's (1993) analysis of community violence, successful families appeared to be those that somehow prevented the stressors associated with living in a multidisadvantaged environment from taking a toll on their stability. These families did not let the violent community contaminate their children's family lives.

With notable exceptions (like chronic maltreatment), there is little we can say with confidence about why most environmental risk factors are correlated with negative outcomes in children. There are few, if any, known neighborhood factors that can be characterized as inevitable determinants of negative child outcomes (Richters & Martinez, 1993). Still, environments with substantial poverty and violence often interact with troubled family characteristics and contribute to child abuse and neglect.

Domains of Children's Welfare: Affective, Cognitive, and Physical

Decision making in child welfare services has been heavily influenced by child welfare service providers' interest in the psychological—especially, affective—aspects of development. Certainly, the most influential theoretical works that have shaped the field since the 1970s have been Goldstein, Freud, and Solnit's (1973, 1979) books, which focused on the psychological relationships between parents and children. The basic notion that has emerged from these works is that a child's relationship to his or her primary caregiver is the major contributor to the child's well-being. We agree that this relationship is important but argue for a broader view of children's developmental needs.

Affective. Clearly, child welfare services must attempt to protect the capacity of children to grow into productive adults and this endeavor requires that major threats to children's psychological well-being be minimized. The major vehicle for understanding the possible impact of child welfare services on affective development has been attachment theory. Bowlby (1969), the originator of attachment theory, contended that infants are born armed with cries and other behaviors that are likely to elicit comforting and protective behaviors in their caregivers. According to him, newborns will look at any face and be comforted by anyone; they begin to show signs of the ability to discriminate between their caregivers and others at about three months. For the next few months, infants tend to vocalize and smile more to people they know, and at about six or seven months, they begin to be cautious about strangers. From then until the second year, they show a clear preference for specific people, particularly their mothers; may protest when their mothers leave their sight; and will greet their mothers when they return. Infants are increasingly likely to feel anxious about strangers during this phase. Attachment is related to cognitive development, which forms as children become able to think about absent objects (Skolnick, 1986). Eventually, children learn to anticipate how caregivers will react to events and begin to influence and manipulate their caregivers' behavior.

Attachment theorists contend that as children mature, their expectations (internal working models) about the world will be based on the quality of their early experiences with caregivers. If young children are responded to in a sensitive manner, they will develop a model of themselves as lovable and view the world as an accepting place. Conversely, if they receive inconsistent, neglectful, harsh, or rejecting care, they may be more likely to view themselves and the world with anxiety and uncertainty (Ainsworth, Blehar, Waters, & Wall, 1978; Matas, Arend, & Sroufe, 1978).

Attachment in perspective. Attachment theory is popular among child welfare workers and trainers (McMillen, 1992). The need to allow a child to develop and maintain a secure attachment is often cited as the central reason for leaving a child in his or her current home environment—whether the biological or foster home. Although consistent parent-child relationships are important to children's well-being, they are not the only important contributors to children's future, and the continuity of the children's relationships with their parents (whether biological parents or foster parents) should not be valued without weighing other considerations.

Poor attachment processes have been shown to be associated with behavioral problems in young children, yet it is unlikely that insecure attachment is either a necessary or sufficient cause of later psychopathology. Much of attachment theory and research has been misunderstood as stating that early attachment relationships are stable and *always* lead to either positive or negative outcomes (Greenberg, Speltz, & DeKlyen, 1993). Attachment theory is sometimes used in an erroneous, mechanistic fashion and generates terms like *attachment disorder* and *attachment impaired* that can be used to justify a hopeless view of a child's future.

Instead, attachment must be considered in the context of a child's biological factors, family ecology, and parental socialization practices (Greenberg et al., 1993). Johnson and Fein (1991, p. 406) provided a useful working definition of attachment as it applies to child welfare services:

> Attachments initially develop through interactions with primary caretakers and continue to develop and stabilize as the child ages. Through the attachment relationship the child develops a sense of security, expectations about others which form the basis for subsequent social relationships, and conceptions of the self. *Although these expectations become more stable with time, they are subject to change with appropriate interventions. Attachment is a developmental phenomenon that occurs not only within early dyadic relationships between parent and child, but also as people form new relationships with those who nurture them and enhance their security and protection* [italics added].

When an early secure attachment between a young child and his or her foster parent exists, there is good reason to expect that the child can develop secure attachments with other caregivers. It is not a good reason to leave the child in the foster parent's care if the foster parent is not willing or able to provide a permanent home for the child. *Certainly close relationships should not be unnecessarily disrupted, but children may need to be moved to ensure their protection or secure their lifetime position in a family.* Although disrupting an early attachment is unfortunate, we believe that it is generally more harmful for a child to be placed in multiple settings or to leave foster care at age eighteen without the benefit of a lifetime family. As we discuss later in this volume, young children who remain in planned long-term foster care have a shocking number of placements within their first six years in care. Maintaining close relationships for young children is essential, but must be placed in a lifetime perspective.

Infants' emotional development and changes in relationships. There does not appear to be a biological basis for the emotional attachment between a parent and a child. Attachment arises from experience, not genetics. Eyer (1992) called *bonding* a "scientific fiction," and Lamb and Hwang's (1982) careful review of research on bonding concluded that strong claims concerning the relationship between early contact and mother-infant attachment are not supported by empirical evidence. A biological parent-child relationship is "neither necessary nor sufficient to guarantee that children grow and develop normally in all spheres—physical, cognitive, emotional, and social" (Schor et al., 1993, p. 1007). Thus, *bonding* should be added to our growing list of terms that should be stricken from the child welfare vernacular.

This in no way diminishes the importance of the parent-child relationship. Since attachment is an interactive process, not an individual characteristic, separation during the first six months of life, if followed by good-quality care and the opportunity to develop a relationship with an alternative long-term caregiver, may not be damaging to the development of a child's capacity or functioning. Evidence suggests that children are more likely to be distressed when they are separated from their mothers after six months. According to Schor et al., (1993, p. 1008, citing Wolkind & Rutter, 1985):

> Separations during the subsequent 2 to 3 years [after the first six months of life], especially if they are prompted by family discord and disruption, are more likely to result in subsequent emotional disturbances. Partly this results from the stranger-anxiety characteristic and levels of language development at this age. Children 3 or 4 years of age placed for the first time with a new family are more likely to be able to use language to help them cope with loss and adjust to change. These young children are able to develop strong attachments and, depending upon the circumstances from which they are removed, may benefit psychologically. *The emotional consequences of multiple placements or disruptions are likely to be harmful at any age.* (italics added)

Yarrow (1979, p. 911) concurred, indicating that although much is not known about children's capacity to withstand negative experiences, developmentally compromising conditions should, in general, be avoided:

There is much we do not know about alternate caregiving—for instance, whether there is an upper limit to the number of persons with whom the infant can establish meaningful relationships, even if these persons are sensitive and responsive. We only know . . . that having many changing caregivers . . . is likely to impair the child's capacity to establish meaningful relationships.

This statement has a direct practical significance for considering the timing of removing a child from his or her home or for moving the child from foster care to an adoptive home.

Cognitive Development

Understanding that child development involves the interaction of the affective, cognitive, and physical domains, child welfare workers must also consider these other determinants of a child's well-being. Even newborns are actively involved in cognitive development. Much of a person's cognitive style is genetically determined, but most cognitive development is a product of the family and environment. Children clearly need responsive, reciprocal interactions with caregivers to develop enhanced language and cognition (Rutter & Rutter, 1993). Thus, environments in which such characteristics exist support the development of early cognition and intelligence (Capron & Duyme, 1989). Being brought up in families where parents are depressed or have diminished communication with their children, in socially disadvantaged homes, and unusually large families all contribute to lags in cognitive development for most children (Rutter & Rutter, 1993).

The economic conditions under which young children grow are perhaps the greatest predictors of children's achievements and abilities in later life, and early childhood is when economic conditions matter the most. In their study of five-year-old children born prematurely and with low birthweights (as many children in foster care are), Brooks-Gunn and Duncan (1996) found that poverty alone accounted for 52 percent of the reduced IQ for African American compared to Caucasian children and that the home environment reduced the difference by another 28 percent—in essence eliminating the gap. They wrote: "Social science is rarely so direct: It's poverty, stupid!" (p. 4). These researchers called for social policy approaches that would help families redistribute their lifetime incomes from the high-income adolescent years (when children benefit less from their families' better economic status) to the early years. Child welfare services can, at least, focus their resources on the youngest children.

How could socioeconomic status (SES) have such a strong effect on infants' development? Genetic and environmental factors are at work in developing cognitive templates and in establishing the rate of intellectual growth curves. One body of research (Columbo, 1993) indicates that infants from better-educated families may be exposed to a wider variety of experiences in and outside the home and soon develop the "software" that enables them to take in new information more readily and recall it more rapidly. The information-processing analogy is that infants with high cognitive abilities and good educational exposure have many templates set up that they can use to create meaning more easily than infants who are starting from scratch. Thus, SES appears to be related to cognitive development through exposure to a variety of verbal and nonverbal experiences. With support and education, such experiences could, of course, be provided by families of all backgrounds.

McCall and Carriger's (1993) meta-analysis concluded that there is an interaction between heredity and the environment so that extremely poor environments interrupt the otherwise consistent and fairly high genetic correlations between infant and childhood IQs. Whereas infants who score poorly on standardized IQ tests may be more likely to come from low-SES homes, infants who are sick score poorly because of temporary medical problems and, with extensive medical care and a rich environment, recover to have average or above-average IQs as children. But poor-scoring infants who are reared in unstimulating circumstances may not recover. Infants with prenatal problems and depressed performance on standardized IQ tests are more likely to remain low scoring on tests of mental performance during early childhood if they are reared in impoverished or other environments that are less likely to support cognitive development (Sameroff & Chandler, 1975).

There are also long-term effects on educational attainment of growing up in families and environments that are unstable and do not offer adequate educational models. Kramer, Allen, and Gergen (1995) found that lower income, minority status, and lower education of parents were strongly and independently related with poorer performance on all cognitive subtests for children aged six to sixteen. The effects on eventual graduation from high school of living in a household with a mother only, a mother and stepfather, a father only, or grandparents were all significantly negative (Wojtkiewicz, 1993). Having parents with less than a high school education has a substantial negative impact on children's own educational achievement (Haveman & Wolfe, 1995).

As biological, economic, maternal, family-structural, and parenting risk factors increase, children's IQ scores decrease (Liaw & Brooks-Gunn, 1994; Sameroff, Seifer, Baldwin, & Baldwin, 1993). Early childhood is a period of unparalleled plasticity and malleability in behavioral systems that eventually develop into more stable intellectual functions that form the basis of personal and academic skills. Enhancing these early cognitive capacities is essential to optimizing the development of each child, irrespective of the individual's level of cognitive capacity or skill (Columbo, 1993).

Given the multiple factors that determine the cognitive ability of young children that, in turn, have substantial direct effects on the children's intelligence as adults, how should we use this information? Child welfare workers should be aware that in addition to ensuring stable, loving relationships between children and their caregivers (parents, kin, or foster parents), they should also make efforts to promote children's cognitive development. Cognitively stimulating infant, toddler, or preschool programs may be necessary for some children who have not had opportunities to participate in enhancement activities. Parental education and support may also be required to help parents, kin, and foster parents to facilitate children's cognitive growth. For children who cannot return home and who need permanent alternative families, these families' willingness and ability to contribute to the children's cognitive growth (or to participate in a program that may offer such opportunities) should be considered.

Physical Development

Young childhood is an unparalleled time for physical growth and development. The early years require a balanced diet and adequate physical activity to support cognitive and affective development. Children whose temperament is compromised by poor nutrition or health will have more difficulties thriving in their caretaking environment (Scarr & Ricciuti, 1991) and, therefore, may be less likely to develop productive social and cognitive styles. Nutritional interventions have recently been shown to have a powerful effect on learning by improving concentration and increasing exploration by children (Brown & Pollitt, 1996).

Injuries are also a major threat to the well-being of young children. According to Gallagher, Finison, Guyer, and Goodenough (1984), children from birth to age five have non-sports-related injury rates that are $1\frac{1}{2}$ times those of elementary school-age children. Although the deaths of children are much more noticed events, the authors found 45 hospitalizations and 1,300 emergency room visits for every child's death they recorded from injury (which included intentional injury by a parent or caregiver). Injuries are often inflicted by family members. The highest likelihood of physical punishment is experienced by children aged four to six, yet very severe violence (being kicked, bitten, hit with a fist, beaten up, burned or scalded, or threatened with a gun or knife or having a gun fired on them) is more common against even younger children (Gelles, 1992).

The significant growth and development during the early years and children's vulnerability to physical harm underscores the value of encouraging safety, nutrition, and physical exploration for children who are served by the child welfare services system. Mastery of new tasks that require fine- and gross motor skills should be actively encouraged; young children will lose countless opportunities if they are left to discover these skills entirely by chance.

Contributors to Developmental Outcomes

A developmental perspective combines attention to the growth of a child's affective, cognitive, and physical capacity to determine a child's functioning as an adult. Having a developmental perspective requires some understanding of what will ultimately add to the well-being of a child across his or her lifetime. Although the enhancement of development is not a primary goal of child welfare services, it deserves consideration when it is consistent with the mandates to protect children, to make reasonable efforts to support families, and to promote legal permanent homes for children. Developmental considerations cannot be incorporated into practice and policy without some understanding of research about what enhances long-term development.

Haveman and Wolfe (1993) reviewed hundreds of studies by economists, sociologists, and developmental psychologists to identify the determinants of children's social success—that is, by the criteria of children's ultimate education, earnings, and avoidance of destructive behaviors. In addition, they conducted a landmark analysis of predictors of success in young adulthood. Although other criteria (such as psychological maturity) could be chosen, these indicators are highly relevant to public policy goals and are clearly related to the positive health and mental health of individuals.

According to Haveman and Wolfe's (1993) review, the most important determinant of children's future success is their parents' education—especially their mothers'. In this case, more is certainly better. Having more siblings in the family has a persistently negative effect on children's success, perhaps because family economic and time resources often are stretched too thin. The negative impact of large family size is often overlooked by child welfare service providers. Children whose parents divorce or choose nonmarital childbearing tend to do worse. Changes in family structure have negative effects on young children. Furthermore, disrupted families and single parents are less likely to provide the necessary ongoing educational support during young adulthood. Children whose immediate family members have had serious scrapes with the law also do less well.

Protective factors are another important determinant of children's development. The amount of parental time spent nurturing or monitoring children has a beneficial impact on children. Children from religious families tend to do better. Economic circumstances have a persistent linkage to children's success, although this relationship is not quantitatively large in Haveman and Wolfe's analysis. In addition, the quality of the neighborhood and the characteristics of peers appear to affect children's attainment, apart from economic factors. School characteristics—especially teachers' skills, parents' levels of involvement, small classes, and the socioeconomic composition of the student body have effects. Opportunities in the community (such as for recreation and employment) may influence attainment for older children as well. These factors should weigh heavily in child welfare workers' decisions regarding young children in foster care, yet as we discuss later, they usually do not.

Affective, Cognitive, and Physical Functioning and Child Abuse

Just as affective and cognitive development are severely hindered by poor environments, they can also be diminished by child abuse. Yet, attempts to study the relationship between social-cognitive functioning and maltreatment have been inconclusive, perhaps because they have barely taken developmental issues into account. Starr, MacLean, and Keating (1991) reviewed the available research on the long-term effects of child maltreatment. They concluded that there is no clear evidence of a high probability of intergenerational transmission of maltreatment and that professionals' fascination with intergenerational transmission as a direct cause of most child maltreatment is misdirected. Evidence suggests that physically abused children are at a higher risk of growing up to commit criminal offenses and that children who are subjected to greater violence are more likely to commit more-violent offenses as adults (Rivera & Widom, 1990). Although Starr et al., suggested that the link between neglect and delinquency was related to the strong association between neglect and poverty, subsequent research found that neglect has an independent, significant effect on delinquency (Zingraff, Leiter, Myers, & Johnsen, 1993). Starr et al. concluded that the connections between childhood maltreatment and later outcomes are the result of multiple interactive factors, but that there are significant adult sequelae of child abuse and neglect. They stressed that services and research must consider the role of developmental timing in preventive and interventive efforts. As they put it:

> [D]ynamic models of development recognize not only that there are multiple determinants that interact in a complex system but also that the cause-effect relationship is often nonlinear. Events that appear small in magnitude may have major effects on subsequent outcomes, depending on the timing of those events. Similarly, a self-system that has settled into a stable but dysfunctional organization may be resistant to seemingly major efforts at intervention. (Starr et al., 1991, pp. 25–26)

No specific profile fits all abused and neglected children. Developmental stage, environment, experiences, and type of maltreatment are all likely to be associated with disabilities and vulnerabilities in many age-specific ways (Cicchetti & Rizley, 1981).

There are many current and historical definitions of child abuse, ranging from extremely narrow (only severe intentional physical abuse) to extremely broad (anything that interferes with optimal development) (Zigler & Hall, 1989). However child abuse is defined, it is necessary to take a developmental perspective when considering and attempting to ameliorate its effects (Aber & Zigler, 1981). Young children are less able to protect themselves and more vulnerable to the absence of food, clothing, or support. Although there has been interest in the observable physical effects of maltreatment for some time (see Kempe, Silverman, Steele, Droegemeuller, & Silver 1962), contemporary researchers have turned their attention to the psychological consequences of abuse and neglect as well. "Regardless of the occurrence of physical trauma or injury, the legacy of maltreatment in its various forms is damage to the child's sense of self and the consequent impairment of social, emotional, and cognitive functioning" (Erickson, Egeland, & Pianta, 1989, p. 648).

When young children who experienced various types of maltreatment were compared to nonmaltreated children from the same poor, high-risk sample, the maltreated children showed social and emotional problems that were greater than those related to poverty alone (Erickson et al., 1989). In addition, specific types of maltreatment tended to be related to particular behavioral problems. The physically abused children tended to be impulsive, to be unable to organize their behavior effectively, and to function less well than the children in the comparison group on cognitive tasks. Many lacked the skills necessary for kindergarten, so almost half had been referred for either special intervention or retention in grade by the end of their kindergarten year.

Children of psychologically unavailable mothers showed a dramatic decline in cognitive and socioemotional functioning as they were followed from infancy through the preschool years, but appeared less deviant when they began school. Although they still functioned more poorly than the control group academically and socially, it was the neglected children who had the severest and widest variety of problems at the time of kindergarten. Their ratings on cognitive assessments were lower than those of the control group, the group with psychologically unavailable mothers, and the sexually abused group. They were anxious and inattentive, lacked initiative, and had trouble understanding their work. Socially, they were both aggressive and withdrawn. They were uncooperative, insensitive, and rarely had a sense of humor. By the end of kindergarten, nearly two-thirds of the neglected group had been referred for intervention or retention in grade.

The problems of the children in each maltreatment group, though consistently greater than those in the control group, seemed to vary in different situations and as the children aged. Among the maltreated children of all age groups, the "lack of nurturance" was a major predictor of their difficulty in school, being angry and unpopular, and having difficulty functioning independently. After a review of other work and their own studies, Erickson and Egeland (1987, p. 164) concluded: "It is that pervasive insensitivity to the child's needs rather than the incidence of abuse per se which is the primary factor accounting for long term psychological consequences."

Carol George and Mary Main (1979) observed the social interactions of ten abused toddlers (aged one to three) and ten matched controls in a day care setting and found that even at that early age, abused children were more aggressive and responded negatively to friendly overtures. These findings were confirmed for preschoolers by Herrenkohl and Herrenkohl (1981), who found that physical abuse was associated with increased measures of aggression. Controlling for family structure, economic status, and mother's education, their findings held steady. Other studies have shown that maltreatment increases the incidence of insecure, particularly avoidant, relationships (Egeland & Sroufe, 1981; Gaensbauer, 1982). Carlson, Cicchetti, Barnett, and Braunwald (1989) found that maltreated infants were much more likely than matched comparison infants to be rated as insecurely attached and were particularly likely to demonstrate disorganized-disoriented attachment. Main and Hesse (1990) suggested that fear is the essential ingredient for the development of disorganized-disoriented attachment. Infants who have been abused or neglected may have strong conflicting motivations to approach their caregivers and may retreat from them to safety.

Aber, Allen, Carlson, and Cicchetti (1989) compared learning outcomes for children from maltreating families, AFDC families, and middle-class families. They developed outcome measures that signified "secure readiness to learn" (competence related to the successful integration of cognitive, social, and emotional functioning required to complete a developmentally appropriate task) and "outer directedness" (a reliance on external cues, rather than cognitive resources, compliance). The maltreated children scored lower than did the AFDC children, who, in turn, scored lower than the middle-class children in secure readiness, and both the maltreated and the AFDC children scored higher than the middle-class children in outer directedness. Maltreatment appeared to have an effect over and above SES on competence, yet was similar to poverty in its effect on conformity. The researchers also compared the maltreated and poor groups to a normative sample on behavioral symptomatology. Of the preschool children, both the maltreated and poor samples had more behavioral problems than did the middle-class sample. Of the children in their early school years, the maltreated ones had more problems than did the poor nonmaltreated children, who, in turn, had more problems than did the normative sample.

Much more is at stake than a child's individual adjustment following abuse or neglect; the physical consequences can be substantial, persistent, and permanent. Children may be scarred, physically disabled, or left developmentally delayed as a result of physical abuse. Reports to the child welfare services system for protective intervention do not now guarantee a childhood free of physical harm; as we will show, young children are reported again and again for maltreatment at disturbing rates—sometimes after their families have received early intervention services from child welfare workers and sometimes after they have been returned home following a stay in foster care. A thirteen-year follow-up study of abused children in Washington state found that they were three times as likely to die from all causes during the study period than were children in the general population and almost twenty times more likely than the general population of children to die from homicide (Sabotta & Davis, 1992). In Illinois, infants and young children are at the greatest risk of dying from the effects of child abuse, accounting for 50 percent of the deaths of infants under one year and over 90 percent of the deaths of children aged five and younger (Department of Children and Family Services, 1995). For the eight years of the Illinois study, about one-third of the fatality victims were being served at the time of their deaths or had been served by the child welfare services system before their deaths.

Developmental Issues and Child Placement

Since the 1970s, a number of studies have documented high rates of psychopathology among foster children (Fanshel & Shinn, 1978; Hochstadt, Jaudes, Zimo, & Schacter, 1987; Howing, Wodarski, Kurtz, & Gaudin, 1993; McIntyre & Keesler, 1986; Swire & Kavaler, 1978). This finding is not surprising—even without considering that placement may upset a child's mental health—because chronic or severe abuse or neglect is almost always a prerequisite for foster care.

Roy (1983, described in Rutter, 1989) compared the classroom behavior of children in foster families, institution-reared children, and children living at home using observations, interviews, and questionnaires. All the children came from "severely disadvantaged backgrounds with much parental deviance and disorder" (Rutter, 1989, p. 337). The institution-reared children were more overactive, inattentive, and aggressive; displayed more inept social behavior, and related less well with their peers.

Tizard and Hodges (1978) studied children in residential nurseries and found that at two years, these children were more physically needy than were children who lived with their families; at four years, they were more attention seeking and indiscriminate with strangers; and at eight years, they showed a lack of close attachments and engaged in unpopular behavior at school. However, most children who were adopted after age four had developed good, stable, affectionate relationships with their new parents, and few had behavioral problems at home, although they still had problems at school. The authors concluded that a lack of early attachment opportunities does not preclude the ability to form attachments later, but it does seem to affect the quality of other relationships.

Hodges and Tizard (1989) revisited the children they had studied a decade earlier and used teacher questionnaires and interviews with the adolescents and their parents to gather information. Although they found no effect due to early institutionalization on the adolescents' IQs at age sixteen, they observed that behavioral and emotional difficulties were more common in the formerly institutionalized group than in a matched comparison group. Strong and lasting attachments with parents were more likely in the adopted group than in the reunified group, but both groups were more oriented toward adult attention, had more difficulties with peers, and had fewer close relationships than the comparison group. The institutions where the children spent their early years had high staff–child ratios and an enriched environment of toys and books. However, close personal relationships between the staff and the children were discouraged, and the children had many caretakers. Hodges and Tizard stated:

> The study gives evidence that children who in their first years of life are deprived of close and lasting attachments to adults can make such attachments later. But these do not arise automatically if the child is placed in a family. They depend rather on the adults concerned and how much they nurture such attachments. Yet, despite these attachments, certain differences and difficulties in social relationships are found over 12 years after a child has joined a family. Whether these differences are now permanent, or further modifiable, we do not know. (pp. 96–97)

Rutter (1989, pp. 338, 334) agreed that early experiences can have a profound impact on later relationships but suggested that interventions may be successful at almost any point:

> [T]he overall pattern of circumstantial evidence suggests that early parent-child relationships may have a particular importance for later relationships with other people. The usual consequence of early adversities is, however, vulnerability and not necessarily a lasting capacity. . . . *There is very little that is unalterable even with respect to the sequelae of severe and prolonged maltreatment in childhood.* (italics added)

When young children are in foster care, close relationships with foster parents may help overcome early abusive relationships. Marcus (1991) studied 52 foster children by obtaining information from child welfare workers, foster parents, and the children. Children who felt more secure with their foster parents, who had more emotional ties with them, and who received physical affection were better adjusted and had fewer achievement problems in school. There was little predictive value in previous attachments with birth parents. Marcus suggested that early attachments may lose predictive power as they are replaced by later ones and that foster children may retain remnants of old attachments but begin to re-form relationships with current caregivers, who become more important. This reorientation of attachment may be facilitated by the lack of nurturance that often exists in birth homes before children are placed in foster care (Erickson & Egeland, 1987). According to Lamb, Gaensbauer, Malkin, and Schultz (1985), it can also be impaired when the quality of foster care is suboptimal—perhaps when foster parents protect themselves against future disappointment by avoiding close relationships with the children in their care.

Kates and her colleagues (1991, p. 584) noted that interventions with foster children are often constrained by "complex and confusing interpersonal and systemic network[s]," which include the birth family, foster family, child welfare workers, and attorneys. The roles of individuals and agencies easily become confused, so the child welfare worker's task must be "to clarify whose child this is not only for the child, but for all those who interact with the child" (p. 585). The experience of placement is not likely to be the same for the child as it is for others. Children of different ages are likely to experience placement differently as well. While child welfare workers, foster parents, and clinicians view the abuse or neglect that precipitated the child's removal as the primary threat to the child's survival, the child may consider placement itself to be the primary threat.

The absence or loss of affectionate maternal care may be felt immediately, but may also have lasting effects on mental health. Rutter (1990, citing a study by Harris, Brown, & Bifulco, 1986) questioned what it is about maternal loss that causes the increased vulnerability to psychiatric disorders in the presence of provoking agents in later life. He argued that the key is a severe lack of affectionate care in childhood (similar to Erickson and Egeland's (1987) "lack of nurturance" mentioned earlier). However, he listed several possible mechanisms in the protective process, including reduction of the impact of risk and the reduction of negative chain reactions, that may ameliorate this vulnerability.

Reduction of the impact of risk. Using an example of admission to a hospital, Rutter (1990) pointed out that the stress inherent in this situation may be less for infants under six months because they lack the attachments that could be threatened by separation and for school-age children because they have the cognitive capacity to maintain relationships for a time while separated. He suggested that the risk could be reduced by trying to avoid admitting children to hospitals during the period of greatest risk. When it is not possible to do so, as it may not be in all child welfare circumstances, he recommended thoroughly preparing the child for the separation experience. In child welfare, avoiding poorly timed changes in placement should also be a primary goal, with the emphasis on making lasting placements before six months of age. Similarly, closely monitoring in-home family maintenance services during the first few months of a child's life may be especially important to avoid possible foster care placements during the next eighteen years.

Reduction of negative chain reactions. An obvious chain reaction that is set into motion for many children are the multiple placements they experience when they receive services from a system that is stretched far beyond its means. "The implication is that protection should be found in the support necessary to enable the . . . parent to function adequately or in the provision of high quality alternative care that will ensure continuity in relationships" (Rutter, 1990, p. 205).

Short- and Long-term Effects of Foster Care

Little is known about the relative affective, cognitive, and physical results of placing young children in foster care. A look at the relatively poor adult outcomes for children who leave foster care—critiqued later in this chapter—suggests that these children would have been better off if they were left at home. There is no direct evidence to suggest that conclusion, however we can draw inferences about ways to make sure that children who do require foster care achieve better outcomes.

Some perspective on foster care can be gained from interviewing youths who are or formerly were in foster care about their experiences. We know from practice experience that many older children in foster care run back home, which suggests that the pull of family is strong. Yet interviews with children who have left foster care indicate that there is another view—that many are grateful to have been removed from home during childhood (Barth, 1990; Courtney, Piliavin, & Grogan-Kaylor, 1996); this may also be true for the majority of children in foster care, despite their occasional horror at the way the removal was handled (Johnson, Yoken, & Voss, 1995).

In a study of 300 children living in kin and nonkin homes in Illinois, over half described their living conditions in out-of-home care as "better" or "much better" than in their parents' homes (Wilson, 1996). Well over three-quarters of the children were "happy" or "very happy" with their current living arrangements, and when asked if there was someplace else they would rather live, about one-third reported that they would prefer to return to their biological parents. The youngest children in this sample were aged five at the time of the study, although the findings were not reported by the children's ages. Little is known about the opinions and thoughts of young children in foster care because researchers have often not asked about them. From experience, however, we know that young children greatly miss familiar surroundings and people when they are removed from home, but that they learn to benefit from new opportunities.

Just a few studies have compared the outcomes for children in foster care versus children who remain at home. These studies have uniformly agreed that placements in foster care have better *measurable* and *short-term* outcomes (Dumaret, 1985; Fanshel & Shinn, 1978; Lahti et al., 1978; Leitenberg, Burchard, Healy, & Fuller, 1981; Wald, Carlsmith, & Leiderman, 1988). That is, on the whole, children who enter foster care leave it with better health, education, and well-being than children who remain at home. The research on the developmental vulnerability of young children to their environment suggests the need to ensure that young children do not have long exposures to marginal or hazardous living environments. Still, in the long run, these developmental gains may be for naught if the intervention completely and permanently disrupts their family circumstances so they enter adulthood without meaningful connections to their biological, foster, or adoptive families.

There are few empirical data on long-term outcomes for children in placement. The characteristics of adults who were formerly foster children or children in group care was the focus of a review of twenty-seven studies published between 1960 and 1990 (McDonald, Allen, Westerfelt, & Piliavin, 1993). Most of the studies looked broadly at the outcomes of foster care versus group care, included multiple outcome measures, and used face-to-face interviews as the primary means of collecting data. The following findings are excerpted from this review.

The adults who were in family foster care as children functioned better than those who spent time in group care: They had more education; were less likely to be arrested or convicted of a crime, to report drug or alcohol problems, to have no close friends, to be single parents, or to be divorced; had stronger informal support networks; and were more likely to be judged by interviewers to be satisfied with their lives (Ferguson, 1966; Festinger, 1983; Jones & Moses, 1984). Whereas these differences may be explained, in part, by the fact that children with fewer problems are more likely to be placed in foster care, rather than in group care, they nevertheless support the conclusion that "more effort must be made to develop family foster home placements that can accommodate the special needs of these children" (McDonald et al., 1993, p. 126).

Age at placement. There is no convincing evidence that age at placement is in itself a good predictor of adult functioning, since the findings of the studies reviewed were highly variable and there are no pure studies of outcomes for children who were placed when younger. There is much evidence, however, that age at placement increases the risk that an adoptive or foster care placement will fail (Barth, Berry, Carson, Goodfield, & Feinberg, 1986)—chapter 4 suggests that this is still true. This variability is predictable from our transactional approach to child development, which identifies numerous other possible contributors to adjustment following placement in foster care.

Festinger's (1983) follow-up study of adults who had been in foster or group care found that males who had been discharged from group care settings and who were older at the time of initial placement had a stronger sense of well-being. In contrast, men who had been discharged from foster homes had a stronger sense of well-being if placed when they were younger. McDonald et al. (1993, p. 128) summarized the significance of these results as follows: "This finding, coupled with the general finding that negative outcomes are associated with group rather than family settings, suggests that early placement in the right setting can be beneficial, and that early placement in the wrong setting may be damaging." Although the results of studies have not been unanimous, it is safe to say that multiple placements were more clearly associated with poorer outcomes than were most other variables: Poorer school achievement, less education (Palmer, 1976; Zimmerman, 1982), more criminal activity (Zimmerman, 1982), less informal social support (Jones & Moses, 1984), decreased life satisfaction (Jones & Moses, 1984; Triseliotis & Russell, 1984), less stable housing (Meier, 1965), and less adequate parenting (Zimmerman, 1982). Of course, children who are difficult to care for tend to have more placements. Still, changes in placements are likely to set off a negative chain reaction requiring children to expend substantial efforts to adjust to new adults, siblings, teachers, and surroundings. Just as we know that children who change schools frequently are likely to have lower grades, we assume that moving from placement to placement takes its toll on children.

In the reviewed studies, longer stays in foster care were associated with a higher degree of life satisfaction (Jones & Moses, 1984) and other measures of adult functioning (Fanshel & Shinn, 1978; Frost & Zurich, 1983; Palmer, 1976; Zimmerman, 1982). This was most clearly the case when the long-term placement was in a stable foster family and when the child maintained contact with the foster family and received support in adulthood (Zimmerman, 1982).

Increased closeness with foster parents while in care was associated with better academic and social progress during care, fewer emotional and behavioral problems after leaving care (Palmer, 1976), and a greater sense of well-being and life satisfaction (Festinger, 1983; Jones & Moses, 1984; Zimmerman, 1982). McDonald et al. (1993) concluded that former recipients of foster care are at a high risk of "rotten outcomes" as adults. These poor outcomes are not simply slightly diminished functioning or the failure to reach their full potential, but involve the failure to meet minimal standards of self-sufficiency (homelessness, dependence on welfare, and the like) and acceptable behaviors (criminal activity and drug use, for example) (McDonald et al., 1993, p. 129). Children in foster care do worse than the general population of children and than poor children in general (Cook, 1994), but some children in foster care may do better than others who receive less protective interventions—foster care may be a protective factor against mortality (Barth & Blackwell, 1996). It should be a fundamental responsibility of the child welfare service system to ensure that children in foster care have outcomes that closely approximate those of children in the general population.

Discussion

One great challenge for child welfare services is to try to predict which biological parents will be able to use the assistance offered to resume the provision of a minimum sufficient level of emotional, cognitive, and physical care for their children (Ruff, Blank, & Barnett, 1990). Another challenge is to try to discern when infants and young children will be best served, developmentally, by moves from one caregiver to another in pursuit of the most beneficial short- and long-term arrangements. Given young children's significant vulnerability in the early years, living in extremely deteriorated settings, repeated placements, and placements in group or institutional care pose developmental risks.

In the chapters that follow, we present a large volume of evidence that suggests that many young children are not currently faring well in the hands of their parents. When they are placed under the jurisdiction of the child welfare system, their lives may continue to be compromised. Even when a permanent placement is achieved, the accumulated affective, physical, and cognitive insults that children have received may require continued rehabilitative efforts. We end with a challenge to reconsider the relative importance of child protection, supporting families, promoting lifetime permanence, enhancing development, and fostering cultural continuity in child welfare practice from the first child abuse report onward. Social workers, lawyers, and judges regularly make decisions about the fate of young children on the basis of poor knowledge of future outcomes and inconsistent views about the most critical issues. We believe that these young children deserve better.

2

Child Abuse and Neglect of Very Young Children

Maltreatment affects a significant proportion of all children each year, and very young children's lives are touched most profoundly. Children under age six are the subjects of about 40 percent of the confirmed reports of maltreatment, even though they represent about one-third of the population of children in this country (National Center on Child Abuse and Neglect, NC-CAN, 1996). Reports of the abuse of young children appear to be escalating; the Third National Incidence Study of Child Abuse and Neglect (NIS-3) indicated a 67 percent overall increase in the incidence of maltreatment since 1986 (Sedlak & Broadhurst, 1996). Among all abused and neglected children, the youngest are the most likely to be the victims of severe injury or death (Sorenson & Peterson, 1994; Straus & Gelles, 1992)—almost half of all the deaths from maltreatment in 1994 were of infants under one year (Wiese & Daro, 1995). For obvious reasons, physical maltreatment is especially serious because its consequences can be severe and long lasting or fatal. Yet young children are most frequently reported for neglect. This fact is far from a cause for relief, however, since young children's absolute dependence on their parents or guardians means that neglect can compromise their physical health and safety and may also cause significant developmental harm (Cicchetti & Toth, 1996; Finkelhor, 1995).

In 1994, over 2.9 million children were reported for maltreatment in the United States (NCCAN, 1996), a sizable proportion from California. Home to an estimated 12.8 percent of the U.S. population under age eighteen, California contained 15.3 percent of the children reported nationwide—about half a million children (NCCAN, 1996).

To take a closer look at the young children who were reported for maltreatment, we examined data from nine California counties (see the Appendix for a detailed description of the study methods). Comparing this population to a sample of cases reported nationally, we found that California's reports mirrored those throughout the nation in several important respects (see Table 2.1). About 6 percent of all reports were for *infants* (from birth to 12 months), 11 percent were for *toddlers* (aged 1–2), and about 19 percent were for *preschoolers* (aged 3–5). As might be expected from the ethnic composition of the state, a higher proportion of the reports were for Hispanic children, which gave us the opportunity to examine this otherwise understudied population. Fewer children appear to be reported for neglect in California than nationally, but these differences may be due to reporting definitions, rather than to actual differences among the states. These data, combined with evidence from NIS-3, suggest that our data are reasonably representative of California's experience with child abuse and neglect, which is important in its own right because of its size and may be relatively representative of the nation.

Throughout the early 1990s, the rates of maltreatment reports in our sample remained higher for infants than for all other age groups; about 50 per 1,000 infants were reported for maltreatment each year. Incidence rates for children over age one declined each year. In 1994, the incidence of maltreatment reports for toddlers was 33 per 1,000 and for preschoolers, 31 per 1,000.

Using NCCAN's data, we estimated the rates of child maltreatment reports for the 11 states that provide unduplicated counts and found an incidence rate of approximately 28 per 1,000 children (NCCAN, 1996). Thus, the rates of reports for children over one year in our sample were similar to those reported by NCCAN.

Understanding the Types of Maltreatment

The most prevalent form of maltreatment for young children nationwide is neglect. Young children in our California sample parallel this trend, since they are more frequently reported for neglect (48 percent) than for any other type of maltreatment. Infants, in particular, are especially likely to be reported for neglect (62 percent).

Case Characteristics of Young Children Reported for Abuse and Neglect

Although neglect is associated with a variety of problems in children, including aggression, noncompliance, withdrawal, weak impulse control, lack of empathy, and poor peer relationships (Barahal, Waterman, & Martin, 1981; Egeland, Sroufe, & Erickson, 1983; George & Main, 1979; Hoffman-Plotkin & Twentyman, 1984), the most profound effects are found in the area of cognitive development and later academic achieve-

Table 2.1 Comparison of Study Sample with National
Maltreatment Report Data: 1994

	National	Sample
Age		
< 1	7.0	6.0
1–2	12.8	10.8
3–5	20.0	18.8
6–17	57.0	55.5
18+	1.1	.5
Unknown	2.1	8.4
Gender		
Female	52.3	50.5
Male	46.7	49.2
Unknown	1.1	.3
Ethnicity		
African American	26.4	14.1
Caucasian	56.4	45.8
Hispanic	9.4	29.0
Other	4.0	5.8
Unknown	3.7	5.3
Source of Report		
Schools	15.8	18.2
Law enforcement	13.0	13.1
Social services	11.6	8.2
Anonymous	7.6	8.1
Medical	11.3	12.3
Other	44.3	40.1
Reason for Report		
Neglect	55.4	42.3
Physical abuse	25.5	32.5
Sexual abuse	13.8	19.3
Other	19.5	5.8
Unknown	4.1	.01

Source for national data: *Child Maltreatment 1994: Reports from the States to the National Center on Child Abuse and Neglect.*
Source for study sample: Social Service Reporting System of Alameda, Contra Costa, Orange, San Diego, San Mateo, Santa Clara, Santa Cruz, Sonoma, and Tulare counties.

ment (Eckenrode, Laird, & Doris, 1993; Howing, Wodarski, Kurtz, & Gaudin, 1993).

African American young children are more frequently reported for neglect than are children from other ethnic groups—about 60 percent versus 43 percent. Although rates of neglect are higher in the African American population, these children are less often reported for sexual abuse (12 percent of reports) than are Hispanic and Caucasian children (about 20 percent of reports).

The proportion of young children reported for sexual abuse more than doubles by the time children are in preschool, from less than 9 percent for infants to over 21 percent for preschoolers. These findings were confirmed by Cappelleri, Eckenrode, and Powers (1993); Jones and McCurdy (1992); and Sedlak and Broadhurst (1996). Using data from the NIS-2, Jones and McCurdy found that sexual abuse among three to five year olds was the second most common reason for maltreatment following neglect. Cappelleri et al. found a rate of 2.41 reports for sexual abuse per 1,000 preschool-age children—only slightly lower than the 2.58 reports per 1,000 for young teenagers and 2.87 reports per 1,000 for older teenagers.

Numerous studies have found significantly higher rates of sexual abuse reports for girls. In a review of empirical research before 1985, Alter-Reid, Gibbs, Lachenmeyer, Sigal, and Massoth (1986) concluded that there were four to five times more female victims of sexual abuse than male victims. Cappelleri et al. (1993) stated that the odds of being reported for sexual abuse were 3.74 times as high as being reported for physical abuse for girls.

Physical abuse accounts for about one-quarter of reports for infants and one-third of reports for preschoolers in California. The NIS-3 found that boys were more likely to suffer severe physical injury than girls as a result of physical abuse (Sedlak & Broadhurst, 1996). Other studies have also indicated that boys are somewhat more likely to be reported for physical abuse (NCCAN, 1996).

Who Reports Young Children?

The majority of child abuse reports are now initiated by mandated reporters (NCCAN, 1996). This has not always been the case. In the 1980s, the majority of reports came from nonmandated reporters, according to Giovannoni (1995), who examined 983 reports of child maltreatment. Of mandated reporters nationally, teachers are the most frequent source of maltreatment reports, followed by law enforcement officers, social service personnel, and medical personnel (NCCAN, 1996).

Because young children have little contact with teachers, incidents of maltreatment are more often discovered by medical professionals (Hampton & Newberger, 1985; O'Toole, O'Toole, Webster, & Lucal, 1993). Several studies have confirmed mandated reporters' special sensitivity to the vulnerabilities of young children. In a study of teachers' reporting practices, Ards and Harrell (1993) discovered that teachers may be more likely to report younger children than older children, physically abused children more than neglected children, and children from urban areas more than children from less dense communities. With regard to nurses, O'Toole et al. (1993) noted that they may be more likely to report maltreatment in cases of young children, sexual abuse, serious injury, and uncooperative parents who are suspected of being the perpetrators. And Zellman (1992) found that younger children are more likely to be reported; other factors that are involved in the decision to report include knowledge of a previous incident of abuse and the type of injury the child has sustained.

Mandated reporters also play a significant role in referring young children to the child welfare system in California. Because of the numerous reporting sources, no single group is responsible for the majority of child maltreatment reports. Of all professionals, however, medical personnel play a significant role in reporting young children. Fifty-four percent of all reports made by physicians and hospitals are for children under age six—almost one-fifth of all reports for children in this age group.

Maltreatment and Ethnicity

Reporters, whether mandated or nonmandated, are more likely to refer African American children to child welfare services than children from other ethnic groups. Figure 2.1 presents incidence rates by age and eth-

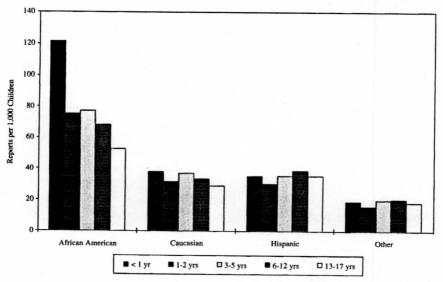

Figure 2.1 Maltreatment reports (Incidence per 1,000 children in California)

nicity for 1994 for all nine counties in California. It shows that the rate for African American infants is approximately three times that of Caucasian and Hispanic infants and almost six times higher than for infants in other ethnic groups. By the time African American children who were born in 1990 reached kindergarten, 39 percent were reported for maltreatment, compared to 15 percent of Caucasian children, 17 percent of Hispanic children, and 9 percent of children from "other" ethnic groups.

There is much debate about whether these ethnic differences reflect real differences in the rate of maltreatment, are a matter of reporting bias, or are an artifact of the poverty of many African American families (Ards, 1989; Chaffin, Kelleher, & Hollenberg, 1996; Coulton & Pandy, 1992; Kruttschnitt, McLeod, & Dornfield, 1994; National Research Council, 1993). Some researchers argue that the variation in reporting rates among ethnic groups may be attributed to reporting bias. Examining a sample of African American children, some of whom were abused and others who were hospitalized for accidents, Hampton and Newberger (1985) reviewed the reporting patterns of hospital personnel in twenty-six counties in nine states. Comparing child abuse reports by hospital personnel to medical diagnoses, they found that the children of lower socioeconomic status (SES) were more frequently reported. The NIS-3 found no difference in the actual incidence of maltreatment for various ethnic groups, although there were large differences in reporting patterns (Sedlak & Broadhurst, 1996).

In a review of studies concerning child welfare and ethnicity, Courtney and associates (1996) pointed out that the impact of race is difficult to separate from the impacts of poverty and substance abuse. Communities of color are disproportionately represented in inner-city neighborhoods and are disproportionately poor (Massey & Denton, 1993; U.S. Department of Health and Human Services, DHHS, 1996). Families in these communities are more likely to have contact with a large number of mandated reporters, including social workers, law enforcement personnel, and medical professionals.

Garbarino and Ebata's (1983) review of the early literature on ethnicity and child maltreatment concluded that differences in the types and incidence of maltreatment seemed to be connected to demographic risk factors, including poverty. Chaffin et al.'s (1996) prospective study of 7,102 parents, which examined the onset of maltreatment, found that race was not significantly related to maltreatment after family size, SES, substance abuse, and psychiatric disorders were controlled.

Research on child abuse reporting at the community level has born similar results. Spearly and Lauderdale (1983) studied the effects of ethnicity and community characteristics on maltreatment reporting patterns in 246 Texas counties. They found that urbanization, which has frequently been linked to poverty in other research (DHHS, 1996; Massey & Denton, 1990), was a strong predictor of maltreatment reports for African American and Hispanic children. Ards (1989) examined various means of estimating child abuse rates at the community level and discovered that 84 percent of the variance initially explained by race could be explained instead by measures of density, urbanization, income, age, and crime. In her later work, Ards (1992) found that the proportion of African Americans in a community was negatively associated with the rate of maltreatment when density, urbanization, income, and unemployment were controlled. Coulton and Pandey (1992) stated that the effect of the percentage of nonwhite families in a census tract on various measures of risk to children became nonsignificant after measures of crime, out-of-wedlock births, and poverty were held constant. In a more recent study of child maltreatment rates across census tracts, Coulton, Korbin, Su, and Chow (1995) were unable to separate the effect of the proportion of African American residents from measures of poverty (residents of color and indices of poverty had to be combined in analyses because of the correlations between factors). Taken together, these studies generally suggest that ethnicity and culture alone are poor predictors of child maltreatment. When large differences in child abuse reporting rates are found among ethnic groups, the explanation is usually found in correspondingly large differences in family or community circumstances.

Maltreatment and Substance Abuse

The association between maltreatment and ethnicity is not only confounded by issues of poverty and community characteristics, but is made further complex by problems of substance abuse. Data from the 1991 National Household Survey on Drug Abuse and the 1991 Drug Abuse Warning Network (DHHS, 1991) indicated that in 1990, 12.8 million children (18 percent of all children) lived with a parent who used drugs; children under age three were disproportionately found in substance-abusing families.

Variations in the use of drugs among ethnic groups may have an impact on reporting. One study of substance abuse among pregnant women in California indicated that African American women were more likely than women of other ethnic groups to use drugs (Vega, Kolody, Hwang, & Noble, 1993); therefore, African American children may be at a greater risk of prenatal exposure to drugs. In particular, cocaine and crack cocaine appear to be the drugs of choice among substance-abusing African American women (Vega et al), and hospital staff may be more likely to report infants' exposure to cocaine than to other drugs (Sagatun-Edwards, Saylor, & Shifflett, 1994). Because criminal penalties are higher for the possession of crack cocaine, these infants may also risk losing their parents to incarceration, thereby being reported for "parental incapacity." At least one study suggested that the rate of women arrested for drug-related crimes is strongly associated with rates of child abuse reporting (Albert & Barth, 1996).

Jaudes, Ekwo, and Van Voorhis (1995) studied 513 children who were born between 1985 and 1990 exposed to drugs in utero. They found that the rate of maltreatment reports was almost three times higher for these children than for children in a corresponding neighborhood. Toddlers were more likely to be maltreated than infants, and neglect was the primary reason for reports. Walker, Zangrillo, and Smith's (1991) study of African American children in foster care indicated that neglect was the primary reason for placement among substance-abusing families; in these families, the children were younger, and the families were twice as likely to be poor and to have housing problems. Murphy and associates (1992) found that 50 percent of 206 child maltreatment cases that resulted in court involvement had alleged substance abuse problems and that neglect was the primary reason for reports among cases involving substance abuse. However, unlike Walker et al. (1991), they did not find a significant difference in SES between substance abusing and non-substance-abusing maltreatment cases (perhaps because of the large number of alcohol users in the sample, who often have higher incomes). At the aggregate level Coulton et al. (1995) found that it was possible to predict drug-related offenses using the same neighborhood indicators used to predict child maltreatment rates, thus highlighting the close association between substance abuse and child maltreatment.

Although substance abuse has been associated with neglect (Chaffin et al., 1996; Jaudes et al., 1996), little information is available regarding the impact of substance abuse on other forms of maltreatment. Famularo, Kinscherff, and Fenton (1992) reported that alcohol was specifically associated with physical abuse, whereas cocaine was associated with sexual abuse. In their study, the use of two or more drugs did not increase the likelihood of physical or sexual abuse compared to the use of a single drug.

Substance abuse may be associated with an increased risk of maltreatment for many reasons, including the diversion of monetary resources and time from parenting to acquire drugs; involvement in criminal activity to support the habit; and poor parenting skills, particularly because many of these families are socially isolated and have unrealistic expectations of children's behavior (Bays, 1990). The following case description, concerning a baby named Patrick, illuminates the circumstances that many of these young children face. The substance abuse of their parents not only brings them to the attention of child welfare authorities, but shapes much of their experience while in foster care.

Joyce, Beth, Crystal, and Patrick

In 1988, Nell had her first baby, a girl named Joyce, who was born exposed to cocaine. Nell had no prenatal care prior to the delivery and had smoked crack throughout her pregnancy. A child welfare investigator interviewed Nell in the hospital and carefully reviewed the case. At the end of her investigation the worker determined that Joyce could go home with her mother.

In 1989, Nell had her second child, also a girl, whom she named Beth. Like Joyce, Beth was born exposed to cocaine. A child maltreatment report was filed, and a social worker investigated the case. Beth, too, was allowed to return home with her mother. No further services were offered.

In 1990, Nell had her third baby girl and named her Crystal. Crystal, too, was born with cocaine in her system. A child abuse report was filed by medical personnel and a social worker investigated the case. This worker also closed the case.

The case file that offers a window into the lives of Joyce, Beth, and Crystal does not describe Nell's family circumstances, her housing situation, the extent of her support network, or the degree of her drug problem. It simply indicates "no action taken" following each report for maltreatment.

In 1991, the child welfare agency received an anonymous complaint that Nell was using crack and was leaving her babies at home unattended. The child welfare worker assigned to the case found Nell's home "messy," but did not find Nell or her children. The case remained open for two months while the social worker "searched" for Nell; this search included two additional unannounced visits to the home when no one was there. When Nell and her children could not be located, the case was closed.

In 1992, Nell gave birth to Patrick, who was also drug exposed and who was reported to the child welfare agency. When this report was received, a social worker investigating the case removed Patrick from his mother's home. Beth and Crystal remained with their mother; four-year-old Joyce had moved in with her maternal grandmother two years earlier through an informal family arrangement.

Three days after Patrick was born, he was placed with his paternal grandmother and remained there for the next 210 days, after which he was moved three times during the following 1½ years. While he remained in care, Patrick's mother and father ostensibly worked on their reunification plans. Nell was required to enroll in a substance abuse treatment program and to submit to drug testing. She was also required to remain free of the law. Prior to Patrick's birth, Nell had been arrested eleven times for theft, receiving stolen property, and assult. During Patrick's stay in care, Nell was incarcerated twice on drug-related charges, and Beth and Crystal went to live with Patrick's father, Gregory, until Nell was released.

Gregory developed a reunification plan with his child welfare worker so that he could get custody of Patrick, who remained with his grandmother. The plan required that he undergo drug testing and attend a drug treatment program, parenting classes, and counseling; that he visit with the child; and maintain a clean record. Gregory, who had experienced several bouts of homelessness, was also required to obtain stable housing. He rarely visited Patrick while he was in care, claiming that he had violated his parole and therefore feared being caught by public officials. His criminal record included selling narcotics, receiving stolen property, and carrying a loaded firearm. Although Gregory tested positive for alcohol and morphine, the case file indicated that if he tested negative for drugs, Patrick would be returned to his care.

When Patrick was two years old, he was reunified with his father and mother. The case file indicates that Gregory "never" participated in the services required in his case plan and that Nell was "seldom" involved. Although Nell participated in some drug treatment, there are no indications in the file that either she or Gregory had resolved their drug abuse by the time Patrick came home.

Since Joyce, Beth, and Crystal were never taken into care, the case file is spare in its information about their well-being. Yet Beth and Crystal experienced their parents' drug abuse and lived in homes of great instability as their mother moved in and out of jail.

Substance abuse was a recurring problem for this family, as it was for many others. Four infants suffered at least from the risk of neglect because of their parents' involvement with drugs, but the evidence of harm was not interpreted as a reason to mandate services until the last child was born.

The fundamental problem underlying Patrick's family was substance abuse and its impact on Nell and Gregory's parenting. But Patrick's dependency petition did not indicate that substance abuse was the reason for removing him from his home; Patrick was removed for reasons of parental incapacity—otherwise known as neglect. The combination of substance abuse, and neglect, set the stage for Patrick's removal from his parents' home. The lack of financial resources contributed to this family's problems.

Poverty and Maltreatment

The close association between poverty and child maltreatment is indisputable. The NIS-3 found that children from families with annual incomes below $15,000 were over twenty times more likely to be maltreated than children from homes with incomes exceeding $30,000 annually (Sedlak & Broadhurst, 1996). Examining the rates of substantiated child maltreatment reports by zip codes, Drake and Pandey (1996) found that family poverty had a significant, positive relationship to neglect, physical abuse, and sexual abuse. In contrast, Spearly and Lauderdale (1983) noted that poverty was associated only with neglect, not with physical abuse. Poverty and neglect may be closely entwined because unique and potentially detrimental parenting choices are imposed on families who lack financial resources (Minty & Patterson, 1994). These families may face greater stress, higher levels of depression, and more profound social isolation.

Although poverty may be implicated in child maltreatment, some argue that reporting bias against poor families may be the cause of the overrepresentation of poor children in child welfare reports. But secondary analyses of two national incidence surveys indicated that income is not influential in the decision to report when type of abuse and age are controlled (Ards & Harrell, 1993). Indeed, the likelihood of reporting among mandated reporters increased between the 1980 and 1986 national incidence surveys, but the role of income in reporting practices was not significant (Ards & Harrell, 1993). Similarly, in studies using hypothetical vignettes, the socioeconomic circumstances of the children were not significant in the decision to report, but poverty dramatically increased the likelihood of children being maltreated (Osborne, Hinz, Rappaport, Williams, & Tuma, 1988; O'Toole et al., 1993; Ringwalt & Caye, 1989; Zellman, 1992).

Although poverty is a significant risk factor for maltreatment, most poor families do not abuse or neglect their children (Pelton, 1989). There is some evidence to suggest that differences in living conditions, parents' health and mental health, and other social risk factors distinguish maltreating from nonmaltreating poor families. In 1979, Wolock and Horowitz studied 380 recipients of child welfare services compared to 180 recipients of Aid to Families with Dependent Children (AFDC), who had not been reported for child maltreatment. Among the nonabusive families, overall housing conditions were better, there was more reciprocity among neighbors, fewer children resided in the home, and parents reported positive recollections of their childhoods.

In a sample of 518 AFDC mothers—119 neglectful, 118 abusive, and 281 nonmaltreating—the nonmaltreating mothers appeared to have better coping abilities and were primarily concerned with financial problems and child-rearing issues (Zuravin & Grief, 1989). Maltreating mothers worried more about relationships, their children, and their health, even when their life circumstances were similar to those of nonmaltreating mothers. They also reported more substance abuse and had more concerns about their children's mental health and success in school. Unplanned childbearing, large families, and poor maternal coping skills also were significantly associated with maltreatment (Zuravin, 1991). Among a sample of mothers receiving AFDC, Polansky, Gaudin, and Kilpatrick (1992) found that neglecting mothers displayed lower levels of relatedness to their children, confidence, impulse control, and verbal accessibility than did nonneglecting mothers. Maternal depression, lower maternal education, the mother's separation from her mother prior to age fourteen, larger family size, and receipt of Medicaid were all important in explaining maltreatment among another sample of low-income mothers of infants (Kotch et al., 1995).

We explored the relationship between poverty and maltreatment reporting in the nine sample counties in California and found that the correlation between poverty (measured by the proportion of families living below the 1989 poverty level per zip code) and maltreatment rates per zip code was modestly strong (.38). Because zip codes in many California counties cover large areas, they mask areas of dense poverty that could otherwise be captured by census-level data. Future analyses that focus on census tracts may reveal more powerful effects.

Discussion

Child maltreatment includes more than single events of abuse or overly punitive discipline. Usually, it is chronic, long standing, and embedded in social and familial circumstances that go well beyond problems of individual behavior. Young children who are reported to the child welfare services system suffer most often from neglect—a form of maltreatment that is difficult to untangle from poverty, substance abuse, family structure, depression, social isolation, and other family problems (Gaudin & Dubowitz, 1997, Hartley, 1989; Hegar & Yungman, 1989; Nelson, Saunders, & Landsman, 1993). Working with families such as these who are overly challenged is especially demanding. Treatment methods for changing patterns of neglect have generally had modest results at best (see Berrick & Duerr, 1997). Success in developing treatment services to help families overcome the tenacious hold of substance abuse has also proved elusive in many instances (Nunes-Dinis, 1993).

Child maltreatment reports for young children represent a call for help for children who cannot care for or protect themselves. Efforts to focus research on and develop innovative and enhanced services for these youngsters is the least that the child welfare community can do. To ignore their appeal shows neglect and disregard for their developmental well-being.

Summary of Key Findings and Recommendations Regarding Child Abuse and Neglect for Young Children

---

Finding	*Recommendation*
2.1. Young children are more likely to be reported for child maltreatment than are older children, and infants are more often reported to child welfare authorities than any other group. Rates of reporting for African American infants are alarmingly high.	2.1. Child welfare workers should be closely familiar with the developmental milestones of early childhood so they can appropriately identify the risks for young children who are reported for maltreatment.
	Reports for maltreatment among infants underscore the need for special efforts to reach substance-

abusing women in the early
months of pregnancy to improve
birth outcomes and the family
circumstances awaiting these babies.

Finding	*Recommendation*
2.2. Infants are more likely to be reported by medical personnel than by any other single group of reporting sources.	2.2. All child welfare jurisdictions should ensure that medical personnel are well trained to identify child maltreatment in young children. Because children aged one to five are less likely to come in regular contact with mandated reporting sources, all mandated reporters should be well trained to ensure that the net of public protection includes all young children.

Finding	*Recommendation*
2.3. There is a sharp increase in reports of physical and sexual abuse of children after the first year of life.	2.3. The physical and sexual abuse of young children reveal significant family dysfunction and should be viewed as critical. Special protocols for expediting permanence should be considered to ensure that these youngsters are protected.

3

From Child Maltreatment to Placement

The proportion of children who receive services after child abuse reports have been filed is relatively small. A significant proportion of child maltreatment reports are screened out immediately, and of the reports that are investigated, even fewer actually receive services or supports from child welfare agencies. Only when tragedy strikes does the general public turn its attention to the service delivery system that constitutes the "front end" of child welfare. When young children die at the hands of their parents despite the fact that child welfare authorities were aware of their circumstances, public ire reaches a crescendo (Pollitt, 1996; Teichert, 1996). Few cases of child abuse and neglect result in such dire consequences, but they are reminders that the initial report is only the first step in a process of determining whether intervention is needed. Information about even the most basic outcomes for young children during this assessment process is scarce. Cases such as the following are far too common in child welfare services; babies like Jeremiah get less than they need from child welfare workers, who fail to determine the degree of their suffering.

Are too many maltreated children going unserved because of the lack of available services, inappropriate risk assessments, or miscommunication? (Milton, 1996; Wells, Fluke, & Brown, 1995). Have we overreacted to rare incidents of children's deaths and injuries without examining the strengths and weaknesses of the child protection system? (Lindsey, 1994; Melton & Barry, 1994). We may not be able to answer these questions definitively, but an examination of reporting, multiple reporting, investigations, and initial services for young children may shed some light on these issues.

Jeremiah

LaTanya was a high school graduate who, at age 28, gave birth to her first and only child, Jeremiah. LaTanya's case file suggests that she was physically abused and neglected as a child, but was never placed in foster care. She had a criminal record for prostitution and drug possession, and she admitted to the heavy use of drugs, including cocaine, amphetamines, and alcohol.

When Jeremiah was born, medical personnel noted traces of cocaine in his body. There were no other special circumstances surrounding his birth; his records indicate that he was healthy and that no medical or physical problems were evident. The day following Jeremiah's birth, medical personnel made a report to the local child welfare agency. Jeremiah's case file indicates that child welfare workers attempted to follow up on the report but were unable to locate him and his mother; his case was closed without an investigation.

One month later, the child welfare agency received a phone call from one of LaTanya's relatives, who said that Jeremiah was being physically abused by his mother. A child welfare worker from the local public agency was assigned to the case and two days later investigated the allegation. She interviewed LaTanya and examined Jeremiah. Jeremiah's temperament was described as "very easy" and "cherubic" in the case file. Notes in the case file show that the worker was aware that Jeremiah was born exposed to drugs and had been reported previously, but she did not see any evidence on this occasion to suggest that intervention with the family was needed. Jeremiah's case file was closed at this point because of "insufficient evidence."

A month later, the child welfare agency again received a report concerning Jeremiah. The case file does not identify who reported the child, but it shows that Jeremiah was reported for "caretaker absence or incapacity." Although the child maltreatment report had merit, the social worker left Jeremiah with his mother and asked that she supervise him closely or ensure that he was in others' care before leaving her home.

Finally, just two weeks later, when Jeremiah was 2½ months old, a fourth report for child maltreatment was logged at the child welfare agency. This time, the man with whom LaTanya and Jeremiah were living—a friend of the family—called the police, telling them that LaTanya had left the house the day before and had not yet returned; he was no longer willing to care for the child. Jeremiah was placed in an emergency foster home, where he lived for a month; he was later moved to his uncle's home, where he stayed for the next seven months. When he was returned to his mother, LaTanya and her son received in-home supportive services from a social worker. Within a few months, however, LaTanya had abandoned Jeremiah, and he was again placed in foster care.

From Report to Intervention

Investigations

When a report of child abuse or neglect is filed, it is received by the child welfare agency or the police, or both. A report is usually screened by phone as the child welfare worker collects information and determines the nature and severity of the incident. The case may be closed immediately if, for example, the report lacks sufficient information to investigate further, is deemed frivolous, or the child is in no apparent danger. The reports that are not closed immediately are referred to investigations workers. (In some states, these staff may be known as intake workers or assessment workers.)

Little research has been conducted on the decision to investigate a report. This lack of information may be due partially to the data collection methods of child protection agencies. For example, in Illinois and Michigan, automated records of maltreatment reports are kept only on cases that are investigated (Goerge, Van Voorhis, Sanfilippo, & Harden, 1996).

Studies conducted in the early 1980s indicated that approximately 85 percent of child abuse reports were investigated. In some states like California, the law required that every appropriate report receive a face-to-face assessment with the child and family. Exceptions to the general rule to investigate were made largely when information was missing or reports were from anonymous sources or absent parents (Barone, Adams, & Tooman, 1981). A more recent study (Wells et al., 1995), based on 1986 data recorded by intake workers from twelve sites in five states, found that investigations are now rare; only 58 percent of the cases from that study were investigated. Of the cases that were screened out, about 9 percent were closed because the families could not be located; 20 percent lacked specific allegations of maltreatment; and 70 percent contained clear allegations, but were screened out for other reasons, such as missing information. Factors influencing the decision to investigate included age (particularly children under age two), the report of an injury, an allegation of sexual abuse, and complete information given at the time of the report. Reports from nonmandated reporters were less likely to be investigated. A recent study of child abuse investigations by Gilbert, Karski, and Frame (1996) examined decision making in one California county. Of the 17,566 reports of child abuse that were reviewed, 46 percent were subsequently investigated. Children who were reported for sexual abuse and African American single-mother families who were collecting AFDC were most frequently investigated. Families who were the most likely to be investigated suffered from housing problems, financial strain, and drug use.

In our examination of nine California counties, we found that a higher proportion of cases are investigated than may be the case in other studies, although differences in data collection methods, mentioned earlier, may explain some of these disparities. About three-quarters of the reports of young children are investigated, compared to about two-thirds of the reports of older children's reports (76 percent versus 66 percent); infants are more often investigated than any other age group. Hispanic children are also more likely to have their cases investigated than are children of other ethnic groups. (See Figure 3.1 for the proportion of children investigated from 1992 to 1994.)

In addition to age, the type of maltreatment the child has sustained has bearing on whether the report will be investigated. Young children who are reported for physical abuse are more likely to have their cases investigated (79 percent of physical abuse reports versus 73 percent of sexual abuse reports and 74 percent of neglect reports), and infants who are reported for physical abuse are more often investigated than any other group (82 percent). Figure 3.2 shows the relationship between the type of maltreatment children sustain and the rate of investigations.

Upon investigation, most cases are rapidly closed for reasons ranging from the inability to find the child or parent to being classified as "no longer at risk" (as in cases of abuse by an individual with whom the child no longer has contact). California, like many states, does not collect information on whether the case was substantiated. The fact that a child who is reported to the child welfare agency is then investigated does not mean that the report was substantiated.

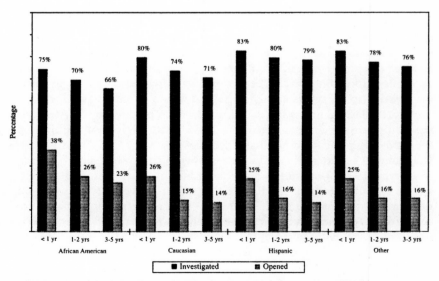

Figure 3.1 Investigations and cases opened for services in California by age and ethnicity (1992-'94)

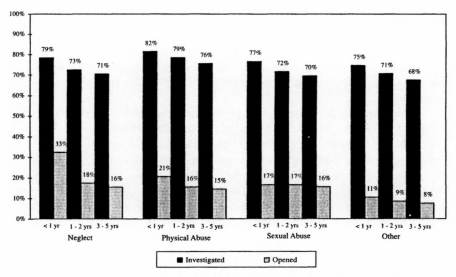

Figure 3.2 Investigations and cases opened for services in California by age and type of maltreatment (1992-'94)

Early Intervention Services

Among the cases that are investigated, some families receive services from child welfare agencies. Variation among states in the proportion of families who receive these services is great; widely divergent definitions of the term *open for services* also cloud state-to-state interpretations of the data. For example, in Illinois, about 5 percent of the investigations resulted in case openings, whereas in Michigan, 100 percent of investigations resulted in services (Goerge et al., 1996). These differences were attributed to the states' interpretation of the terms *services* and *open*. In the latest national summary of state child welfare reports (National Center on Child Abuse and Neglect, NCCAN, 1996), 15 percent of the substantiated cases received court intervention, which, at a minimum, indicates that the cases were opened. In a large New York county, 30 percent of the cases were substantiated and, of those, 40 percent (12 percent of all the investigated cases) were provided services beyond the investigation (Freeman, Levine, & Doueck, 1996).

In California, 16 percent to 38 percent of young children who are reported for maltreatment for the first time receive services beyond the investigation. These services range from brief intervention and referral to in-home services to foster care. For the purposes of our study, the term *open for services* refers to any case still receiving services beyond the investigation ten days following the initial report. African American children are somewhat more likely to have their reports opened for services, and these differences are most pronounced for African American infants (see Figure 3.1). Children who are reported for neglect are somewhat more likely to have their cases opened for services (22 percent) than are children who are reported for physical abuse (17 percent) or sexual abuse (16 percent) (see Figure 3.2). The cases of infants reported for neglect are opened for services at a higher rate (33 percent) than are those of any other group.

A logit model was constructed to examine the odds of a case being opened for services (See Table 3.1). African American children were about two times as likely to receive services as Caucasian or Hispanic children. Infants were more likely to have their cases opened than other young children, particularly if they were neglected.

Too little is known about the outcomes for children who are investigated or do not receive services. Are they more likely, for example, to be rereported for maltreatment? Our data suggest that young children who are *not* investigated are equally likely to be rereported as are those who *are* investigated (about 45 percent). Figure 3.3 depicts children's pathways to services through the front end of the child welfare system. A significant proportion of children who are initially reported for maltreatment have later contact with the child welfare system in a variety of ways. The figure shows that Jeremiah's case is not unusual; having a child maltreatment report does not guarantee an investigation or services, nor does a subsequent report necessarily warrant assistance.

Table 3.1 Odds Ratio of the Likelihood of a Case Being Opened for Service in California at First Report ($n = 8,751$)

Variable	Odds Ratio
Age at First Report	
Less than 1 year	*1.00*
1–6 years	.65
Ethnicity	
Caucasian	*1.00*
African American	2.10
Hispanic	1.10 NS
Reason for Report	
Sexual/physical abuse	*1.00*
Neglect	1.88
Interaction	
Neglect/1–6 years	.62

Note: Served: 2,454. likelihood ratio chi-square = 4.926, 61 *df* ($p = .55$).
*Italics denote reference categories.

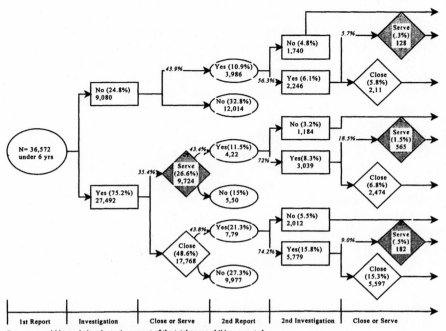

Figure 3.3 Service pathways of young children first reported in 1992 in California

Multiple Reporting

When a child is reported to child welfare authorities more than once, the circumstances of that child and family should be of concern. Infants like Jeremiah should not endure four reports before their cases are considered serious by child welfare authorities. Recurrent reports may indicate newly developing problems in a family, a failure in the system to protect the child, or the failure of the services provided (Eamon, 1994; Fryer & Miyoshi, 1994). Some studies indicate that children who are repeatedly victimized by maltreatment may experience social and developmental outcomes that are significant (Ney, Fung, & Wickett, 1994; Wolfe & McGee, 1994). In addition to the effects on the child, multiple reports have an impact on a system that is already overwhelmed by new referrals (Fryer & Miyoshi, 1994).

An early study of multiple reporting among 120 randomly selected open cases of physical abuse (Johnson & L'Esperance, 1984) indicated that 46 percent had a second report within two years. Studies of court-involved cases (Murphy et al., 1992) and foster care placements (Zuravin

& DePanfilis, 1995) have also shown that approximately one-third of these cases had more than one report prior to their current involvement with services. Three studies of substantiated maltreatment reports found that repeat reports were more likely to occur for reasons of neglect and that ethnicity was not a significant factor in recurrent abuse (DePanfilis, 1995; Fryer & Miyoshi, 1994; Levy, Markovic, Chaudry, Ahart, & Torres, 1995); 10 percent to 25 percent of the substantiated cases in these studies included multiple reports.

Fryer and Miyoshi (1994) examined the revictimization of 24,507 Colorado children with substantiated maltreatment reports between 1986 and 1989. They found that the risk of a second report was greatest within thirty days of the initial event. DePanfilis (1995) confirmed these findings elsewhere. Both studies suggested that younger children (under age six) were more likely to experience multiple reports.

Several characteristics of the maltreating parent and the household appear to be related to the likelihood of a subsequent report. Johnson and L'Esperance (1984) found that the amount of time the child spent with an abusing adult, the mother's parenting skills, the reasonableness of the mother's expectations of the child, the family's ability to use agency resources, and the presence of more than one child in the home were significant predictors of a second report. Among 239 families whose cases were closed following an investigation, Wolock and Magura (1996) found a dramatic increase in second reports among those who were identified as having substance abuse problems. Over half the substance-involved families had second reports compared to one-quarter of the other families. Other characteristics associated with second reports include high maternal stress, domestic violence, and low social support (DePanfilis, 1995).

In California, more than half the young children who were reported during the study period (1992–1994) had only one child maltreatment report within three years. Infants had the highest rate of multiple reports (42 percent). Hispanic children were less likely to receive a second report, and children who were reported for neglect once were more likely to have more than one report. For young children who were reported to child welfare authorities more than once during the study period, the median time to a second report was four to five months, depending on their ages.

Multiple types of maltreatment. Child abuse and neglect reports in our data indicate only one type of maltreatment, so we could not determine whether children are experiencing multiple types of abuse at any point in time. However, by examining multiple reports, we made a rough estimate of children who are experiencing more than one type of maltreatment over time. Over half the children (57 percent) with multiple reports who are initially reported for neglect are also reported for neglect in their second reports. Among the remaining cases, about half are first reported for neglect and are subsequently reported for physical abuse. The results are similar for those reported for physical and sexual abuse; 47 percent and 45 percent, respectively, are reported again for the same reason. About one-quarter to one-third of physical and sexual abuse cases are rereported for neglect (25 percent and 31 percent, respectively) and about one-quarter of sexual abuse cases are rereported for physical abuse (25 percent).

Placement in Foster Care

A small but important proportion of young children who are reported for maltreatment are ultimately placed in foster care. In the thirty-five states that provide data on placement, almost one-fifth of the children whose cases are substantiated are placed in care (NCCAN, 1996). Goerge et al. (1996) found that among cases that were investigated, children reported for neglect were slightly more likely to receive services and to be placed in foster care than were children reported for physical or sexual abuse.

Families whose children are placed in foster care appear to have more significant or multiple problems. Sagatun-Edwards, Saylor, and Shifflet (1994) reported that 93 percent of the cases of drug-exposed infants in their study were opened for investigation, and for 62 percent of those who were investigated, petitions for removal from the home were filed in court. A study of 1,035 families suggested that the characteristics that affected placement in foster care are similar to those implicated in the substantiation of maltreatment, but the risk factors are cumulative for foster care (Zuravin & DePanfilis, 1995). Furthermore familial problems, such as parents' substance abuse, developmental delays, mental health difficulties, and domestic violence may predict placement, regardless of poverty, ethnicity, and prior reports.

Information on children entering foster care in California were combined with our data on maltreatment reports ($n = 15,872$). As described in Chapter 2, infants constitute about 6 percent of all child maltreatment reports, yet, as we will show in later chapters, they include about one-quarter of the first entries into foster care statewide. Figure 3.4 shows each decision point in the child welfare system and confirms that infants are more likely to be investigated, served, and placed in foster care. As we will show, infants constitute a unique group among all children; they are viewed as especially vulnerable by child welfare workers and their reports for maltreatment are treated with special sensitivity.

When we examined young children's pathway to services by ethnicity, we found that African Americans are overrepresented in maltreatment reports and are heavily overrepresented in foster care caseloads. Figure 3.5 illustrates the differences in pathways to services, from maltreatment report to foster care placement, for various ethnic groups. Although reports on Hispanic children are more frequently investigated, few Hispanic children actually receive services or are placed in care, and the same ap-

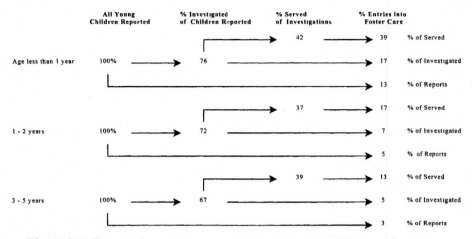

Figure 3.4 From maltreatment report to placement by age (Percentage of previous case decisions in California)

pears to be true for children of other ethnic groups. The situation of African American young children stands in stark contrast: A relatively low proportion of these children are investigated, yet they are much more likely to be served and placed in foster care.

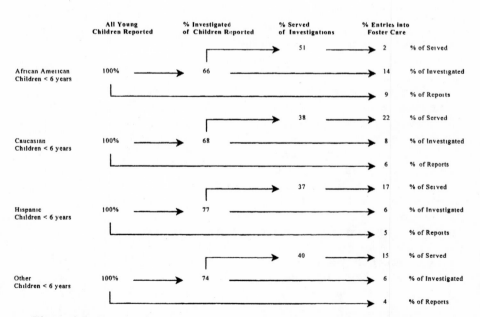

Figure 3.5 From maltreatment report to placement by ethnicity (Percentage of previous case decisions in California)

Discussion

The current child welfare system is overwhelmed by the number and complexity of the cases it encounters and is plagued by inadequate resources to address families' needs (Howard, 1994; Lindsey, 1994). Some critics of the system have proposed such changes as relegating investigations to law enforcement (Pelton, 1989), eliminating poverty by refocusing child welfare resources on income assistance (Lindsey, 1994), and restricting child welfare services to child protection (Besharov, 1992). Although our data do not allow us to assess the viability of these proposals here, they show a system that is heavily weighted by young children of color who are reported mainly for neglect. Many of these young children are investigated by child welfare authorities, but only a small proportion of their families are offered services. Data are sparse about the nature and intensity of services when they are provided; if we knew more, we might build better predictive models of the characteristics of families who are most likely to benefit from services.

Instead, we know that among the cases investigated by child welfare authorities, a relatively large number continue to cycle in and out of the system. Young children who are placed in foster care do not represent a success by any means—from the children's standpoint, they have suffered a fundamental insult by their removal from home—but at least foster care provides some assurances that children have been protected from further harm. The children for whom the child welfare system is clearly not working are those who are reported and are later maltreated again by their parents; almost half the young children who were reported once are failed by the current system in this way.

Summary of Key Findings and Recommendations Regarding the Abuse and Neglect of Young Children

Finding	*Recommendation*
3.1. The younger the child, the more likely he or she is to be investigated or served, to experience multiple reports, or to be placed in foster care. Overall, a relatively small proportion of young children who are investigated are provided services.	3.1. Given the extreme vulnerability of young children, more intensive services may be needed to support and supervise their well-being immediately following reports of their maltreatment.
Finding	*Recommendation*
3.3. A large proportion of young children are reported for maltreatment more than once, yet young children are no less likely to be rereported if they are provided services after investigation.	3.3 Clear definitions and screening guidelines are needed to help reduce the number of cases that cycle in and out of the child welfare system.

Finding	*Recommendation*
3.4. African American children are more likely to have their cases opened and later to be placed in foster care.	3.4. It is important to conduct additional research to understand whether the higher levels of service to these children reflect more severe circumstances among African American children, fewer informal resources among African American families, or biases by child welfare workers.

4

Foster Care, Reunification, and Adoption

Foster care is an extreme intervention for maltreated children who cannot remain safely at home. Although its intent is to protect, children who are placed in foster care may be denied the opportunity to grow up with their parents and siblings and to absorb the unique sounds, sights, and smells of their biological homes. When they lose their children to foster care, parents may forfeit the chance to hear their babies' first words or to watch them learn to walk. Others remain closely involved but miss days and weeks with their children that they might otherwise have shared.

Relatively few reports of child abuse or neglect result in foster care placements; nevertheless, the foster care caseload is growing. During placement, a child welfare professional coordinates services with the goal of reunifying the family. If this goal cannot be achieved in a specified period (eighteen months in most states, but twelve months in California), the Adoption Assistance and Child Welfare Act of 1980 (P.L. 96-272) mandates the implementation of an alternative permanent plan—specifically adoption, guardianship, or long-term foster care. An additional six months of foster care can be added if it is highly probable that reunification will occur by extending the time limits.

The time limits are based on elapsed court time—not just calendar time. So, a child's six-month hearing may occur twelve calendar months or more after placement, depending on delays, continuances in the scheduling of reviews, and the resolution of issues related to the dependency decisions that occur at the beginning of the case. As we will show, a sizable proportion of children will be reunified eighteen months or more after they first enter care.

Foster Care Performance Indicators

A preliminary analysis of data from the Adoption and Foster Care Reporting System (AFCARS, 1996) set the 1994 national foster care caseload at 469,073. Westat estimated there were 502,000 children on the basis of a national probability sample (Maza, 1996). Over a third (35%) of these children were under age 6. African American children constituted a larger proportion of the caseload (47 percent) than did the children of any other ethnic group (Caucasian, 32 percent; Hispanic, 14 percent; American Indian, 1 percent; Asian, 1 percent; and ethnicity unknown, 6 percent).

California's welfare-supervised foster care caseload rose from 62,336 in 1989 to 87,010 in 1995 (See Appendix for a description of the data source). The prevalence rate (number of children in care per 1,000 children in California) grew from 8.2 in 1989 to 9.5 in 1995. Similar to national estimates, 37 percent of the children in foster care in California are under age six. A smaller proportion of the caseload in California is African American, and a larger proportion is Caucasian or Hispanic (African American, 37 percent; Caucasian, 36 percent; and Hispanic, 25 percent).

As shown in Figure 4.1, the growth in foster care is mirrored by an increase in the number of children placed with kin and in specialized foster care homes (SFC homes, also known as treatment foster care). The number of children in foster homes and group homes has not increased.

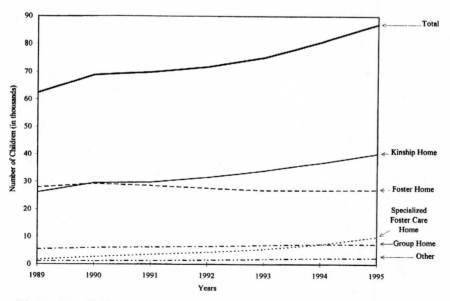

Figure 4.1 Children under age 18 in foster care, by type of placement in California

The growth in formal kinship care can be attributed to a number of factors (Courtney & Needell, 1997). Many child welfare agencies have taken steps to follow the policy mandate of P.L. 96-272 by promoting the support of children by family members. California law (S.B. 243) clarifies that kin are a placement of choice. Also, the dwindling number of non-related foster families has led many child welfare agencies to seek other types of placement. Last, the U.S. Supreme Court decision in *Miller v. Youakim* (1979) provided the basis for the federal government's reimbursement of foster care payments made by states and localities to kin in certain circumstances. Whether the state pays foster care funds to the kinship caregiver, a child in court-ordered kinship foster care is entitled to the same permanency protections as are other children. A look at one family whose relatives helped during troubled times exemplifies the important role that many relatives play in the foster care system.

Janice and Douglas

Renee, aged 15, and Kevin, aged 17, were both in high school when Renee gave birth to their baby, Janice. Renee and Kevin dropped out of school at the time and started collecting Aid to Families with Dependent Children (AFDC) to care for their new baby. Their rent was cheap, and some of their family members helped out, but tension was high between the two adolescents. Kevin was physically abusive to Renee and became agitated when Janice fussed. When Janice began to cry, Kevin would hit her out of anger and frustration. When Janice was four months old, Kevin beat her severely, telling Renee that he thought she was spoiling the baby. Renee fled with the baby to her aunt's home in an adjoining county, where they took Janice to the hospital for care. Medical personnel identified that the baby had a fractured skull and bruises across her body. Renee was reported to child protective services for child maltreatment because she had failed to protect her daughter.

Before the child welfare agency could send a social worker to investigate the case, Renee returned home to Kevin. When the social worker located Renee and saw Janice's injuries, she took the baby into custody. Janice was initially placed in an emergency foster home for eleven days; she was then transferred to a second emergency foster home for one day (for reasons that are not made clear in the case file) and was finally placed with her maternal grandmother.

When Janice was placed with her grandmother, Renee left Kevin and moved in with her older sister. Pregnant with her second child, she enrolled in an anger-management class and a parent education class, met with her social worker regularly, and frequently visited her daughter. About a month after Renee began to work on her reunification plan, the social worker who was attending to the case wrote in

Janice's case file that she seemed to be doing well:

The mother seems to have good bonding with the baby and seems to be re-
lating well to her. The minor appears to be relaxed, with fine grasping ability,
and appears to be in a normal developmental range.

While Renee was making progress in her case plan, Kevin had
more difficulties. He, too, was required to attend an anger-management class and a parenting class, to attend counseling, and to visit
Janice, but he did not comply with any of these demands. Instead, on
his only visit to see Janice, he became violent and broke down the
grandmother's door. Janice's grandmother reported the incident to
the police, and Kevin subsequently refrained from all contact with his
daughter.

Seven months after Janice was placed, Renee had a second child
whom she named Douglas. Renee's sister helped raise Douglas, and
Renee's mother encouraged her to visit Janice often. The social
worker arranged for Janice to stay with Renee on weekends under the
aunt's supervision, and these weekend visits became regular in time.
After fourteen months in care, Janice was returned to Renee. Renee,
Janice, and Douglas continued to live in her sister's home and to receive supervision from a social worker for an additional four months.

In the twenty-nine states with the ability to identify kinship care
placements, almost 80,000 children, or 31 percent of the foster children
in legal custody of the states, were placed with relatives in 1991 (Kusserow,
1992). These figures are likely to grow in light of federal mandates included in the Personal Responsibility and Work Opportunity
Reconciliation Act of 1996. This welfare reform bill requires states to consider relatives when making foster care placements; these requirements
will push states that have not yet embraced kin as a placement resource
to do so. In 1993, the percentages of days that children spent in kinship
care compared to all other child placements in California, Illinois, and
New York were 45, 54, and 36, respectively (Goerge, Wulczyn, & Harden,
1994). The use of kinship foster care varies greatly among localities. In
1994, two-thirds of the children in foster care in Baltimore were living
with kin, compared to 2 percent of the children in Norfolk, Virginia
(Curtis, Boyd, Liepold, & Petit, 1995). In 1995, 41 percent of the infants, 47 percent of the toddlers, and 53 percent of the preschoolers in
California's foster care caseload were living with kin (see Figure 4.2). The
merits of and problems associated with kinship care continue to stir debate (see Berrick & Barth, 1994, and Wilson & Chipungu, 1996, for reviews of recent research).

The use of SFC homes has also increased in the past few years—at
least in California. Whereas less than 3 percent of the children in

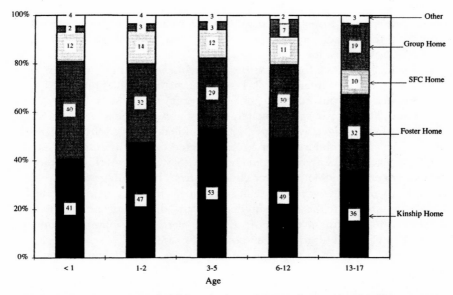

Figure 4.2 Percentage of children under age 18 in foster care in California in 1995, by type of placement

California's foster care caseload were in SFC homes in 1989, nearly 12 percent were in 1995. Moreover, in 1995, nearly one-third of all children in care in the 20 smallest California counties were in SFC homes. It is not clear what proportion of the children who are placed in SFC homes require the more intensive (and more expensive) services that these homes are supposed to provide or the extent to which the growth in the use of SFC homes is a reflection of a shortage of foster families who are willing to provide care at the state-paid rate.

In addition to kin and SFC placements, less than one-third of children in out-of-home care are in what has historically been thought of as foster care—living in foster homes with unrelated caregivers who have little or no training. Group care for young children is examined more fully in Chapter 5.

A prominent trend in foster care is the high proportion of infants in care. Infants are more likely to enter foster care than are children of any other age. Analyses of entries to foster care in five states—California, Illinois, Michigan, New York, and Texas—have shown that the proportion of new cases who were infants rose from about 16 percent in the mid-1980s to 24 percent in the early 1990s (Goerge et al., 1994). From 1989 to 1992, approximately one-fourth of the first entries to foster care in California were under age 1; the proportion decreased slightly to 22 percent in 1995. Toddlers (1–2 years) have consistently made up about 15 percent of the first entries in California. Preschoolers (3–5 years) have fluctuated around 18 percent; 6–12 year olds, about 29 percent; and teenagers, about 16 percent. Therefore, more than 55 percent of the children who entered foster care in 1995 were under age 6. These trends now seem to be stable, and we expect that young children will dominate entries to foster care for some time.

The incidence rate for first entries to care for infants in California was nearly 14 per 1,000 infants (or 1.4 percent) in the population in 1989, but dropped to about 10 per 1,000 (1 percent) in 1995, as Figure 4.3 illustrates. This rate is approximately three times the incidence rate for children of other ages. Three per 1,000 toddlers and preschoolers and about 2 per 1,000 children over age six entered care for the first time in 1995. In each of the five states in the Multi-State Data Archive studied by Goerge et al. (1994), younger children (from birth to age four) were more likely to enter foster care than were older children. Incidence rates have been shown to be much higher in some distressed communities. Wulczyn (1994), found that more than 10 percent of infants in some New York City neighborhoods entered foster care.

African American children, regardless of age, enter foster care at a much higher rate than do other children in each of the states in the Multi-State Data Archive. In California, at least, this is especially true for infants (Figure 4.4): Nearly 36 per 1,000 African American infants in the population entered care in 1995, compared to about 11 per 1,000 Caucasian infants and 6 per 1,000 Hispanic infants. Infants of other ethnic groups entered care at a much lower rate (approximately 2 per 1,000). The incidence rate for African American infants has been declining in the past few years, in that it was 46 per 1,000 in 1993, although the current rate is still alarmingly high.

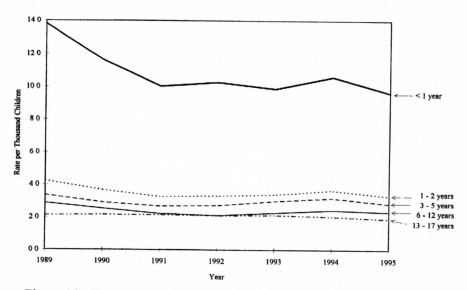

Figure 4.3 First entries to foster care in California by age (Incidence per 1,000 children)

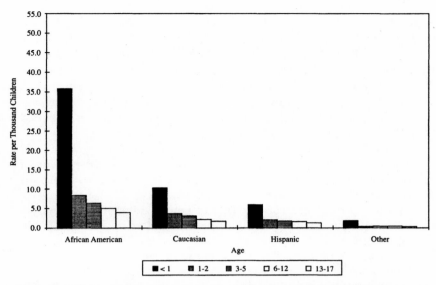

Figure 4.4 First entries to foster care in California in 1995 (Incidence per 1,000 children)

Because of these high incidence rates, many young children's lives are touched by the foster care system. By the time a child begins kindergarten, the chance that he or she has experienced foster care is substantial. Nearly 3 percent of all five year olds in California have been in foster care at some point since their birth, and over 10 percent of African American children! Foster care does not, then, represent a marginal degree of family problems; rather these data suggest that in some communities, rates of fundamental family disruption are high. That is, foster care is not isolated to individual children whose relationship with their parents has been disturbed, since children often come into care with their siblings. In California in 1995, about 70 percent of the children in kinship care and 55 percent of those in nonkin care were members of sibling groups in care. Over 25 percent of the children in kinship care and nearly 20 percent of those in nonkin care had at least three siblings in care.

Most young children who enter foster care have been removed from their homes for reasons that fall into the broad category of neglect. In 1995, neglect was the reason for 80 percent of the entries of children under age six, compared to 11 percent for physical abuse and 3 percent for sexual abuse. Relatively small proportions entered care because of exploitation, disability, voluntary placement, or relinquishment.

Exits from Foster Care

Kinship care. Although foster care is designed to be temporary, how temporary is it? In California, as shown in Figure 4.5, about half the infants who enter kinship care are still in their first spell of care after two years. (A spell is a continuous period in care and can involve one or more placements.) By four years, about one-third of the children placed as infants remain in care, and after six years, one-fourth have still not exited their first spell. About 10 percent of young children with kin exit to guardianship within six years. Six years after placement, only 11 percent of infants, 6 percent of toddlers, and 4 percent of preschoolers are adopted from kinship care (see Figures 4.5, 4.6, 4.7, and 4.8).

Nearly one-half (47 percent) of African American young children in kinship care are still in care after four years, and about 40 percent of African American young children are reunified, compared to about 60 percent of children from other ethnic groups.

More than one-third (35 percent) of young children who were removed from their families because of neglect and were placed with kin are still in care at four years. A smaller proportion of children who were removed because of physical or sexual abuse remain in care.

Some children who are placed in kinship care remain in care longer than others. In California, kin who care for children who are not eligible for federal Title IV-E (of the Social Security Act) foster care funds may receive welfare (AFDC or Temporary Assistance to Needy Families) to care for foster children. Children who are eligible for federal foster care payments and are placed with kin are much more likely to still be in care after four years than are those who are not eligible for federal funds (41 percent of the eligible children versus 25 percent of the not-eligible chil-

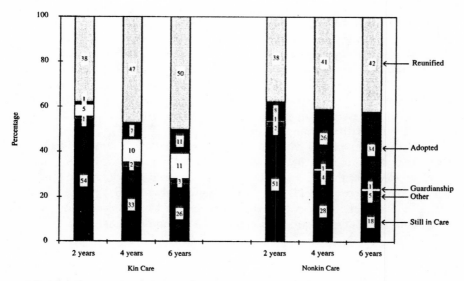

Figure 4.5 Exits from first spell of foster care in California at 2, 4, and 6 years (Children under 1 year at entry)

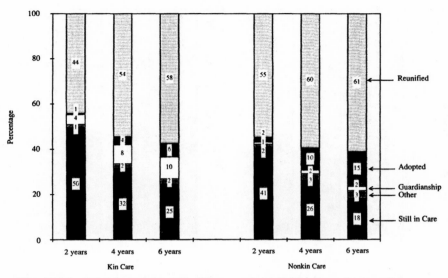

Figure 4.6 Exits from first spell of foster care in California at 2, 4, and 6 years (Children aged 1–2 years at entry)

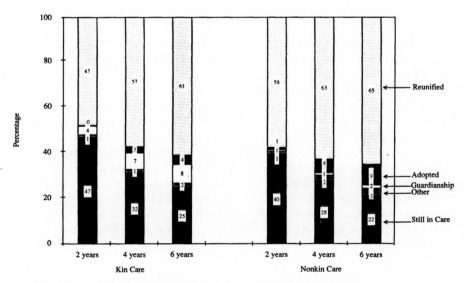

Figure 4.7 Exits from first spell of foster care in California at 2, 4, and 6 years (Children aged 3–5 years at entry)

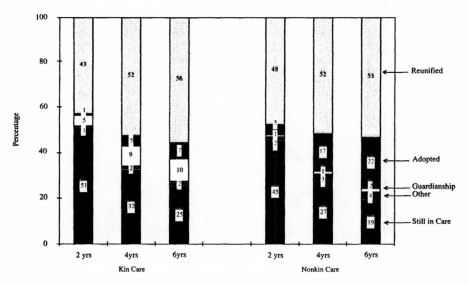

Figure 4.8 Exits from first spell of foster care in California at 2, 4, and 6 years (Children from birth to age 5 at entry)

dren in kinship care). Taken together, these findings suggest that when young children are placed in foster care with kin, they are not particularly likely to leave care via adoption, and their opportunities to leave foster care are highly dependent on their ages, ethnicity, the reasons they were placed in care, and whether their caregivers receive higher foster care subsidies or lower welfare payments.

Nonkin care. Like young children in kinship care, about half the infants who enter nonkin care are still in their first spell after two years. By four years, one-fourth remain in care, and after six years, nearly one-fifth. Like infants in kinship care, these infants are less likely than toddlers or preschoolers to go home, yet unlike those who are placed with kin, only about 1 percent of young children who are placed with nonkin exit to guardianship within six years. Since nonkin who assume guardianship may receive state-funded subsidies, some remain on the foster care rolls, receiving support and supervision. (Kin do not have this option in California.) Although reunification is unlikely after four years, many adoptions that do occur are finalized after this time. Six years after placement, more than 33 percent of the children who entered nonkin care as infants are adopted. For young children who enter after infancy, the likelihood of adoption is much lower; 15 percent of toddlers and 9 percent of preschoolers in nonkin care are adopted six years later.

More than a third (37 percent) of African American children in nonkin care are still there after four years, and reunification rates mirror those for African American young children in kinship care (about 40 percent).

Children who are placed in care because of neglect are more likely to still be in care (27 percent) than are children who are placed for other reasons.

Studies of children's length of stay in foster care and their various means of exit have, until recently, been plagued by severe methodological problems (see discussion in Barth, Courtney, Berrick, & Albert, 1994). In general, cross-sectional point-in-time studies (see, for example, Maas & Engler, 1959; Shyne & Schroeder, 1978), tend to overrepresent children who stay in care for a relatively long time. Other retrospective or longitudinal studies (like Fanshel & Shinn, 1978; Jenkins, 1967), while instructive, are of limited usefulness today because children in their samples were in care before the structural changes in foster care associated with P.L. 96-272.

Still, a brief mention of findings from Fanshel and Shinn's (1978) study is all but obligatory in any discussion of outcomes from foster care, since it remains the most comprehensive longitudinal study of foster care ever conducted and provides a benchmark for the performance of child welfare services for young children. The 624 New York City foster children in this study entered care in 1966, were under age 12 at entry, and were in care for at least ninety days. After five years, the children who were the youngest at entry (from birth to age 2 years old) were the most likely to still be in care. African American and Puerto Rican children were less likely to be discharged than were Caucasian children, and children who had been abandoned or neglected were less likely to be discharged than were children who were removed for other reasons. After identifying a subset of "adoptable" children (those who were aged 6 or younger at entry, whose mothers were unwilling to assume care, or for whom agency interviews indicated that adoption was a possibility), Fanshel and Shinn found that 16 percent had been adopted within five years, 42 percent had been discharged (presumably by returning home), and another 42 percent were still in care. Although 46 percent of the "adoptables" were under age 3 at entry, almost three-fourths of the children who were actually adopted were from this youngest group. However, 35 percent of the youngest group went home compared to 49 percent of the preschoolers. Therefore, age at entry for children younger than 6 years was not associated with remaining in care, since very young children were more likely to be adopted, while older (but still young) children were more likely to go home. This study highlights the importance of understanding the different caseload dynamics for children of different ages—and the likelihood that children of different ages may have similar lengths of stay for different reasons.

Other studies have found no association between age and outcomes from foster care. In a study of 185 foster children in the Children's Aid Society in Pennsylvania, Lawder, Poulin, and Andrews (1986) found no relationship between age and the likelihood of reunification. Benedict and White (1991) studied 689 foster children in Maryland who entered care between 1980 and 1983 and found no association between age at entry or ethnicity and length of stay. Placement with kin, developmental delays, and poor school grades were associated with longer lengths of stay, as were previous referrals to the child welfare system and the social workers' perception that the children's families needed to participate in parenting education and regular visits.

Some research indicates that the longer children remain in care, the less likely they are to return home at all. In a study of 1,196 foster children in Illinois who entered care between 1976 and 1984, Goerge (1990) found that the probability of reunification decreased over time and as the number of placements increased. Children who were 4 to 7 years old at entry were more likely to return home than were children of other age groups (although the youngest group was not restricted to infants, but included children from birth to age 3). Children placed in Cook County (Chicago), especially African American children, and those placed with kin were less likely to reunify than other children.

Using separate models for children in kin and nonkin care, Courtney (1994) found that infants and teenagers in nonkin care were less likely to go home than were children who entered care between ages one and thirteen, particularly if they were African American. Age was largely insignificant in the kin model, except for a decreased likelihood of reunification for Hispanic infants. Courtney considered eligibility for federal foster care funds a proxy for children's poverty prior to entry into foster care. Although he did not consider the interaction between type of placement and eligibility for federal funds directly, his separate kin and nonkin models indicated that eligibility was more strongly related to remaining in care for children who were placed with kin than for those placed with nonkin. (As was mentioned earlier, eligibility has an effect on whether kinship caregivers receive foster care funds, whereas nonkin providers are funded regardless of eligibility.) Overall, Courtney found that children who were placed with kin go home more slowly than those who were placed with nonkin, particularly in the first few months after placement.

Currently, children in California who enter foster care as infants stay in their first spell for a median of about two years, regardless of whether they are placed with kin or nonkin (see Figure 4.9). The median length of stay for toddlers and preschoolers who live with kin is somewhat shorter than it is for infants and is considerably shorter for those who live with nonkin. However, echoing Courtney's (1994) findings, young children who live with nonkin are much more likely to leave care quickly; for instance, it takes eight months for 25 percent of the toddlers who live with kin to leave care compared to only two months for those who live with nonkin).

In a study of 775 children who had been in foster care for at least six months in Arizona (McMurtry & Lie, 1992), age was not significantly associated with the likelihood of reunification, but increasing age was in-

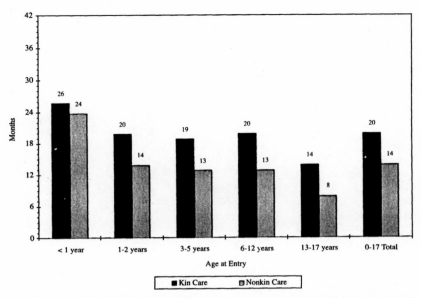

Figure 4.9 Median length of stay in foster care in California (by age at entry)

versely related to the likelihood of adoption. Since only about half the foster children in Arizona at the time of the study had stays longer than six months, it is not known how the inclusion of children with short stays in foster care would have altered the results. The main finding of this study was the much lower likelihood of reunification for African American children, regardless of age. Courtney and Wong (1996) further clarified the ways that selected variables contributed to distinct types of exit from care, using a "competing risks" partially parametric regression model (known as a proportional hazards model) to consider reunification, adoption, and running away for a sample of 8,625 children in foster care in California.

Goerge et al. (1994) considered hazard ratios associated with several variables on length of stay in California, Illinois, and New York. For all three states, infants were less likely to leave a first spell in care than were older children, as were children in kinship care and African American children compared to all other children.

Modeling exits from care. Drawing on Courtney and Wong's (1996) work, we examined the hazard ratios for reunification and adoption in California with a proportional hazards model. This approach offers a powerful way to examine the independent contribution of case characteristics to outcomes. Risk ratios larger than 1 suggest a greater likelihood of the outcome (reunification, adoption, other) for children in that category compared to the reference group (see Table 4.1).

Table 4.1 Hazard Ratios for Reunification, Adoption, and Other Exits in California ($n = 58,057$)

Variable	Reunification	Adoption	Other
Age at Entry			
Age less than 1	*1.00*	*1.00*	*1.00*
Age 1–2	1.39	0.42	0.80
Age 3–5	1.35	0.23	0.75
Ethnicity			
Caucasian	*1.00*	*1.00*	*1.00*
African American	0.74	0.37	0.95 NS*
Hispanic	1.02 NS*	0.81	1.19
Other	0.99 NS*	0.74	1.30 NS*
Reason for Removal			
Neglect	*1.00*	*1.00*	*1.00*
Physical abuse	1.40	0.87	0.95 NS*
Sexual abuse	1.47	0.88 NS*	1.36
Other	1.22	3.17	1.23 NS*
Primary Placement**			
Nonkin	*1.00*	*1.00*	*1.00*
Kin—IV-E eligible	0.96	0.20	0.72
Kin—Not eligible	1.27	0.71	0.74
Size of County			
Large	*1.00*	*1.00*	*1.00*
Small	1.27	0.52	1.72
Los Angeles	0.76	0.27***	0.78

Note: Reunification: 29,236 events, -2LL model chi-square = 3316.955 12 df ($p = .0001$). Adoption: 6,005 events, -2LL model chi-square = 7026.433, 12 df, ($p = .0001$). Other Exit: 1,430 events, -2LL model chi-square = 109.858, 12 df, ($p = .0001$).
*NS = $p > .05$.
**time varying variable: Kin—IV-E eligible usually receive the AFDC Foster Care subsidy; Kin—Not eligible usually receive AFDC/TANF (welfare).
***Los Angeles County does not record many of their adoptions in FCIS—according to other adoption sources—so the true odds ratio is almost certainly larger.
Italics denote reference categories.

Reunification. Infants were less likely to be reunified than were children who entered care between the ages of one and six. Controlling for age, reason for removal, type of placement, and size of county, we found that young African American children were less likely to be reunified than were Caucasian children and that there were no significant differences in the likelihood of reunification for Hispanic or "other" children compared to Caucasian children. Children who were removed for neglect were less likely to be reunified than were children who were removed for all other reasons. Children in kinship homes who were eligible for federal foster care (Title IV-E) funds were less likely to be reunified than were those who were not receiving foster care payments (not eligible for federal funds). Reunification was less likely for young children in Los Angeles County than in the other thirty-seven large California counties and was most likely for children in the twenty smaller counties.

Adoption. Caucasian children were more likely to be adopted than all other children. African American children were only about one-third as likely to be adopted as Caucasian children, and Hispanic children were 80 percent as likely, controlling for other factors. Neglected children were somewhat more likely to be adopted than were physically or sexually abused children. A small number of children who were removed for other reasons (primarily voluntary placements or relinquishments) were much more likely to be adopted than were other children. The type of placement and eligibility for federal funds had a large effect on the likelihood of adoption. Children in kinship homes were less likely to be adopted than those in nonkin homes, particularly if they were eligible for federal foster care funds while in care. Children who were eligible for federal funds were less than one-third as likely to be adopted as were noneligible children in kin homes and were one-fifth as likely to be adopted as children in nonkin homes.

Our review of the factors associated with reunification and adoption highlights the importance of age in work with children. Neglected infants appear to be particularly challenging, yet these are the children who are most likely to come to the attention of child welfare workers.

Reentry to Foster Care

Reunification of children and their biological parents can usually be considered a successful outcome only if they are not subject to abuse and/or neglect following their return home. The few studies on reentry to foster care that have been done have found that 15–30 percent of children who are reunified come back into foster care at some point and that children who experience short first spells in care have the highest rates of reentry (see Rzepnicki, 1987). Shorter stays in foster care appear to be related to higher likelihoods of reentry. In a study that examined caseload dynamics of children in New York's foster care system between 1984 and 1986, Wulczyn (1991) found that children who were discharged from care within ninety days were more likely to reenter than were other children. (Children who were first placed when they were between ages ten and twelve had the highest reentry rate.) Festinger (1994) reported that limited parental skills (such as problems communicating with children, understanding child development, and handling discipline) and less support from family members, friends, and neighbors were the strongest predictors of reentry for 254 children who had been reunified with their families in New York City. The study included only children who had been in care for at least two months and who were younger than fifteen when they left care; the reentry rate was 13 percent within a year of discharge. Age alone was not significantly associated with reentry, but children aged six or older who had caregivers at home with at least two problems were more likely to reenter than were all other children (younger children regardless of caregivers' problems, or older children with caregivers who had no more than one problem).

Some research has suggested that infants are more likely to reenter care than are older children. Using a large sample of children in California who had been returned to their families from foster care, Courtney (1995) found an association between exiting care as an infant and a higher hazard of reentry after controlling for type of placement, ethnicity, health problems, eligibility for federal foster care funds, number of placements, and time in care before discharge. However, the only age group with a significantly lower risk of reentry than infants was the group that exited from age seven to twelve. Children who had been in care for three months or less before reunification were more likely to reenter than were children with longer first spells in care. Courtney also reported that eligibility for federal funds increased the likelihood of reentry, while placement with kin (rather than in foster or group care) was associated with lower reentry rates. The analysis did not consider the interaction between type of placement and eligibility for federal foster care funds.

We used event-history analysis to study reentry to a second spell in foster care for children who had left their first spell in care via reunification. Children who were returned home from kinship care appeared to be less likely to reenter than were those who spent all or most of their first spell in nonkin care (Figure 4.10). Infants and toddlers were more likely to reenter than were older children; an estimated 19 percent of young children who were placed with kin and 28 percent of those who had been with nonkin reentered care within three years of returning home. For children who went home between the ages of three and five, 16 percent of those who had been with kin and 25 percent of those who had been with nonkin reentered foster care. Young children who reenter foster care often have prolonged stays at home before they come back into care; at three years after reunification, the cumulative probability of reentry is more than double what it was six months after children return home.

Modeling reentry. Statistical models that simultaneously control for several factors help explain the complexity of reentry to the foster care system. Ethnic group membership, age category at exit, reason for removal, primary placement and type of funding, and size of county in the first spell were included in a reentry model (see Table 4.2).

Children who were infants or toddlers when they left foster care were slightly more likely to reenter care than were children who left care between three and five years old. Being African American slightly increased

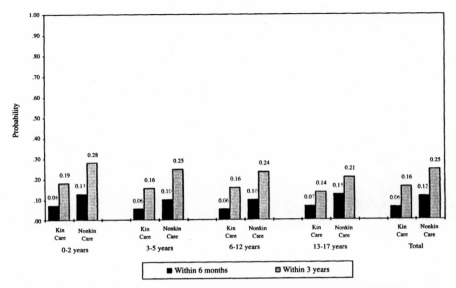

Figure 4.10 Cumulative probability of reentry to foster care for children in California who were returned home from first spell (by age at exit)

the probability of reentry compared to being Caucasian, while being Hispanic or "other" ethnicity lowered it. Neglected children were considerably more likely to reenter than were children who were removed for other reasons. Children who spent less than six months in care in a first spell were more likely to reenter than were those who had longer first spells. Children who had been in kinship homes without federal foster care funds were much less likely to reenter than were either those who lived with kin and had federal funds or those who lived with nonkin. In other words, the protective effect of kinship care against reentry, seen at the bivariate level, was apparent only for children who were not receiving federal foster care funds in the multivariate model. Two possible explanations for this finding are that the families of the children from nonfederally eligible homes have more resources to ease reunification or that there is more financial incentive for the kin of federally eligible children to resume care of their children.

Courtney and Piliavin (1996) explored the issue of how the characteristics of children who go home—as opposed to those who remain in care—may influence estimates of the likelihood of reentry to foster care. The bivariate probit method they used included a model of reunification before the reentry model. Their findings suggest that children who leave foster care as infants are not more likely to reenter than are older children, and there are no significant differences in reentry by ethnicity, when sample selection bias is controlled for in this manner.

Table 4.2   Hazard Ratios for Reentering Care Following Reunification
in California ($n = 37,455$)

Variable	Reentry
Age at Reunification	
Age 0–2	1.00
Age 3–5	0.93
Ethnicity	
Caucasian	1.00
African American	1.09
Hispanic	0.82
Other	0.85
Reason for Removal	
Neglect	1.00
Physical abuse	0.64
Sexual abuse	0.64
Other	0.76
Length of Time in First Spell	
Less than Six Months	1.00
Six Months–two years	0.83
More than two years	0.59
Primary Placement*	
Nonkin	1.00
Kin—IV-E eligible	1.01NS**
Kin—Not eligible	0.43
County Size	
Large	1.00
Small	1.15 NS**
Los Angeles	0.97 NS**

Note: Reentry—7,125 events, -2LL model chi-square = 1034.396 13 df ($p = .0001$)
*Kin—IV-E eligible usually receive the AFDC Foster Care subsidy; Kin—Not eligible usually receive AFDC/TANF (welfare).
**$NS = p > .05$.
†Italics denote reference categories.

Stability of Placement

An important element of permanency planning is reducing children's moves from residence to residence, yet this topic is little studied. Prior to the Adoption Assistance and Child Welfare Act of 1980, at least two studies determined that the instability of foster care placements was considerable. After examining all children in care, Wald (1976) estimated that half the foster children had more than one placement and one-fifth had three or more placements. Knitzer and Allen (1978) found a high degree of unstable placements and showed that approximately 30 percent of the children they studied had moved three or more times while in care. One of the goals of the landmark federal legislation was to reduce children's experience of instability by offering permanence within strict time frames. Yet estimates from the Voluntary Cooperative Information System, conducted by the American Public Welfare Association, representing 15 states nationwide, indicated that little has changed: More than 57 percent of the children in care at the end of fiscal year 1990 had multiple placements during the previous three years, and nearly 30 percent had three or more placements (U.S. House of Representatives, 1994).

When young children are involved, moves from caregiver to caregiver may be particularly problematic. To examine the stability of these youngsters' placements, we concentrated on children who remained in a first foster care spell for two, four, and six years in all California counties excluding Los Angeles (see the Appendix for an explanation). Children with kinship care as their primary placement had significantly more-stable placement experiences than did children who were placed with nonkin. Considering age at entry, only 20 percent of the infants, 24 percent of the toddlers, and 21 percent of three to five year olds had been in three or more homes after two years in kin care (Figures 4.11–4.14). In addition, most of the moves that occured for children in kinship care were either from a nonkin placement to a relative's home or from one relative's home to another. Although moves are often disruptive, changes of placements among relatives may be different and less traumatic for a child than moves from one stranger to another.

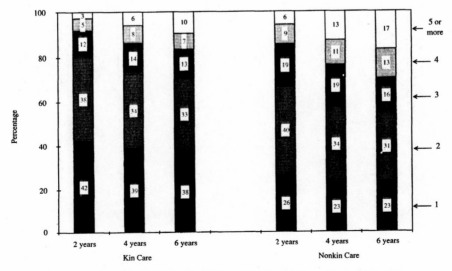

Figure 4.11 Number of placements for children under 1 year old at entry who were still in care in California at 2, 4, and 6 years

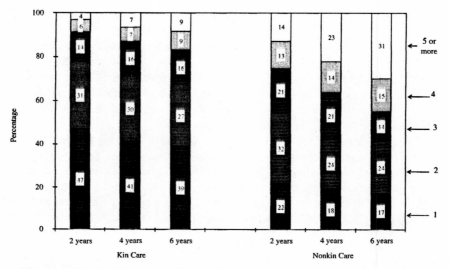

Figure 4.12 Number of placements for children aged 1–2 at entry who were still in care in California at 2, 4, and 6 years

In contrast, children in long-term foster care with nonkin were much more likely to have been in at least three different homes after two years (34 percent of the infants, 48 percent of the toddlers, and 49 percent of the three to five year olds). For young children who are growing up in foster care—that is, those who have been in a first spell for at least six

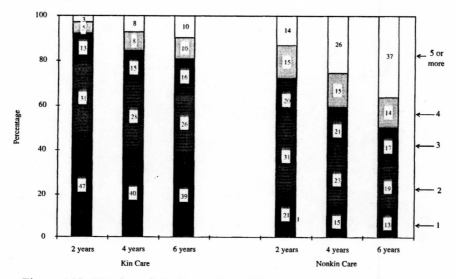

Figure 4.13 Number of placements for children aged 3–5 at entry who were still in care in California at 2, 4, and 6 years

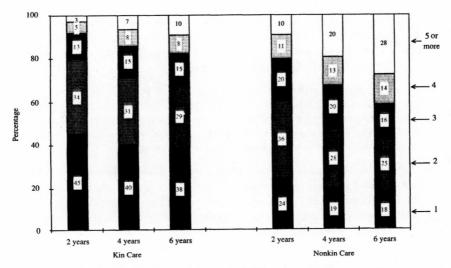

Figure 4.14 Number of placements for children from birth to age 5 at entry who were still in care in California at 2, 4, and 6 years

years—moves from one placement to another continue well beyond the two years when permanent long-term foster placement was apparently the court-ordered permanent plan. This occurs especially with children who are placed with nonkin. For children in nonkin care, 46 percent of the infants, 60 percent of the toddlers, and 68 percent of the preschoolers had at least three placements. In fact, 31 percent of the children who entered nonkin care as toddlers and 37 percent of those who entered as preschoolers had five or more placements within six years! These data make it clear that we should not allow inertia or sentiment to interfere with a child's need for a permanent *exit* from foster care by permitting long-term foster care to be a permanent plan. Long-term permanent foster care is an oxymoron.

Discussion

Infants enter foster care at a much higher rate than do older children and find themselves in a system that was not designed with them in mind. Until recently, the average age of children in foster care was dropping annually in California and in several other large states (Goerge et al., 1994). Now, many children who entered care at or shortly after birth are growing up in foster care—a situation that is again raising the average age of children served by this system. Furthermore, an estimated 10 percent of African American children have a brush with foster care before they enter kindergarten. Therefore, child welfare has become an essential program—one that touches the lives of a larger proportion of the population than was once thought. Placement rates such as these must be examined critically as an indicator of significant social and family disruption. Studying New York's foster care system, Wulczyn (1994, p. 181) sensitively portrayed the implications of high placement rates:

> [C]hild placement represents a fundamental break in the continuity of the traditional parent-child relationship much like the dissolution of two-parent families into single-parent families. When viewed as part of the changes transforming the family experience of American children, the placement trends observed in the past few years take on an added significance.

Family dissolution, at the rate seen in many California communities, is alarming and is likely to worsen as social services are cut, community economics worsen, family structure places greater burdens on single mothers, and substance abuse remains a dominant escape from deteriorating neighborhoods.

While thousands of children may find themselves part of the foster care caseload, many are placed with relatives, including grandparents, aunts, and uncles. Children who are placed with kin may have a different kind of placement experience. They may also have distinct outcomes in the child welfare system, partly because of the structural limitations in the current law (Berrick, Needell, & Barth, 1995).

The findings presented in this chapter tell only part of the story of young children in foster care. Along with the case outcomes we measured, there are other important indicators of child welfare performance. In particular, our analyses lack data on children's health and development, which some would argue are the most critical indicators of programmatic success or failure. However, few would contest that safe reunifications, adoptions, and stable placements are better for young children and their developmental progress than are lengthy spells in nonkin foster care, multiple placements, and reentry. Yet, the latter are common occurrences in the foster care system.

Summary of Key Findings and Recommendations Regarding Foster Care, Reunification, and Adoption

Finding	*Recommendation*
4.1. The foster care caseload is increasing because there are fewer exits from than entries into care each year.	4.1. Three related but distinct issues must be tackled to reduce the foster care caseload. Prevention and early intervention services must be improved to lower the number of children who require removal from home, the number of children exiting foster care must be increased via enhanced reunification and adoption efforts, and the number of children reentering care following reunification must be de-

creased, perhaps by continuing comprehensive services for a period following reunification.

Finding	*Recommendation*
4.2. The considerably elevated incidence and prevalence rates for African American children, far above differences that can be explained by poverty or type of placement, are major sources of concern. African American children are dramatically more likely to enter and stay in care longer; are less likely to be reunified, adopted, or placed in guardianship; and are more likely to reenter care than are Caucasian or Hispanic children. Our multivariate analyses demonstrated that African American children have much poorer outcomes than other children, even when other key predictors (such as age and kin versus nonkin placement) are held constant.	4.2. More research is needed to explore the reasons for the disparities between African American children and other children. The interplay of factors contributing to higher rates of service use also suggests that intensive and lasting interventions may be needed to protect African American children. Foster care is, of course, embedded in a society that is still struggling with enormous racial inequalities. Still, it is imperative that we understand the reasons why the child welfare service system is failing African American young children and work to revise policy and practice so, at a minimum, they do not increase the disparities.

Finding	*Recommendation*
4.3. Kinship care is the placement of choice for a higher proportion of children each year. Children who are placed with their relatives are less likely to be adopted than are those placed with nonkin. Kinship placements also appear to be more stable than do other placements. For children in kinship care, federal eligibility for foster care funds is associated with longer stays in care and higher reentry rates.	4.3. Since the foster care system was not designed with kinship caregivers in mind, practice and policy need to evolve so they can adequately address the needs of kinship families. Kinship care is not the same as foster care, and policies and programs that were specifically designed to promote permanence in the extended family system are needed. Kinship parents should be able to exit the dependency system when there is no longer an issue of child protection that requires monitoring. Developing alternatives for children to leave foster care to live with their kin caregivers without a reduction in monthly subsidies will ensure greater permanence for children outside the child welfare system.

Finding	*Recommendation*
4.4. Too many (about one-fourth) young children who are placed in nonkin foster care remain in care permanently.	4.4. Foster care should be time limited for almost all young children. Barriers to reunification, guardianship, and adoption, whether socioeco-

nomic, systemic within the child welfare service system, or political, must be dismantled. In addition to six-month court reviews, administrative reviews should be made at three-month intervals for all cases involving young children to expedite permanence.

Finding	*Recommendation*
4.5. Children who are removed from their biological families as infants are less likely to return home and are much more likely to be adopted than are other young children.	4.5. More intensive efforts to reunify families (including the greater length and frequency of visits) may be required to increase reunification rates for infants and parents. In addition, greater emphasis should be placed on adoption for toddlers and preschool-aged children. Lessons from agencies that provide special-needs adoption services may be instructive for public child welfare agencies.

Finding	*Recommendation*
4.6. Most young children in foster care have been removed from home because of parental neglect. Neglected children are less likely to go home and are more likely to come back into care than are children who have been physically or sexually abused.	4.6. We believe that neglect is strongly associated with substance abuse in many families. Therefore multidisciplinary collaboration between child welfare and the drug and alcohol service community is essential to make an impact on the tenacious hold that substance abuse can have on many parents. Developing an array of treatment methods that work with substance-involved families is one of the greatest challenges of the service delivery system.

Finding	*Recommendation*
4.7. Young children often have lengthy stays in care. The median length of stay is well over one year.	4.7. At this critical juncture in life, healthy development is essential for young children. Child welfare agencies should identify early childhood specialists on their staffs who are available to provide consultation regarding placement, case planning, and specialized developmental enhancement services for young children, including Head Start and early intervention under Part B of The Individuals with Disabilities Education Act, as amended (P.L. 99-457).

Finding	Recommendation
4.8. Multiple placements are common for even the youngest children in nonkin foster care.	4.8. Placement moves may be damaging to young children. Caregivers should be trained so they are prepared for the types of issues that abused and neglected young children bring with them to care. Emergency shelter placements should be short (one month or less), so that workers have time to assess children adequately and place them in what should be their final foster care placement.

5

Group Care

Steve and Ron

When Steve was born in 1988 to Barbara and Tom, he tested positive for cocaine, but the social worker who was assigned to the case determined that there was insufficient risk to the baby for child welfare services to be provided to him and his parents. Barbara and Tom had an extensive family support network, and when family members were contacted by the child welfare agency, Steve's paternal grandmother and maternal aunt stepped forward to offer their help and support.

A year later, Barbara gave birth to Ron. He, too, tested positive for cocaine, but the agency again declined to provide services for the family. Barbara was fourteen years old when she gave birth to Steve, and Tom was twenty. Neither were employed, neither had graduated from high school, and Tom had already developed an extensive arrest record.

A year after Ron was born, Barbara brought him to the Eastside Children's Hospital because he was having severe seizures and drifted in and out of consciousness. When questioned about her child's condition, she claimed that she could not comprehend his behavior. According to her, she had been driving her car, when Ron "slumped over in his car seat" and lost consciousness. Medical tests determined that Ron was suffering from a drug overdose of cocaine; his mother also tested for high quantities of cocaine in her body. Doctors were able to revive Ron after they pumped his stomach, but he was immediately placed on a police hold and was not returned to his mother.

Adapted from Group Care and Young Children, *Social Service Review*, 1997, v. 71, n. 2, University of Chicago, with permission. © 1997 by the University of Chicago. All rights reserved.

The police arrived at Barbara and Tom's home shortly after the hospital incident and removed Steve. Both children were placed in protective custody in an emergency foster home.

Shortly after Ron and Steve were placed in care, both were moved to their paternal grandmother's home. Mrs. Young was concerned about the children's well-being and was determined to offer them a "better" home than their parents'. She cared for the two young boys for the next four years. During that time, Barbara and Tom did not comply with any of the stipulations in their case plan. Neither submitted to drug testing, enrolled in a drug treatment program, attended parenting classes, kept in contact with the social worker, nor visited the children. Over the course of their four-year placement, the children were visited by their parents no more than a handful of times.

During the permanency planning hearing, the judge determined that the children would remain in long-term foster care. The children's placement with Mrs. Young was stable and loving, and it was evident that the two would not return to either of their parents. The child welfare worker initially recommended that Mrs. Young be granted legal guardianship for the two boys, but after discussions with her supervisor, she recommended that the boys remain in long-term foster care. The children's case file indicates that although the worker was aware of Mrs. Young's significant commitment to the children, she also had concerns that had not yet been addressed. Mrs. Young was collecting Supplemental Security Income owing to alcoholism, although she told the worker that she was no longer drinking. And several of Mrs. Young's relatives, who frequently stayed at her home, had committed serious criminal offenses. These issues and others pointed to the importance of maintaining supervision through long-term foster care, so the children might be afforded somewhat more protection and oversight than they would receive under legal guardianship.

In 1994, the boys' behavior began to grow increasingly difficult. The boys' social worker was called early in the year by another social worker assigned to Steve's school. The school social worker indicated that in kindergarten, Steve was "constantly in motion," had "an inability to focus," had "kicked a teacher," and had threatened another child by making "stabbing motions with scissors." Ron was too young for school and was on a waiting list for the local Head Start program, but his behavior was equally difficult. His social worker's assessment of his behavior was as follows: "Ron's behavior is very difficult. He constantly touches and pulls everything in sight. He hits walls and his speech is extremely difficult to understand. The children bite and fight with each other frequently." Shortly after the social worker wrote these observations in the children's case file, Mrs. Young's apartment was destroyed by fire. She claimed that the fire was due to an electrical problem, but the apartment manager insisted that one or both boys had started the fire in their bedroom. (Mrs. Young was subsequently assessed $35,000 to pay for the damage and was billed monthly.)

The boys' behavior was indeed challenging, but the child welfare worker was surprised when Mrs. Young called her two days after Christmas. Mrs. Young said that she could no longer control the boys and that they must be removed immediately; the social worker did so that afternoon. Because of the immediacy of the issue, Steve and Ron were placed in two separate emergency group homes, Golden West and Sunshine House. There was no time for a thorough assessment or a careful match between the boys' needs and the various placement alternatives in the community. It was the middle of a long holiday week, and few staff were even working in the office. Thus, no effort was made to find a county foster home or a specialized foster home to care for the two boys. Instead, the boys were placed in two group homes, each of which had one bed available. The boys remained in their respective group homes for the next two months.

A specialized placement worker reviewed the boys' cases and selected a new placement for both children. Steve was sent to New Hope group home, and Ron was sent to Opportunity Place—a group home in a nearby city. It does not appear from the case file that the worker attempted to locate a suitable foster home or specialized foster home for either boy. Steve's assessment form for New Hope read as follows:

Steve has a history of fire setting, destroying property, stealing and aggressively acting out in school. He interacts negatively with peers, throws things at them, spits at them, hits them without provocation, and attempted to urinate on another students' leg.

The case file went on to state that Steve suffered from hyperactivity and extreme distractibility; exhibited unprovoked, negative, and aggressive behaviors toward adults; may have sexually molested a peer; and showed no remorse for his actions. He was, according to his case file, "defiant, rebellious, and unwilling to follow instructions."

At age five, Ron's assessment differed little from his brother's. His case file at Opportunity Place noted:

The minor's behaviors include fire setting, climbing on furniture, running away, poor impulse control, aggressiveness with peers, prolonged tantruming (sic), inability to tolerate limits, and problems in school. [The child has] low self-esteem and requires one-on-one supervision. He engages in high-risk behavior, for example, trying to jump out of a moving car going 55 miles an hour.

The semiannual court reports, completed by social workers at both of the group homes, suggested few changes for these boys over time. Both were placed on medications shortly after their placement, yet according to social workers, the effectiveness of these drugs is not clear. Some months the boys seemed to do better than others, but overall, the social workers' case reports indicate a high degree of concern about these children's well-being.

Two years after their initial placement, both children are still in their group homes. Steve is now a rapidly growing eight year old, and Ron is seven. Ron, in particular, appears to have developmental delays in addition to his behavioral problems; he has much to catch up on in his short life.

Neither Ron nor Steve's behavior has improved considerably since they were placed even though both children receive therapy weekly, are in special recreation programs, are enrolled in special education classes, and are in homes with a small staff-to-child ratio. The cost of Steve's care while living at New Hope is approximately $4,100 per month (not including non-public school costs, funded by the local school district), and Opportunity Place receives about $3,000 a month for Ron's care.

Until recently, the boys were reunited at their grandmother's home twice a month for weekend visits. For some time, Mrs. Young also visited them regularly in their group homes, stating her wish that they might one day return to her home. But Mrs. Young was reluctant to bring them home too soon. She knew that the boys were a handful—about a year ago, the boys began stealing from her during their home visits and she threatened never to take them again—and she was concerned about her ability to care for them well. Her concerns were well founded. About six months ago, Mrs. Young had a stroke. She is gradually recovering, but it seems unlikely that Ron and Steve will be able to return to her care.

It is unlikely that the boys will be able to return to their parents, either. The boys' father was released from prison some months ago and visited the boys at their grandmother's home. Shortly thereafter, he was arrested and again imprisoned. Barbara last visited her boys about two years ago. With a new baby in her arms, she appeared reserved and did not touch the youngsters. Steve was keenly interested in his half-sister, but Ron ignored both his mother and his half-sister. Since that time, Barbara has not attempted to make contact with her sons. Whether these boys will remain in their group homes until they are released at age eighteen is uncertain. If they do, the cost of their care may approach $1 million.

As we discussed in earlier chapters, young children now dominate the child welfare caseload and the majority of out-of-home placements are made to relatives (kinship care) and to foster family homes. Of those in nonkin care, a small but substantial group of young children are placed in group or congregate care.

The number of young children who are placed in group care, though limited compared to children placed in foster care, is not a trivial matter from a philosophical standpoint, nor is it inconsequential to the children in these settings. The Adoption Assistance and Child Welfare Act of 1980 (P.L. 96-272) laid out certain philosophical constructs for developing child welfare practice and principles; among them was the standard of using the least restrictive, most family-like setting when making a foster care placement. Kinship foster care clearly fits this guideline, since no setting can be more family-like than family itself. Foster family care is the second-best alternative for children whose relatives are not able or willing to care for them. But congregate care stretches the conventional wisdom of "least restrictive" and "family-like"; particularly when young children are involved, group care should be viewed with a critical eye as to its capacity to achieve the fundamental goals of the child welfare system: to protect children from harm, to support families, and to promote lifetime permanence of care.

The debate over the merits of group care has long been an undercurrent in the child welfare literature (Ashby, 1984; Lerman, 1982; Wolins & Piliavin, 1969). According to Fanshel, Finch, and Grundy (1990), group care should generally be avoided. As they stated: "The least desirable outcome is a group care placement, the placement of last resort and essentially a failure of the system" (p. 110). But many scholars and professionals in the child welfare community have noted that group care is best used as one of several placement alternatives; they have suggested that it should be used sparingly for adolescents, severely emotionally disturbed children, and children who are otherwise difficult to place (Wells, 1993). However, Zeitz (1969, p. 71) described group care as an advantage for some children under specifically circumscribed conditions:

> The institutional community provides the child with opportunities to work through many problems and manifest various kinds of behavior that would not be permissible in most foster homes. Since these are children who have been damaged by emotional deprivation and rejection, they have need for warm but casual relationships with a variety of adults in whom they can find continuous acceptance.

These conditions are less likely for young children. Whether any young child would benefit from "warm but casual relationships" is highly questionable.

Group care has often been used when there are crises in placements, particularly after wars or epidemics have left thousands of children without parents (Costello, 1995). Today, the crisis is less obvious. The placement of young children in group care may be driven by higher foster care caseloads, fewer available foster parents, or an increase in the specialized needs of young children.

There is little empirical evidence to confirm or disconfirm the notion that young children may be better off in placements other than group care. Data on the long-term outcomes of children who were raised in the child welfare system are sparse, in general. No studies have been conducted that have *definitively* found differences in outcomes on the basis of type of placement. Instead, differences that have been seen in the outcomes of children placed in group care as opposed to foster family care often have not been differentiated according to the levels of behavioral, emotional, or psychological problems the children had upon entering care. Similarly, the data have not indicated the types of home environments or abuse the children sustained before placement (McDonald, Allen, Westerfelt, & Piliavin, 1993). These significant caveats aside, as we discussed in Chapter 1, most studies point to somewhat more negative effects for children who spend all or part of their childhoods in group care settings as opposed to children who are cared for in foster homes.

Whether group care placements for young children are right or wrong may depend on one's philosophical perspective, one's view of developmental theory, or the actual outcomes measured during care. The following is an attempt to analyze the placement experiences of young children in group care versus foster family care in California. These findings also have implications for other states that allow young children to be placed in congregate settings.

Group Care for Children in California

Group care accounts for a relatively small proportion of all out-of-home placements. Since 1988, the group care population has been relatively stable, averaging approximately 9 percent of the total placements annually. However, the cost of these placements is high. In 1994, the median monthly payment for young children in group care was $4,091, compared to the standard rate for young children in foster family care of about $360. While group care represents a small proportion of all placements, it consumes a large proportion of the foster care budget.

As might be expected, the majority of children in group care are adolescents, aged thirteen to seventeen. But a surprising number of young children are also placed in group care. As Figure 5.1 shows, the growth in the use of this placement alternative for young children peaked in 1989, decreased, and then held steady for the remainder of our study period (see the Appendix for a description of the methods used to obtain this information). From 1989 to 1995, young children under age six made up 13 percent to 18 percent of the total group care population in California.

Concern about the growth of group care for young children was recognized by the California state legislature in 1993, and as a result, legislation was introduced to curb its use. Assembly Bill 1197 (AB 1197, Chapter 1088, Statutes of 1993) directed counties to minimize the use of group care for young children and provided guidelines regarding the length of stay for these children once such placements were made. The legislation allowed for 60-day placements, with extensions under certain conditions up to 120 days. But did this law have the intended effect? Analyses of 1995 data do not show a decrease in the use of group care

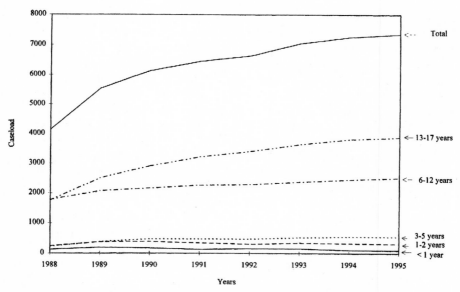

Figure 5.1 Group care caseload in California by age of child (on July 1 for each year)

for young children, as the legislation might have indicated. Recently, a youth advocacy agency filed a law suit against the California Department of Social Services for failing to develop standards for young children who are placed in group care. The advocates in this case highlighted the disparities in regulations for infants placed in group care and in regular day care, citing, for example, staffing ratios for infants in day care of 1:4 compared to staffing ratios for infants in group care of 1:10. Similarly, although feeding schedules for infants in day care are regular and frequent, those in group care settings are not specified; if group home operators were so inclined, they would not be required to feed infants more frequently than once every 15 hours (Moore, 1996).

Unless the utilization of group care for young children diminishes considerably in the next few years, these trends should be examined carefully against the conventional standards of child welfare practice. If young children are placed in group care settings, these arrangements should be sufficiently more effective than foster family care in protecting their physical well-being, supporting their growth and development, and offering stability of caregiving. They should also be judged by their ability to facilitate permanence for young children—through more rapid reunification with biological parents, expedited adoptions, and lower rates of reentry to care. If group care is not demonstrably more protective and facilitative of permanency, child welfare professionals should actively guard against the use of this expensive placement resource for youngsters through policy, administrative regulations, or restrained practice.

Protection

Physical well-being. As was shown in earlier chapters, the large majority of children who are taken into protective custody in California and most other states are placed because of reasons associated with general neglect, severe neglect, or the absence or incapacity of caregivers. Age is related to the reasons for placement. Young children are more likely to be placed because of neglect, but there are no differences between children placed in group care or foster care. As children age, they are more likely to be removed for reasons associated with physical abuse and sexual abuse, but again, differences in type of placement are not apparent.

Data on the extent to which the category neglect may mask other factors are limited. For example, the data do not indicate the extent to which children may be medically compromised because of prenatal exposure to drugs or other medical conditions, so we can not determine whether young children who are placed in group care settings are more fragile, on average, than children who are placed in foster family homes and therefore may need the higher level of protective supervision afforded by around-the-clock staffing. A critical piece of data, missing from most administrative data systems, would indicate the severity and duration of children's maltreatment prior to placement. Without this information, the broad indicators of neglect, physical abuse, and sexual abuse provide the best window into the circumstances that brought these children to the attention of child welfare authorities.

We do not know whether children who reside in group care are better protected from harm than those who are placed in foster care. The only available proxy for this information—quality of care—can be examined in the general child welfare literature to consider the protection afforded to children in various types of placements. Colton (1990) compared specialized foster homes with group care facilities in Great Britain, examining each facility's orientation to children or institutionally oriented practices and environments. The study reviewed the home environment, routine, disciplinary practices, and community involvement of twelve specialized foster homes and twelve residential homes. Although staff in both settings were child oriented in their outlook, these attitudes were not adequately translated in the group home settings. Specialized foster homes scored well above group homes in their ability to communicate a child orientation to the children. The sample for the study was small and the children studied were over age twelve, but the findings may point to differences in facilities that may be found for younger children as well, even when the group care setting is developed with young children in mind.

Cohen's (1986) small-scale study of group homes in Los Angeles showed that congregate care offered basic supervision and care, but that the overall quality of the homes (as characterized by the administrators) was either "fair" or "poor." Cohen found that the cost of care was not associated with quality or with the difficulty of the children who were served.

A study of group care providers by Barth, Courtney, Berrick, and Albert (1994) found that staffing in group homes can be a problem. The administrators noted that they have a number of difficulties locating and hiring qualified staff; 27 percent of them said that there were "very few" qualified workers available to fill positions in residential care. Turnover in group homes was also high, exceeding the rate of turnover noted in the National Child Care Staffing Study (Whitebook, Howes, & Phillips, 1989). (Day care staff have an annual turnover rate of about 41 percent.) A number of studies of day care have noted that the quality of care diminishes as a result of staff turnover (see, for example, Anderson, Nagle, Roberts, & Smith, 1981), high turnover in group care settings is likely to have similar effects.

Growth and development. As was described in Chapter 1, the early years are essential for children's healthy growth and development. Child welfare agencies that are charged with temporarily raising children may not be able to provide an optimal alternative to a caring parent, but they should at least be able to reduce the likelihood of developmental harm to children. Since young children who are placed in out-of-home care have already experienced a significant disruption in their family relationships, child welfare agencies should work to optimize stability and relationship building at this critical developmental stage. Whether group care, which offers shift-parents and regularly changing caregivers, provides the greatest stability possible to vulnerable youngsters is certainly questionable. In the day care literature, some have argued that the critical developmental milestones of early childhood may be compromised by multiple alternative caregivers (Belsky, 1988; Clarke-Stewart, 1988). Research has also shown that infants who frequently change caregivers are less "socially competent" as toddlers, preschoolers, and young school-age children (Howes, 1988; Howes & Stewart, 1987). Other research on the effects of day care for infants and young children has found that quality of care is one of the strongest determinants of healthy development (Anderson et al., 1981; Howes, Rodning, Galluzzo, & Myers, 1988). And the characteristics of the caregivers, including the ratio of caregivers to children, are the most significant indicators of the quality of care for young children. Some group care settings may indeed provide high-quality care for young children (see Howes, 1989, for a description of some qualities associated with high-quality infant care); however, the vast majority cannot ensure that children will experience the predictability of a single, stable caregiver.

Stability of caregiving. Some evidence suggests a link between early and prolonged residential care and later breakdowns in foster placements (Conway, 1957; Pringle & Bossio, 1960; Trasler, 1957). Multiple placements are arguably inappropriate and often deleterious to the well-being of children (Fanshel et al., 1990). We examined the issue of stability of placements for young children in group care compared to children in foster family care in California (see the Appendix for details on the methods used for analysis). Studying a cohort of young children placed in either setting, we found that instability of young children's placements in group homes was high. Differences were pronounced across age groups. Most notably, 54 percent of preschoolers whose primary placements were in group care settings experienced five or more placements within four years of care, compared with 19 percent of preschoolers who lived primarily with foster families.

Were these group care placements brief? Our data indicate that although many providers state that young children are placed in group home facilities for short-term assessment periods, many young children actually had extended stays in group homes, the median length of stay being well over a year. As Figure 5.2 shows, children leave somewhat more quickly from group care during the first year of placement, but thereafter have similar or slower rates of exit compared to foster family care.

Permanency

Placement in group care has been touted as a means toward reunification because parents may feel less competitive toward the staff of a group home than a foster family. In addition, group care has been thought to facili-

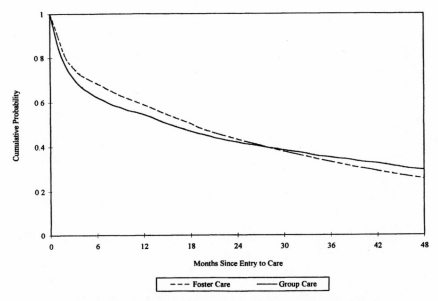

Figure 5.2 Cumulative probability of young children continuing in care in California

tate adoption because there may be more services available to show that reasonable efforts have been made. We examined the questions of reunification and adoption through analyses of the California data.

Reunification. As Figure 5.3 shows, our analyses indicated that four years after placement, infants and toddlers are somewhat more likely to reunify with their biological parents if they are placed in group care settings than in foster homes (e.g., 59 percent versus 42 percent for infants). Accounting for children's later reentry into out-of-home care after a return home, however, the adjusted reunification rate for infants is 41 percent for group care and 32 percent for foster care.

From event-history analyses of reentry, we found that three years after returning to their biological parents, 25 to 30 percent of young children (depending on their age) had reentered care. The likelihood of reentry for infants whose primary placement was a group home was the highest, with a cumulative probability of .31, compared with a cumulative probability of .28 for infants who were placed in foster care. The greatest likelihood of reentry occurred during the first year after returning home, regardless of type of placement.

The reunification rates for children in group care and in foster care were roughly similar, but the findings are difficult to interpret. Given the limitations of administrative data, we cannot know the family circumstances or the characteristics of the children placed in either setting. The somewhat stronger reunification rates for children in group care may be

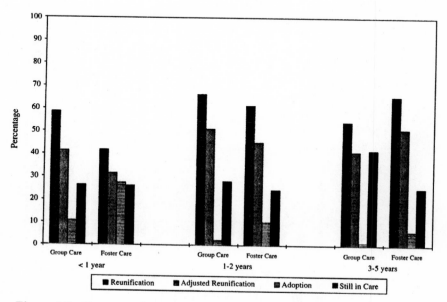

Figure 5.3 Outcomes four years after placement in California

explained by the greater services and supports offered in many group home placements, although other reasons are equally plausible.

Adoption. Although children who are primarily placed in group care are somewhat more likely to reunify with their parents, they are much less likely to be adopted. Six percent of the children in group care, compared to 17 percent in foster care are adopted. (Children who are placed in kinship homes have the lowest rates of adoption, as shown in earlier chapters, and were not included in these analyses.) Although not evident in the data, a possible explanation for this difference is that foster parents become attached to foster children and choose to adopt them if reunification fails. One may also surmise that children in group care may be more troubled or medically needy than those in foster homes and are therefore less adoptable than other children in care. In addition, child welfare workers may view children in these placements differently and make fewer efforts to explore adoption alternatives. Data from a study of group care and specialized foster care providers support these findings regarding the potential impermanence of group care placements (Barth et al., 1994). When asked to describe the long-term prospects of randomly selected children in a group care setting, the providers identified only 3 percent of the children as being likely to be adopted. In contrast, many of the specialized foster parents had adopted in the past (18 percent) or were eager to adopt their current foster children (38 percent).

Alternatives to Group Care

Group care has traditionally been reserved for difficult older children. It has the potential to focus all activities on helping change the behavior of behaviorally disordered youths so they can be transferred to less controlled and more family-like settings. Group care providers and researchers describe the difficulty of their clientele in such terms as "children of action and impulse" (Ekstein, 1983, p. vii) and "their records are replete with litanies of behavior so dangerous that one marvels that they have so far survived physically intact. These are children who throw chairs at their teachers, dismantle principal's offices when sent there; and strike out with fists, rocks and teeth at other children, at parents, at grandparents" (Small, Kennedy, & Bender, 1991, p. 328). These descriptions do not normally fit most young children. Although Steve and Ron (in the vignette at the beginning of this chapter) show evidence of extreme problem behaviors such as those just mentioned, it is not clear that they could not thrive in a specialized care setting—especially considering their tender age.

Young children who are placed in group care settings may have a great need for services, but the literature on group homes and residential treatment does not provide assurance that consistent placement criteria are used to determine which children will be placed in foster care or group care or whether the group homes in which they may be placed are considered to have sufficient good-quality services. Criteria for placing children in group care settings have been categorized by Wells (1991) as "vague" (Apsler & Bassuk, 1983), "varying widely across centers" (Marsen, McDermott, & Minor, 1977), and "defy(ing) categorization" (Maluccio & Marlow, 1972). Wells (1991) noted the importance of basing decisions to place children in group care on general principles, emphasizing placement in the "least restrictive setting possible, in community-based programs, and in family-focused programs appropriate to age and development" (p. 341); she also stressed the importance of "deinstitutionalization and normalization," goals that are not met when young children are placed in group care environments. Our review of group care placements for young children in one county in California and the message from participants in focus groups was that some children are placed in group care because of convenience or error, not because they have special behavioral or health care needs.

It is difficult to determine the minimum age at which group care may be appropriate for children. Admission criteria, developed by the National Association of Psychiatric Treatment Centers for Children (1990) suggest that a combination of psychobiological, psychosocial, developmental, and environmental problems should be taken into account. Children with severe behavioral problems meet these criteria, but the criteria do not specify the age at which placement in residential care is either optimal or acceptable. Research on the effectiveness of group and residential care cannot yet clarify whether group care is effective in providing a lasting reduction in problem behaviors, and it is far from conclusive on the ages of children who require group care (Whittaker, Overstreet, Grasso, Tripodi, & Boylan, 1988).

Foster care, especially specialized foster care in which foster parents are well trained, has been found to be at least as effective as group care in reunifying children with their biological parents, although studies on this topic have generally focused on older children. An experimental study (Chamberlain & Reid, 1991) with children aged nine to eighteen who were hospitalized clearly indicated this effect. In this study, youths who were ready to be discharged from the hospital were randomly assigned to a specialized foster care program or, primarily, to residential treatment. At seven months, those in specialized foster care had somewhat better behavior and spent significantly more days in the community than the children who were in group care. Although the study population differed from the population of concern in our analysis, the ability of specialized foster care to maintain this highly disturbed group of children at a rate that is at least equivalent to group care suggests that specialized foster care may be viable for young children.

Discussion

If older children, who can present challenging physical, psychological, and emotional problems, can be maintained and improve in specialized foster care settings without posing a risk to themselves or others, the viability of this placement alternative for young children deserves special consideration. In theory, group care offers continuous safe care from the time of placement to young adulthood—a phenomenon that is not seen in its entirety in foster care. In theory, placement in group care would also avoid the pitfalls of children living in overburdened foster care, the potential harms of unsafe reunifications, and the frequent shifting of children from foster home to foster home as they age (Proch & Taber, 1985). But the evidence from California's administrative data do not match the theoretical assumptions that drive the placement of young children in group care. These data, coupled with philosophical support for family-like settings, suggests that all group care for young children should be critically examined and that stringent restrictions should be placed on its use nationwide.

Summary of Key Findings and Recommendations Regarding Group Care for Young Children

Finding	*Recommendation*
5.1. Between 13 and 18 percent of the total group care population includes children under age six.	5.1. Young children should not be placed in group care settings. Young children placed in specialized foster care or in foster family care accompanied by additional services—such as parent training and behavioral treatment—should be able to achieve substantial benefits. Group care should be called on to change problem behavior only if it can be expected to offer considerably greater advantage than placement in a supported foster care environment.
	All states should endeavor to recruit and train specialized foster parents for work with young children who have special needs. Such efforts would be fiscally sound and would reflect appropriate developmental considerations for this special population.

Finding	*Recommendation*
5.2. Young children experience a high degree of placement in group care settings.	5.2. Because of their developmental vulnerability, young children, in particular, should be sheltered from the experience of multiple placements. By design, group care promotes multiple placements because social workers seek to place children in less and less intensive and restrictive settings. Owing to their inherent instability, group care placement should be prohibited for young children except in extraordinary circumstances.

Finding	*Recommendation*
5.3. Although group care placements for young children are designed for short-term assessments with quick transfers to less restrictive settings, the median length of stay in care for young children is over one year.	5.3. When group care placements can not be avoided for young children because of the need for thorough physical and/or developmental assessments or for the treatment of severe medical conditions, stays in these settings should be especially brief. Social workers should be required to abide by strict time limits of one to two weeks while alternative, developmentally appropriate placements are located.

Finding	*Recommendation*
5.4. Children younger than age six who are placed in group care are much less likely to be adopted four years after placement than are young children placed in foster care.	5.4. It is likely that the differences in adoption outcomes for young children in group care and foster care have more to do with the considerable problems that youngsters in group care bring to their placements, rather than to the greater efforts that social workers make on behalf of children in foster care. Nonetheless, since group care settings do not appear to expedite adoption for children who are unable to go home, this situation adds to the general concern regarding this placement alternative.

6

Focus on Infants

Before their first birthday, babies learn to grasp small objects, sit up on their own, and crawl. They coo at their caregivers, smile in response to others, and make their needs for food, comfort, and sleep known. The first year is an incredible journey during which infants explore the world and learn about their place in their families. The special circumstances of infancy demand a sensitive foster care system, since foster care for infants is unlike that for children of other ages. Leaving an infant in the home of a maltreating parent poses a significant danger, but placing an infant in foster care may also cause significant developmental harm. The decisions made by parents, social workers, and the courts weigh especially heavily when infants are involved and can have lifetime implications. The case of Damon shows how much infants may have to lose.

Shaneesh, Derek, and Damon

In 1987, Stella gave birth to a girl named Shaneesh in Santa Clara (California) County General Hospital, who tested positive for cocaine. A child abuse report was filed, and the case was investigated and closed. Shortly thereafter, Shaneesh was sent to live with her father, and her mother moved to San Mateo County.

In fall 1989, Stella gave birth to a boy named Derek at San Mateo County General Hospital who also tested positive for cocaine. Derek was reported to the child welfare agency and a social worker investigated the case. Before any action could be taken, Derek and Stella moved to Alameda County, and the San Mateo investigation was closed.

A year later, Stella gave birth to a boy named Damon at Alameda County General Hospital who also tested positive for cocaine. Damon had no other special circumstances associated with his birth; he was born within the normal range for weight, although his mother did not receive any prenatal care before delivery. Damon was reported to the child welfare agency, and a social worker visited the hospital to investigate the case.

Stella was twenty-two when Damon was born. She had finished high school and had taken a few vocational education courses, but two years earlier, when she discovered she was pregnant with Shaneesh, she had left school. Stella had a lengthy criminal record, mostly related to her drug problem. She had been arrested for drug possession on a few occasions, theft, and receiving stolen property. She collected Aid to Families with Dependent Children (AFDC) and had a history of significantly instable housing, with several spells of homelessness in recent years. Damon's father, Mike, was twenty-eight years old, had completed high school, and was working part time at a gas station when Damon was born. He used crack-cocaine and had a lengthy criminal record, including the possession and sale of drugs. When the social worker initially investigated the report, Mike asked that Damon be taken from Stella and placed in his care. But because Mike and Stella were not married, the social worker denied his request, first suggesting that a paternity test be given to verify his relationship to the child.

The social worker and the courts determined that Damon could be sent home with his mother as long as she participated in the Family Maintenance program from which she would receive in-home supportive services. Stella agreed, and Damon was sent home. At this time, Mike moved in with Stella, and the two of them received visits from their social worker once a month. Four months later, a new report for maltreatment was filed on Damon. At four months old, his mother and father had left him alone at home for most of a day. The child abuse report indicated "caretaker absence/incapacity" as the reason for his referral.

Damon was placed in shelter care for about three weeks and was then moved to an emergency foster home. He stayed in the emergency foster home for the next eight months until, at age thirteen months, he was moved to a foster family home for continued care.

During the first month, when Damon was living in shelter care, Stella never visited him. She and Mike split up, and she was having a series of difficulties locating stable housing; she told her social worker that it was just "too difficult" to visit Damon during this period of her life. When Damon was moved to the emergency foster home, Stella visited for about an hour, three times a week. After about three months, she stopped visiting him altogether, never responded to calls from the social worker, and never attended court hearings thereafter.

Mike was also initially involved with Damon during placement, but after four months in care, Mike only occasionally telephoned the foster mother; he never visited his son.

When Damon was thirteen months, an adoption assessment was conducted by a county social worker. Damon had not had any contact with his mother for over five months, and there was nothing to suggest that he would again; he also had not had any personal contact with his father in five months. In addition to their reluctance to visit, neither the mother nor father had made any progress on the case plan. Both were required to enroll in a drug treatment program, to submit to regular drug testing, and to participate in counseling and parent education classes, but neither had done so. Damon was living in an emergency foster home placement that was, by design, temporary, and no efforts had been made to consider his long-term permanency needs until he was over a year old. Nevertheless, Damon's adoptability assessment suggested that he could not be adopted. It reads:

It does not appear likely that the minor can or will be adopted. The parents have maintained regular visitation and contact with the minor and the minor would benefit from continuing this relationship. Grounds to free the minor do not exist.

Shortly after the assessment was completed, Damon was moved to a foster family home, and reunification services for the family were continued. Four months after the adoption assessment and the change in placement, Mike began visiting his son. Visits were difficult because Mike had moved to San Francisco County and Damon was living with his foster family in Alameda County. Nevertheless, Mike attempted to call Damon weekly and visited every other week. In addition, Mike began to call Damon's social worker regularly, angry that his child remained in care and asserting that Damon should have never been placed at all. Around this time, Mike was reported to child welfare for physically abusing his eight-year-old daughter. The case was investigated and closed because of "insufficient evidence." Two months later, Damon was allowed to spend unsupervised weekends with his father. Although Mike never completed any of the requirements of his case plan, Damon was reunified with him, three months shy of his second birthday. The judge in Alameda county recommended in-home Family Maintenance services for the family, but since Mike lived in San Francisco county, the judge had no jurisdiction to enforce his ruling. Mike angrily refused services when a San Francisco County social worker visited his home, and his case file was closed.

Although one of the goals of the child welfare system is to attain permanence for children, it is unclear from this case whether the fundamental goal of child welfare—protecting children's safety—was first considered. Unless there is evidence that was not captured in Damon's case file, there is nothing to suggest from the record that he was re-unified with a caregiver who was any more safe than the caregiver from whom he was initially removed. Because Mike was not mandated to receive Family Maintenance services, he refused the voluntary services offered to him, and Damon's safety was no longer monitored by the continued surveillance of the child welfare agency. In fact, jurisdictional boundaries, artificially created by county lines, may allow families to escape the services, supports, and scrutiny of the child welfare agency simply by moving to an adjoining county where a different child welfare agency is unlikely to pick up their case.

In addition to compromising Damon's safety, this case illustrates the ways in which the permanency of children's living arrangements may sometimes be compromised. That is, at age one, a door to legal permanence was closed. The child had little or no relationship with either parent and no other known relatives in his life. He was not living with a foster family who might have considered adopting him, but was still living in an emergency foster home where caregivers are trained to consider their services temporary. At the age of about one year, Damon would have been de facto relegated to long-term foster care if he had not been returned to his father. In fact, the closed adoption opportunity may have forced the resumption of reunification when it would not otherwise have done so. Cases like Damon's illustrate how a few wrong turns and simple phrases in a case file may add up to lost opportunities for children.

Infants and the Child Welfare System

Maltreatment in the Early Months of Life

Of the 50 infants per thousand in California who were reported to child welfare authorities in 1994, many were reported during the first month of life. African American infants are more likely than other groups to be reported as newborns; indeed, they made up almost 36 percent of the newborns reported for maltreatment (see Figure 6.1).

Almost all newborns (92 percent) reported to child welfare agencies are reported for neglect (see Figure 6.2). Our data do not include specific categories for maternal substance abuse, but a report of neglect for a newborn probably indicates the infant's prenatal exposure to drugs or the mother's substance abuse at the time of the birth. Additional support for this hypothesis may be found in the fact that most newborns (78 percent) are reported by medical personnel. By age six months, neglect comprises only about half of the reports. This dramatic increase in reports for physical abuse after one month of age is of significant concern, given infants' great vulnerability to severe injuries.

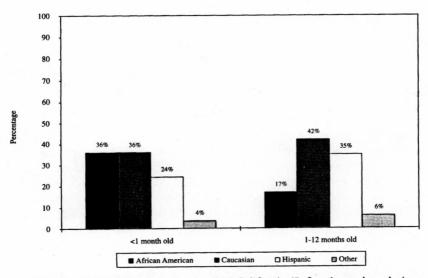

Figure 6.1 Child maltreatment reports in California (Infants' age, by ethnicity)

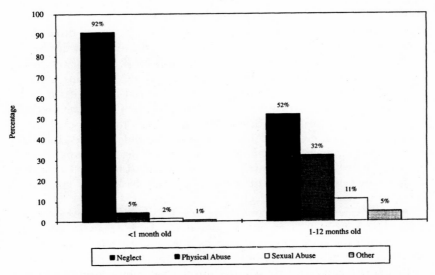

Figure 6.2 Child maltreatment reports in California (Infants' age, by reason for report)

From Maltreatment Report to Case Opening

Mirroring the results we described in Chapter 3, the younger the child, the more likely a report will be investigated and the more likely a case will be opened for service. The reports of most newborns (78 percent) are investigated, and of the investigated cases, about half (50 percent) are opened for services. However, for infants older than one month, slightly more than one-quarter of the cases are opened for services even though it is unlikely that older infants who are reported for child abuse live in circumstances that are only half as threatening as those for newborns. As we have mentioned in some of the case descriptions presented throughout this book, many investigations are closed because of insufficient evidence. This evidentiary-based system thus closes the door to potential services for families who might otherwise benefit from them. Clearly, many infants remain at risk whether or not they receive services. Like other young children, about 40 percent of the infants who are reported during the first month of life are subject to at least one more report during their early years. The large proportion of these infants who are reported for neglect suggests that they may be living in environments that pose chronic threats to their healthy development in the crucial first months when nutrition and caregiving lay the foundations for healthy development and secure attachments.

From Maltreatment Report to Foster Care Placement

Virtually all the newborns who are placed in foster care are reported for neglect, and almost three-quarters of them are reported by medical personnel. Among the older infants (aged one to twelve months) who are placed in foster care, over 25 percent are reported for reasons other than neglect—primarily physical abuse. African American newborns are heavily overrepresented in the entries to foster care; 38 percent of the newborns and 25 percent of the older infants are African American.

About 20 percent of newborns who are reported in the first month of life have had at least two reports prior to placement, and the median time to placement is six days. Seventy-five percent of the newborns enter foster care within a month of the first report. For older infants, the median time to placement is twenty-eight days, and almost a year passes before seventy-five percent of these children are placed in care. Given the developmental importance of the first year of life, this group's continuation in inadequate care is of deep concern.

African American infants are overrepresented in virtually every phase of the child welfare system, but the differences increase as the children travel though the system's stages (see Figure 6.3). African American infants make up 6 percent of California's infant population, but about one-fourth of the infants who are reported for maltreatment, investigated, or whose cases are opened for services and one-third of the infants who en-

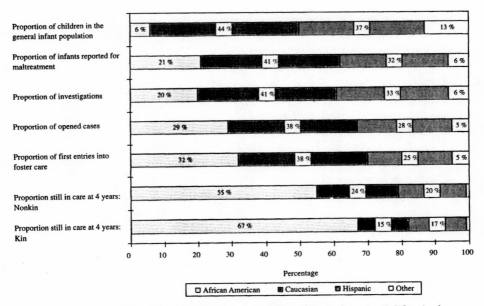

Figure 6.3 Stages of child welfare services delivery for infants in California, by ethnicity

ter foster care are African American. For children who entered foster care as infants and are still in care after four years, more than half of those who live with nonkin and two-thirds of those who live with kin are African American. In stark contrast, Caucasian infants are as likely to be reported and investigated as their representation in the general population would suggest, yet they are less likely to enter foster care or to remain in care four years after entry.

Foster Care

The development and health of many of the newborns who enter foster care are at risk because of their smallness. Infants in foster care are much more likely to have low birthweights (less than 2,500 grams) or very low birthweights (less than 1,500 grams) than infants in the general population, even after ethnicity and poverty are controlled (see Figures 6.4 and 6.5 and refer to the Appendix for information about sources of data). Nearly 30 percent of poor African American infants who enter care were born with a low birthweight, and another 6 percent were born with a very low birthweight, about twice the rate for other poor African American infants. Nonpoor African American children who enter foster care are also much more likely to have been born with a low birthweight than those who do not enter care. Poverty is not strongly related to low or very low birthweights for infants of other ethnic groups, but those poor neonates

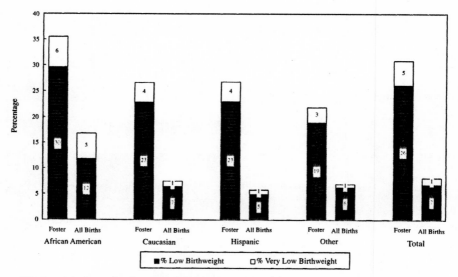

Figure 6.4 Low birthweight neglected infants with poor mothers entering foster care versus all births in California

entering foster care are about four times as likely to have been born with a low or very low birthweight than are other children. Overall, about 25 percent of all infants who enter care were born with low birthweights, and about 5 percent of them were born with very low birthweights.

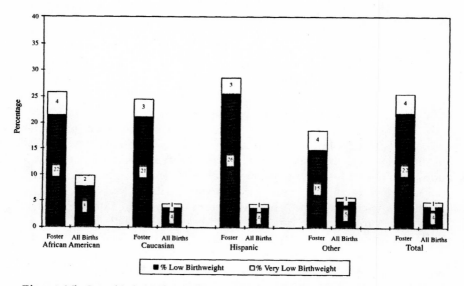

Figure 6.5 Low birthweight neglected infants with nonpoor mothers entering foster care versus all births in California

Parents who lose their infants for reasons associated with drug abuse usually have neglected or abandoned them, rather than physically or sexually abused them (General Accounting Office, 1994; Walker, Zangrillo, & Smith, 1991). Statutes and policies on whether to remove drug-exposed newborns vary from state to state and by practice within states and among workers. There has been little systematic study about this decision. One study of 99 infants born with cocaine positive toxicology screens in New York City (Neuspiel, Zingman, Templeton, DiStable, & Drucker, 1993) found that about one-third remained with their mother after discharge, a third were placed with another relative, and the remaining third were placed in non-relative foster homes. Removal from the mother was associated with being African American and having prior welfare involvement, controlling for parity, sex, and birthweight. Placement outside of the family was associated with being African American, having prior welfare involvement, having no prenatal care, the mother's young age at first delivery or older age at the birth of the study child. Of particular relevance to foster care dynamics is the finding that being African American was associated with placement, even when all mothers in the study were using cocaine.

Wulczyn (1994) merged data from the New York foster care database with vital statistics data, and examined the relationship between birth status and foster care placement (and duration in placement). He considered the joint effects of birthweight, placement type, prenatal care, mother's age, and sibling placements on length of stay in foster care. Results indicate that placement with kin, placement within three months of birth, lack of prenatal care, and low birthweight were associated with increased length of stay.

Schwartz, Ortega, Guo, and Fishman (1994) found that infants in their large Michigan sample were in care for a median of 2.3 years before achieving a permanency outcome. African American infants were in care longer than Caucasian infants, but only if they resided in an urban area. Infants in Wayne County (i.e., Detroit) were in care much longer than those in the rest of the state (2.8 years vs 1.7 years for Caucasian infants and 3.5 vs 1.7 years for African American infants).

In California, approximately half of the infants entering care are removed from their families within one month after birth. The number of newborns entering care peaked in 1989, then declined for a couple of years. Since 1992, entrances have remained relatively constant at slightly over 3,000 per year. More than five newborns enter care for every 1,000 born in California.

Many mothers who neglect their newborns have previously given birth to several other children. Examination of birth records in California indicates that only 17 percent of neglected newborns placed in care were the first born child. Whereas only 12 percent of children born in California have at least three older siblings, 41 percent of newborns entering foster care have at least three older siblings.

Several analyses have demonstrated that the likelihood of adoption for children who were at least a year old when they entered care is much lower than for children who entered as infants. Barth (1997), who followed a sample of children who first entered nonkin care when they were younger than six and who were either adopted or still in care four years later, found that children who entered care as infants were three times as likely to be adopted as to remain in care as were toddlers (aged 1–2), and five times as likely as preschoolers (age 3–5), when their ethnicity was controlled.

Placement Constellations for Infants

Data on the number and timing of placements for infants are scarce, despite the developmental significance of continuity of care. In the Michigan study, Schwartz et al. (1994) found that 55 percent of the infants who entered care in 1981 had more than one placement, but that 61 percent of those who entered in 1987 had multiple placements. This study, although unique in its attention to infants and number of placements, contains no information on the length or type of each placement or on how many infants had more than two placements while in care.

Because of the developmental implications of multiple placements, we examined the duration and type of each placement a child endured within four years of a first spell in foster care in California (see Figure 6.6). (Over one-third of infants who are placed with kin and one-fourth of those who are placed with nonkin remain in care for at least four years.)

Only 29 percent of the infants who are still in care after four years have been in one placement; another 30 percent have had two placements. The constellations displayed in Figure 6.6 account for 75 percent of the children who remained in care for at least four years; all other sets of placements are each representative of less than 1 percent of the infants still in care and are composed of combinations of three or more kin, foster, or group home placements. Thus, of all infants who enter foster care, about 30 percent remain there after four years and 40 percent of that group experience at least three foster family placements or the shift care inherent in group home placements.

The duration of each foster care placement also matters. Infants in their second foster placements were in their first placements for a median of four months. In other words, half the infants in their second nonkin placements spent more than four months in one foster home and then were moved to another foster (stranger) home. An even more striking finding (not shown) was that one-fourth of the children were in one home for more than a year before they were moved to another home. Children with more than two foster home placements almost always experienced moves after they had time to develop close relationships with their caregivers and during a developmental period in their own lives when they needed continuity of care. At this time, multiple placements of young

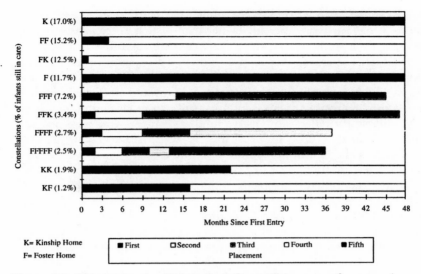

Figure 6.6 Placement constellations for infants still in care at four years in California

children are often the product of malfunctions in the child welfare system, rather than child-specific problems. For example, young children are frequently placed in "emergency shelter" foster homes immediately after birth or upon removal from their biological parents. These placements are intended to be short term, in large part because providers of emergency shelter care are scarce and are reimbursed at a higher rate than are other providers of family foster care. However, children often remain in these homes for many months and are then moved to other foster homes before a decision is made about whether they will be reunified with their families or placed in preadoptive homes. Multiple placements such as these are inappropriate for infants. If an additional placement must occur, it should be made within a few weeks of placement. If not, the extra move should be avoided by earlier permanency planning, thereby keeping the infant in one home until reunification is achieved or an adoptive home is found.

Permanence

The goal of permanence is reflected in federal law and refers to "activities designed to help children live in families that offer continuity of relationships with nurturing parents or caretakers and the opportunity to establish lifetime relationships" (Maluccio, Fein, & Olmstead, 1986, p. 5). Although guardianship and long-term foster care are legally permissible options, it seems reasonable to restrict acceptable permanence for infants to either reunification or adoption.

We studied permanence for a sample of infants, each of whom was followed for four years after his or her date of first entry. Therefore, at the end of the study period, these children were aged four or five years. Several logit regression models were developed to isolate the contribution of such independent variables as age and ethnicity to being in foster care at four years. African American, newborn, and neglected children were compared to those who were not. Children in kinship homes, both those eligible for federal foster care funds and those who were not and therefore who were probably receiving "regular" AFDC payments, were compared to children in nonkin homes. One model considered the likelihood of reunification versus being in care at four years, and the other considered the likelihood of being adopted compared to being in care at four years.

About 90 percent of all reunifications were from a first spell in care, with the remaining coming after the second (8 percent) or third (2 percent) spells. About one-third (32 percent) of the young children who entered a second spell in care were reunified and did not reenter foster care for a third spell. Although lower than the reunification rate from first spells, this rate is still a sizable proportion of second-spell outcomes and suggests the importance of continuing to work toward reunification, even if first attempts fail. Most adoptions (96 percent) were from a first spell in care. More than three-fourths (76 percent) of the infants who were in care four years after they were first placed were still in their first spell, with the rest in a second (22 percent) or third (2 percent) spell.

Reunification versus in care. What are the characteristics of infants and their placements that help explain who is returned home and who remains in care? The model used to address this question was tested on 1,398 infants who had been reunified within four years and 783 who were still in care (infants were 1.78 times as likely to be reunified as to be in care). Whether the infant entered care as a newborn or older infant was not significantly related to reunification (see Table 6.1).

African American infants were much less likely to be reunified than were those of other ethnic groups. Ethnicity is a major factor in reunification, regardless of eligibility or type of placement. Therefore, future researchers must attempt to include other variables (such as the characteristics of child care workers, parents' substance abuse, and parents' compliance with reunification plans) in their studies to gain a better understanding of the dominant role that ethnicity plays in the likelihood of reunification.

Neglect (compared to physical or sexual abuse), decreased the likelihood of reunification by half. Neglect is a complex, often chronic, problem that poses enormous challenges to efforts to reunify infants with their families. In particular, the substance abuse that is usually tied to neglect is often extremely difficult to remedy. In addition, neglect and substance

Table 6.1 Odds Ratios (and 95 Percent Confidence Intervals) for
Reunification and Adoption versus In Care at Four Years in 57
California Counties Excluding Los Angeles

Reunification

Reunified (1,398) = (1,626 from first spell) − (361 reentries) +
(156 from second spell) − (40 reentries) + (17 from third spell)

Newborn versus older infant	**1.10**	(0.91, 1.33)
African American versus other ethnicity	**0.39**	(0.32, 0.47)
Neglect versus physical or sexual abuse	**0.53**	(0.39, 0.70)
Kinship care—IVE eligible versus other placement	**0.96**	(0.78, 1.18)
Kinship care—Not eligible versus other placement	**1.83**	(1.40, 2.38)

Likelihood ratio chi-square = 13.18, $df = 18$, $p = .7808$

Adoption

Adopted (867) = (830 from first spell) + (34 from second spell) +
(3 from third spell)

Newborn versus older infant	**2.14**	(1.70, 2.67)
African American versus other ethnicity	**0.26**	(0.20, 0.32)
Neglect vs. Physical or Sexual Abuse	**0.93**	(0.65, 1.33)
Kinship care—IV-E eligible versus other placement	**0.20**	(0.15, 0.27)
Kinship care—Not eligible versus other placement	**0.53**	(0.39, 0.75)

Likelihood ratio chi-square = 22.57, $df = 18$, $p = .2077$
In Care (783) = (592 from first spell) + (171 from second spell) + (20 from third spell)
for both models

abuse are probably linked to low birthweights and may require special considerations in child welfare.

Kinship care interacted with federal eligibility for foster care funds, so that eligible infants who were placed with kin who were receiving foster care payments were about as likely as were children who were placed with nonkin to be reunified, while children who were placed with kin who were receiving only AFDC were more likely to go home. The relationship between eligibility and lower reunification rates from kinship care is probably connected to the higher payments available to kin caregivers for eligible children while they are in care, which may act as an incentive for a triad (birth mother, child, and caregiver) to maintain court dependency (Berrick & Needell, in press).

Adoption versus in care. If infants are not reunified with their families, they have a substantial opportunity for adoption, although the likelihood of adoption varies by children's characteristics and types of placement. The model sample included 867 infants who had been adopted within four years and 783 who were still in care (infants were about equally likely to be adopted as to be in care after four years).

Infants who entered care as newborns were more than twice as likely to be adopted as were infants who entered after one month or more. It is highly unlikely that infants who are not reunited within four years will ever go home. Newborns are likely to be adopted more readily and more often because they are more frequently abandoned, which means that reunification services and adversarial terminations of parental rights are avoided. Yet, any infant who enters care who is unlikely to be reunified or placed permanently with relatives should be considered at risk of abandonment to long-term foster care and placed in a potential adoptive home as quickly as possible. The need for permanence may be even more urgent for older infants, since they are ready to form attachments with their caregivers and may be more likely to suffer if and when they are moved.

African American infants are one-quarter as likely to be adopted within four years as children of other ethnic groups. Perhaps more than any other outcome, ethnicity plays a major role in the likelihood of adoption.

Four years is too long for any child who enters care as an infant to still be enduring the impermanence of foster care placement or multiple placements, yet our data show that over one-fourth of the infants are still in care at four years, instead of being reunified or adopted.

Discussion

Many infants who enter foster care at birth have been born with the developmental risks associated with low birthweight and often exposure to drugs, and some enter care after months in unsafe homes. Kamerman and Kahn (1995) observed that although some attention has been paid to policy issues affecting preschoolers in recent years (such as Head Start), infants and toddlers are still practically ignored. Our study suggests that there is much work to do to provide a wider net of protection for infants before we can consider foster care as the temporary way station between maltreatment and permanence that it is intended to be.

Infants who will not be going home must be allowed to establish strong and permanent attachments to other adults. When foster care is unavoidable for babies, every effort must be made to minimize separation and loss, and foster parents should be trained regarding the importance of "unconditional commitment to the child in their home so as to facilitate a secure attachment between them and the child" (Kates, Johnson, Rader, & Strieder, 1991, p. 591). For infants who must come into foster care, every effort must be made to prevent all-but-unavoidable multiple placements, and foster parents should provide nurturance, opportunities for physical exploration and growth, and cognitive stimulation to the infants they take into their homes, not just a safe environment. Appropriate training for foster parents in the importance of warmth and affection may be necessary to dispel the outmoded but not extinct notion that it is best for foster parents to remain aloof and detached. Social work training for child welfare workers should include a thorough consideration of the importance of the child-caregiver relationship from various theoretical perspectives, particularly an understanding of attachment that is not mechanistic or deterministic. Training may also be needed to remind caregivers about the importance of cognitive stimulation for infants; warmth and affection are not enough to promote healthy development.

Although stability is important for all children in placement, our greatest concern is for infants who are still in long-term foster care after several years. One-third of these children are living with kin after at most two previous placements. Remaining in care with kin does not necessarily imply impermanence; many relatives plan to keep the children in their care forever (Berrick, Barth, & Needell, 1994). For these families, children may remain in foster care because of a service and support arrangement that essentially penalizes kin for leaving the formal child welfare system. When it becomes clear that there is no longer an issue of child protection, kin should be able to exit foster care in a way that is culturally acceptable and provides the necessary financial and service supports.

The other two-thirds of infants in long-term care—those in nonkin care, are the greatest shame of the current child welfare system. No child who enters foster care as an infant should be in nonkin care after four years. Even if these children have spent their entire spells in the same placements, the system has not afforded them developmental protection. For babies, permanence and protection are inexorably intertwined. Foster parents have neither the rights nor the responsibilities for foster children that they would have for their own biological or adopted children. Even the most well-intentioned foster parents must view themselves as temporary providers, and this perception is bound to place barriers in the path of their forming intimate, loving relationships with the foster children they care for. This situation may partially explain why children in long-term nonkin foster care had an unmitigated accumulation of placement moves during the six years we observed them. Children who are removed from their parents need either to go back home or to be adopted or otherwise placed out of care in a permanent home. Long-term foster care as a permanent plan is not a satisfactory option when babies are concerned.

Many infants are currently reunified with their biological parents after fewer than six months in care. For those who subsequently reenter foster care, the decision to reunify appears to have been the wrong one. But what about the others? If infants are going to be returned home that quickly, perhaps there is some way they can be protected without removing them in the first place. Shared family care (Barth, 1994), in which parents and children are placed together in foster homes, is an option that should be explored, both to avoid placement and to hasten reunification, and other forms of *extended* family preservation services should be available to keep infants safe *and* with their parents. Given the long-term challenges of resolving substance abuse and caring for low birthweight and sick children and large families, *brief* family preservation services are unlikely to be sufficient for parents of infants.

Interpreting the finding that African American infants in kinship care are considerably less likely to be adopted than are other infants in kinship care is complicated. However, the finding almost certainly reflects a strong resistance to formal adoption, which may be incongruous with cultural concepts of the extended family, perceptions of the fiscal disadvantages of adoption, and the lack of options that would allow kin to reverse adoptions should the parents recover. Alternative ways for kin to exit foster care should be made available that support the needs of African American extended families who do not want to adopt but do want to take full responsibility for their relatives' children.

There is no such explanation for the fact that African American infants in nonkin care are unlikely to be adopted. There is a critical need for enhanced efforts to find permanent homes for these infants in the African American community by recruiting and offering the necessary supports to potential adoptive families. One hope is that the Multiethnic Placement Act of 1995 and the Adoption Enhancement Act of 1996 will increase the proportion of African American children who are adopted by families of their own and other ethnicities. There appears to be a growing agreement that children should not be removed from transracial foster families who want to adopt them, and the law now requires that a range of factors—including race—should receive serious consideration in recruiting families and making placements.

Decisions regarding outcomes for newborns in foster care are different from those for older infants and children because it may appear that rapid placement in other permanent homes is best for infants who have not had a chance to get to know their biological mothers. The decision to focus on reunification must come from a belief that children belong, when possible, with their own families and a recognition that many of the problems associated with parental abuse and neglect can be resolved in those families. Special efforts to offer parallel planning for newborns using intensive reunification services along with careful alternative planning would be a welcome change from the "either-or" approach that now dominates child welfare services.

Although our study did not specifically include data on perinatal exposure to substances, it is likely that many of the infants who were placed in foster care in California (particularly those who were removed as newborns for reasons of neglect) were exposed to drugs in utero or have mothers who have substance abuse problems. The confounders of prenatal drug exposure (such as poverty and neglect) that complicate studies on outcomes for substance-exposed infants are not variables we should be trying to control for, but rather scourges we must work to eradicate. The political, economic, and social forces that complicate women's drug abuse must be addressed if the number of substance-exposed infants, including those entering foster care, is to decline.

Analyses of the stability and permanence of placements four years after entry into foster care tell where these infants are when they reach kindergarten age—the age when they are likely to form important new relationships outside the home. There is evidence that the child welfare system is not performing well when babies are placed in care. Transactional theories of development strongly suggest that prenatal substance exposure and/or maltreatment do not necessarily doom infants to compromised lives and that what happens to infants in the months after they enter foster care may be as critical as the events that necessitated placement. If we are truly interested in protecting children, social workers must incorporate knowledge of child development into the child welfare service delivery system.

Summary of Key Findings and Recommendations Regarding Infants

Finding	*Recommendation*
6.1. Newborns are more likely than older infants to be reported for neglect, receive case investigations, and have their cases opened.	6.1. Child welfare workers appear to be exercising good practice in recognizing the increased vulnerabilities of newborns. Many of the newborns have probably been exposed to drugs in utero, which suggests the need to target preventive and interventive services to the identification of women with high-risk pregnancies.

Finding	*Recommendation*
6.2. Although reports for reasons of abuse are rare among newborns, infants with these reports are more likely to receive services and be placed in foster care.	6.2. Child welfare workers appropriately consider reports of abuse seriously. Greater efforts to standardize their responses to reports of neglect are necessary.

Finding	*Recommendation*
6.3. Most children who entered foster care as infants and are still in care after four years have been in multiple placements, and many of them have been moved after months in a first placement.	6.3. Emergency placements should not last for more than one month, during which time a comprehensive assessment should make it likely that the next placement is the last one before a

child leaves foster care. Concurrent planning can reduce the need for children to be moved from placement to placement in the service of adoption.

Finding	*Recommendation*
6.4. African American infants are overrepresented at every juncture in the child welfare system.	6.4. Research that attempts to explain the disparities is sorely needed. Training for caseworkers on the specific needs of African American families, especially extended kinship caregiving families, is essential.

Finding	*Recommendation*
6.5. Infants who enter nonkin care when they are more than one month old are considerably less likely to be adopted than are those who enter as newborns.	6.5. Older infants in nonkin care who cannot go home should be adopted. This may require the increased recruitment of adoptive families whose concerns about the effects of possible prenatal exposure to drugs are addressed.

Finding	*Recommendation*
6.6. A considerable proportion of infants are still in a first spell of foster care after four years.	6.6. There is little justification for any infant being in nonkin care for more than four years. Concurrent planning or fost-adopt programs should be developed so that infants who cannot be reunified with their biological parents are placed in homes where they have an opportunity to be adopted.

7

Understanding Children and Families Served by the Child Welfare System

The performance of the child welfare system has traditionally been judged by state and federal officials through a series of process indicators that reveal whether families have a case plan or how often families receive an administrative or judicial review. More recent interest in developing outcome indicators in child welfare services has focused largely on the performance measures that can be most readily obtained through administrative data. The three general areas of performance in child welfare include the structural characteristics of programs (including staff-to-child ratios and staff qualifications), the process characteristics of programs (the timeliness of assessment and treatment plans and the level of contact between staff and clients, for example), and case outcomes (such as the status of cases, the status of clients, and clients' satisfaction) (Courtney, 1993). In previous chapters, we outlined the system's performance at the case-status level and have shown that on many indicators, young children do not fare well. But what does it mean when the child welfare system and families with young children succeed? And which families are served best by the system? To develop a window through which to view these families' lives, we reviewed the case records of 100 randomly selected infants who were placed in foster care in the first year of their lives to learn about the family situations that typify the cases of young children (see the Appendix for a detailed description of our methods).

Although many issues could have been addressed through the review of case records, we were interested in examining the children and families who might be characterized as the most successful by conventional indicators of performance in child welfare services. For example, infants who were removed from their homes and who were subsequently reunited with their biological parents could be considered the best examples of success that the child welfare system currently has to offer. Some infants in our sample subsequently reentered care (approximately 30 percent, based on the random distribution of the sample—a proportion similar to the statewide figure). These families are important to consider for comparative purposes, since they helped us differentiate between the short-term success of reunification and the long-term success of remaining permanently with one's family.

Who Are the Families Who Succeed?

Infants' Characteristics

About half the infants in our sample who were reunited with their biological parents were under one month old at placement. Somewhat more of them were girls than boys (55 percent versus 45 percent), and the large majority of the cases (67 percent) were African American. (Although African American infants are in care at high rates throughout California, this percentage is higher than expected and reflects the underlying population of the county in which the case records were examined.)

Over two-thirds of the babies were, according to their case files, exposed to drugs prenatally and the large majority of them were exposed to crack cocaine. In earlier chapters, we lamented the lack of information on prenatal exposure to drugs in our administrative data set. The information obtained through case files, however, sheds some light on the prevalence of this problem. If the information was readily available to the child welfare workers, the case files indicated that infants were exposed to drugs. Since in some cases the information could not be discerned, we believe that our estimates of drug exposure underestimate the extent of this problem.

About half the babies had special needs at birth, including problems associated with withdrawal from drugs, special feeding needs, or requirements for apnea monitors; about half were born without the benefits of prenatal care, and approximately one-third had low birthweights. (These data, of course, mirror the information presented in Chapter 6 on infants' low birthweight.)

A review of the written summaries collected in this study point to the array of problems many of these infants experienced when they were initially removed to foster care and shortly thereafter:

• Child seems to be delayed. Born drug exposed, now learning to walk at age $1\frac{1}{2}$ years. Social worker reports that he seems behind in developmental norms. Foster parent also noticed that child seemed to have some developmental problems. Child referred to regional center for developmental testing.

• Baby showed signs of neurological distress for first several months of life but has made many gains with foster care. He is now developmentally on target at about two years old. Baby is small for age.

Factors associated with higher reentry rates for these babies included being African American and having a greater number of problems at or shortly after birth. Table 7.1 summarizes the characteristics of the children and of the families who succeeded by maintaining the children at home once the children left foster care and of those who later reentered care.

Among the more significant aspects of Table 7.1 is the total column, which describes the overall makeup of the families who had infants placed

Table 7.1   Characteristics Associated with Reentry to Care for Infants in California

Characteristics	Nonreentry Cases	Reentry Cases	Total
Infants' Characteristics			
Mean age at removal (in months)*	3.7	1.9	3.0
Mother's Characteristics			
Mean total number of children***	2.9	4.3	3.3
Race (%)*			
African American	59	82	67
All others	41	18	33
Substance abuse (%)*	70	97	84
Previous drug treatment (%)*	39	68	47
Previous criminal behavior (%)**	55	80	68
Housing problems at point of child's return home from care (%)**	25	53	36
Reporting Characteristics			
Mean CPS reports for family***	2.7	5.2	3.4
Mean number of placements during initial spell*	1.8	1.4	1.7
Other siblings in care during initial spell (%)*	49	73	61
Last placement with kin during initial spell (%)*	37	13	30
Mother participated regularly in case plan (%)	67	40	59

* $< .05$, ** $< .01$, *** $< .001$–significance levels show differences between nonreentry and reentry cases.

in foster care and then were reunified. This column shows the extensive involvement of these families in substance abuse, crime, and homelessness and echoes findings from other studies that have pointed to multiple problems among families who receive child welfare services, including domestic violence (Kruttschnitt, McLeod, & Dornfield, 1994), parents' mental health concerns (Kotch et al., 1995), and substance abuse (Chaffin, Kelleher, & Hollenberg, 1996).

Birth Mothers' Characteristics

When infants were initially removed from home and placed in foster care, the average age of their mothers was about twenty-seven years. Two-fifths of the mothers had given birth to their first child during adolescence. On average, women had 3.3 children, including the infants. About half the mothers (54 percent) had not completed high school, and about three-quarters were unemployed when their infants were removed from their care. Twelve percent of the mothers were incarcerated at the point of removal.

A significant majority of the women (84 percent) had substance abuse problems when their infants were removed, and the vast majority of them were involved with crack cocaine. The incidence of drug abuse in the sample of mothers exceeded the rate of prenatal exposure to drugs in the sample of children by some 20 percent, which is not surprising because infants' prenatal exposure to drugs is difficult to assess and is often missed by conventional assessment methods. In addition to drug abuse, 68 percent of the mothers had documented criminal activity, often including arrests for drug-related charges, prostitution, theft, assault, and forgery, prior to their infants' removal. The case records also indicated that half the women were victims of domestic violence and about two-fifths had been abused or neglected as children (these figures reflect only the data presented in the case files and may not capture the full extent of these problems.) Mental health problems were also high: Almost two-thirds of the mothers had some identified mental health problem or educational disability in their case files, most often depression or learning disabilities.

The case summaries that describe these mothers' personal struggles are lengthy and sobering, as the following examples indicate:

• Mother has a criminal history of prostitution, armed robbery, petty theft, and drug abuse. She started heroin at age 22. She was molested as a child by her brother and his friends; was also raped by neighbor children. She finished eleventh grade, then dropped out of high school.

• Mother has bipolar disorder. She has significant problems with uncontrolled rage. She has a bullet in her back from being shot while driving. She is on prescribed drugs and is addicted to them. The mother was stabbed by the father and needed recent surgery. She has an extensive arrest record including robbery, carrying a deadly weapon, and vandalism. Mother is a past IV drug user.

The families whose children were more likely to reenter care included those in which the mothers had given birth to a larger number of children, were substance abusers, had participated in drug treatment, and/or had criminal histories. Many women (73 percent) had problems with unstable housing before their children's removal, and some continued to have unstable housing when the children returned home. Children in families whose housing continued to be unstable when they returned home were more likely to reenter care later.

It is arguable whether the families who "succeed" in the child welfare system, by achieving the goal of having their children returned home and remain at home for at least two years would generally be labeled so by the public at large. Over one-third of the mothers were still using drugs when their children were returned to their care, 55 percent had continued mental health problems, 21 percent had engaged in more criminal behavior during their children's absence, and 36 percent had new or continuing housing problems. Even if the mothers were viewed as successful by virtue of sufficiently meeting the requirements of their case plans, the likelihood that their infants would thrive under such circumstances and become part of a "succeeding generation" is slim.

Birth Fathers' Characteristics

About three-quarters of the infants' fathers were known to the social service agency at or shortly after the infants were removed from their homes. Two-thirds of these fathers were married to or involved with the infants' mothers, and many had at least a minimal relationship with the infants. In spite of their relationship with the infants, less information on the fathers was available in the case files (in general, such information was available for about 75 percent of the cases). Almost two-thirds of the fathers had graduated from high school, and about one-fifth were employed (full- or parttime) when their infants were removed. About one-fifth of fathers were incarcerated at the time of their infants' removal, about two-fifths were unemployed, and about 10 percent were unable to work because of a disability or other condition.

The majority of the fathers (83 percent) had extensive criminal histories. Commonly, these arrests were for such violations as grand theft, drug-related charges, aggravated assault, and the possession of illegal firearms. More than three-quarters of the fathers were substance abusers. About half had previously battered their spouses or partners, and about one-fifth (17 percent) of the case files indicated that the fathers had been abused in childhood. None of the fathers' characteristics were found to be associated with the infants returning to foster care. Summaries of the fathers' characteristics are as follows:

• The father became involved with the child when the mother was incarcerated and she left her daughter in his care. Little information is available about the father's background. There were two sexual abuse reports on the daughter and the father's role is questionable. No abuse was substantiated.

• The father used to work as a mechanic. Unemployment caused more stress on the family and he started abusing his wife and son. He separated from the mother due to increased problems but still remains involved with children through visits and child support.

Reporting and Placement History

The histories of child abuse reports on some families were extensive, with a range of from one to ten reports. (The number of reports, of course, was closely related to the number of children in the family.) The average number of reports prior to placement across all families was 3.4, and the average for the studied infants was 1.6. As we described in earlier chapters, the majority of reports were related to neglect or the caretakers' absence or incapacity—largely associated with the parents' involvement with drugs. Infants remained in care for an average of 8.25 months. (This length of stay is shorter than the median length of stay estimated in previous chapters, since the sample under study included only those who had been reunified).

A factor associated with reentry was a higher number of child abuse reports for the *family* before this spell in foster care; the number of prior reports on the *subject child* was not related to the child's subsequent reentry. Since they were young infants, the number of child abuse reports was quite limited. Similar to our findings reported elsewhere in this book, infants with shorter stays in care during their initial placements were more likely to reenter foster care, and those who were placed with kin were less likely to reenter. About two-thirds of the mothers had two children already in care when their infants were removed from their homes. If an infant had other siblings already in care when he or she was removed, the infant was also more likely to reenter care.

Reunification Plans

The parents were required to maintain regular contact with the social worker and the infant during the reunification phase. In addition, case files included a number of additional stipulations for reunification. Somewhat more than half the mothers were required to attend counseling or therapy (59 percent), submit to regular drug testing (58 percent), enroll in a drug treatment program (52 percent), acquire stable housing (55 percent), and attend parenting classes (49 percent). The case plans for the fathers were virtually the same.

Over two-thirds of the mothers "frequently" or "always" visited their infants during placement, and about half the fathers visited regularly. Similarly, about 59 percent of the mothers regularly participated in their case plans, compared to 48 percent of the fathers. Visits prior to reunification had no notable effect on the infants' reentry, yet it appears that mothers who regularly participated in other aspects of their case plans were somewhat less likely to have their infants reenter care.

In addition to the mothers' and fathers' activities during the placement, the social services agency also provided or ensured that the families received a variety of services. Before placement, about one-fifth of the families received services, such as case management, counseling, drug and alcohol treatment, and/or transportation. During placement, the majority of the families received case management (89 percent), counseling (68 percent), drug and alcohol services (60 percent), and/or transportation (55 percent). Following placement, virtually all the families received some type of postreunification services. These services included case management (72 percent), counseling (53 percent), drug treatment (39 percent), and/or financial assistance (39 percent). Child welfare workers had an average of 8.3 contacts with the families and collateral service providers per month during the time the case files were open. ("Contacts" were calculated by counting the total number of entries in a case record divided by the number of months the case was open. These entries detailed in-person and phone contacts.) Families whose infants reentered foster care received significantly more postreunification services than those families who did not reenter care. These extra services were not apparently effective in changing the path to reentry.

Stacie's story characterizes those of many infants who are placed in foster care. The complexity of her family's problems might have pointed to the challenges her parents would ultimately face in attempting to reunify. Her mother, Angela, had already received services from many agencies before Stacie came to child welfare.

Alex, Lisa, Daniel, Mark, Francis, Gina, and Stacie

Angela was born in 1965 to a teenager mother. In elementary school she began to have trouble, fought with other students, and regularly argued with her mother. In the fifth grade, she stopped attending school, spent time on the streets, and eventually was placed in foster care. During early adolescence, she abused drugs and had many brushes with the law. At age fourteen, Angela gave birth to her first child, Alex.

When Alex was one year old, Angela's mother reported him to the social services agency. She told the child welfare worker that Angela was pregnant with her second child, that she was involved with drugs, and that Angela and her baby could not live in her home. Angela's case file provides few details about the next ten years of her life, but shows that she gave birth to her second child, Lisa, in 1980; to Daniel, Mark, and Francis two years apart; and to Gina in 1987. All her children were removed from her home for "general neglect," "parental incapacity," and "drug abuse." Alex and Lisa were placed in guardianship with a relative; Daniel, Mark, and Francis were placed for adoption; and Gina was in foster care with a plan for reunification with her mother. In 1990, Stacie was born, also exposed to drugs, and was immediately reported to child welfare by medical personnel.

Stacie was placed in her maternal aunt's home six days after her birth and remained there for the next six months. During her stay at her aunt's home, the child welfare agency received an anonymous phone call alerting them to the dangerous conditions of the aunt's home. The complaints were investigated, but they did not appear so bad as to warrant Stacie's removal. In the sixth month, Stacie's aunt was evicted from her home. She called the child welfare agency and asked that Stacie be moved, since she could not handle the added burden of a baby while coping with her personal circumstances. Stacie was then placed in an emergency foster home, where she stayed for the next two months. Later, a foster family home was located, and Stacie was again moved. This time, she stayed in the foster home for ten months. While in care, Stacie had recurring ear infections and was identified as developmentally delayed. The social worker and her foster parent in the emergency foster home noticed that her speech, language, and motor skills were all slow to develop. A social worker from the area's regional center conducted an assessment and identified special services for Stacie to help her catch up.

During Stacie's stay in care, her parents made efforts toward reunification. Her father, Scott, had a history of abusing alcohol, crack, and heroin. He had been arrested for drug possession, forgery, stolen property, and parole violations and was often violent toward Stacie's mother. Shortly after Stacie's birth, Scott married another woman, broke up with her a few months later, and reunited with Angela. Scott and Angela's relationship, however, was punctuated by frequent arguments, fighting, and domestic abuse. Angela moved numerous times, first from Scott's home and then to his mother's home and was homeless on several occasions. After some months, Scott and Angela told their social worker that they had finally ended their relationship, and Scott began to make earnest efforts to gain custody of Stacie.

Scott was required to enter a drug treatment program and to test clean for drugs before he could bring Stacie home. He was also required to acquire stable housing, to meet with the social worker regularly, to attend parenting classes, and to express a consistent desire to make a home for his daughter. He visited Stacie weekly while she was in foster care, and after a year asked that she be sent home to him. Angela was also required to visit with her child, to acquire stable housing, to attend counseling, to meet with the social worker, to enroll in substance abuse treatment, and to attend parenting classes. Both parents appeared to cooperate with their case plans to a large degree and received transportation vouchers, emergency shelter (for Angela), rental assistance, help obtaining Aid to Families with Dependent Children (AFDC), case management, drug treatment, parenting classes, and counseling.

When Stacie was nineteen months old, she was reunified with her father. One month later, Scott was arrested for drug possession. The social worker assigned to the case discovered that Scott and Angela had lived together for the month after Stacie had been returned home. Angela was again using drugs heavily, and Stacie was removed from her care and placed in an emergency foster home. During the next year, Angela visited once every few months. Scott moved to Reno after he was released from jail and never visited his daughter. At Stacie's twelve-month court review, when she was 2½, the emergency foster home provider requested legal guardianship of Stacie.

In reviewing Stacie's case file, it is difficult to determine whether the social worker made the right decision in returning Stacie to her father. There was scant evidence that Scott had complied with his case plan—on several occasions when he was required to submit to a drug test he could not do so. It is also unclear why Stacie was not returned to the foster parents with whom she had spent almost a year prior to her return home. Instead, Stacie had to develop a new set of relationships with a fifth family when she was 2½. Why she was placed in legal guardianship rather than adoption—particularly at such a young age—is probably due to her identified developmental disabilities and the foster caregiver's need for assurance that she would continue to receive support from the county. Nevertheless, there is no adoption assessment in Stacie's case file, which may also suggest that adoption was not seriously considered. If it was, a plan to meet Stacie's special needs could have been developed.

What Makes a Difference for Families?

The majority of families who reunify with their infants do not subsequently reenter care. Yet, in the county in which this study was conducted, about one-third will reenter within three years. Although we have indicators that point to areas of family vulnerability, such as those described here, only parents can articulate the personal strengths and features of services that contribute to change. The discussions in the focus groups we held with some of the families we studied suggested that the hills they must climb to reach a safe and sufficient family life are steep.

• You have to be rich to do everything they want you to do. I had to jump through hoops [to get my daughter back]. I don't have a car, but I had to go to drug treatment. It was almost impossible. I had to borrow money to do it.

• Once you make up your mind [that you can change], you can do it. The worst is over. I appreciated my social worker when I was on the other side. But you have to decide. Do I want my baby? Or do I want the drugs? Which one are you going to choose? It's up to you. They can't make that decision for you.

• My biggest change was my addiction. My biggest blessing is that my kids came home. I was selfish, I was unfit. But their father stuck by me, he was there. I'm stable now, I manage my money, I pay my bills. When I really started to help myself, then they back you 100 percent.

Social workers who made a difference for families were those who pushed and encouraged just enough; they were perceived as allies instead of enemies.

• She became my friend. She explained that she was there to help me get my shit together and get my family back.

• My worker was encouraging. She asked me what *I* wanted. I was in [prison] and she brought me back and forth for court appearances. She came out to see me one day when I was so high I didn't even recognize her, but she didn't hold that against me. I was so sorry, and she gave me a second chance. She was a good woman.

• My worker always had something nice and encouraging to say. She always said there was light at the end of the tunnel.

The services that were most valued by families were simple and concrete. None of the families who participated in our focus groups mentioned therapy as an especially important service, and parent education was considered valuable only after these mothers took ownership of the fact that their parenting had been severely compromised.

• When I got clean, they helped me get an apartment and helped furnish it. They gave me child care, a dentist, and they got me into junior college for cosmetology.

• CPS paid for my [electric bill], deposit, and furnished my apartment. They paid for toiletries and put me back on AFDC a month before my child came back.

Although foster care did not appear to be a feature of the child welfare system that either hindered or helped reunification, many parents in our focus groups had strong feelings about their experience with foster parents.

• My son was in two foster homes and they moved him and they didn't tell me that they moved him. While he was in the first home, I knew the foster mom wanted to keep my baby for herself. The foster mom would make things really difficult for me and made me feel like not visiting. She also did things to him without telling me, like she cut my son's hair without asking first.

• I didn't like the fact that my son didn't know who I was. My baby was two months when he was put in care, and it was six or seven months before I got to visit him.

- [Foster parents] act like you're going to hurt your own child. They stand over you, breathing down your neck. They should just let you have some privacy with your baby. The foster mom just assumed the worst in me.
- Mine was with her for two years. She was praying for me, and I got humiliated. When I got over it, I told her if I didn't get better, I wanted her to keep my son.

In addition to the problems with foster care, many women also complained about communication with their social workers. Many women felt as though they had not been heard by their workers and that much of what they said was taken out of context. This appeared to be an especially prevalent sentiment during the initial stages, when the investigations worker collected evidence for removing the infants.

- I didn't know everything you say to CPS will be held against you.
- I called Parental Stress and said that I was at the end of my rope. They thought I was suicidal; then police came, took me to the Psych ward, and they took my kids. What's Parental Stress for, anyway?
- The court report is the problem. They take things out of context. They put pieces of information together that don't make the whole picture. They talk to people that have nothing to do with the case.

Women who have been through the child welfare services system; who have lost their children; and who have come out on the other side with an honest perspective about their role, the state's role, and the community's role in their experience are few. Even the most successful clients—those who have no future contact with the child welfare agency—have often lost something profound in their journey.

- When I had my first baby, I went into the bathroom and smoked crack in the hospital, right after I had him. Now they would put me in jail if I did that, but then, they gave him to me. Then, on his second birthday, they took him because of drugs. It was my decision to put my first son up for adoption. If you don't have relatives, and I didn't, those are your choices. By the time I was ready, it was too late for him. I volunteered adoption. It was the best thing I could do.
- My second baby was taken due to drug addiction. I shouldn't have got to keep him, except I got clean. In the beginning you see a lot of parents who don't make it. But it's like welfare reform, now—they want you to get your shit together. When I got clean, they helped me get an apartment and helped furnish it. My second baby has deficiencies from all my crack. He's not slow, but he has social skill deficiencies. But he didn't see me smacking or beating on him like I did his older brother. He'll do OK.
- I'm five years' clean now. I'm a miracle. I'm a success. But I used to hate the system when I was in it. I love and miss my baby, and he knows his mother wants him. I have faith I'll see him.

Discussion

Although this study had a relatively small sample, its findings provide otherwise scant information about the case and family-service circumstances of infants who are returned home from care. The data point to a variety of family characteristics that typify child welfare cases involving young children. Most alarming is the complexity of the cases that come to the attention of the child welfare services system. These are not families who need assistance only with their parenting practices. Instead, the majority of these families are deeply troubled by substance abuse, criminal histories, mental health challenges, and housing problems. The women are more likely than most American women to have given birth as adolescents, and they are more likely to have larger families (U.S. Department of Health and Human Services, 1996). The majority have educational deficits, most are unemployed, and some experienced maltreatment as children. Family circumstances in these cases are exceedingly complicated, and problems are often long standing.

What types of services are provided to such families? And is it realistic to expect that many will change their lives significantly? Most families receive case management services from social workers who are already burdened with thirty to forty other cases. The majority of contacts these workers have with the families is by telephone, and these conversations often are brief. The paperwork required to maintain continued documentation of families' progress and children's safety is significant—the average case file we reviewed involving an infant was approximately two inches thick; when older children were also in care or when children later returned to care, several large folders for the family were usually bound together. Given their large caseloads, child welfare workers' appearances in court are also frequent. Could this service accurately be called case management, or is it just case monitoring? We believe that the latter characterizes the child welfare system more accurately. The service delivery system for children and families in child welfare is minimalist in approach, and the obligation for change falls heavily on the individual family. Parents receive limited support and services. Largely, these families must walk the road to recovery alone.

Summary of Key Findings and Recommendations Regarding the Children and Families Served by the Child Welfare Services System

Finding	*Recommendation*
7.1. The children and families who come to the attention of the child welfare services system are a residual population with an extremely great need for services.	7.1. Families who have contact with the child welfare system may need to be provided with an array of services in a saturated fashion, including drug treatment, assistance with housing, income, and parenting.

Finding	*Recommendation*
7.2. Over three-quarters of the fathers were involved in their children's lives at or after placement, yet fathers' characteristics had no bearing on whether children would reenter care.	7.2. Child welfare services are primarily female dominated, with case plans largely reflecting services provided to children's mothers. Focused attention on the role that fathers can and do play in children's lives may be an important step in improving child welfare outcomes.

Finding	*Recommendation*
7.3. About one-fifth of the fathers and 10 percent of the mothers were incarcerated at the time of their infants' removal. Almost two-thirds of the mothers and 83 percent of the fathers had previous experiences with the criminal justice system. Some of their criminal involvement was lengthy and serious.	7.3. Child welfare workers should develop service plans that allow for visits when parents are imprisoned during their children's stay in foster care. Greater collaboration should be developed between the child welfare services system and the probation system so that families who have had brushes with the law can be closely supported to remain free of further legal infractions.

Finding	*Recommendation*
7.4. A large percentage of parents abuse substances, so their parenting is compromised.	7.4. The interface between drugs and maltreatment is a consistent theme in child welfare services. New service technologies that can effectively address substance abuse must be developed before child welfare workers will have much effect on the parenting practices of the majority of child welfare cases.

Finding	*Recommendation*
7.5. Families with multiple prior reports for child maltreatment and infants whose older siblings are already in foster care may be more likely to reenter care.	7.5. Children and families who present these characteristics to the child welfare system should be afforded closer support and supervision. These problems may signal complex family situations that preclude successful family reunification.

8

Public Child
Welfare Practice

Child welfare is a challenging profession; numerous factors influence social workers' decisions regarding risks to children and the optimal delivery of services to families. More important, child welfare work is becoming increasingly complex as forces in the social and political landscape
change dramatically. Issues, such as maternal substance abuse, poverty,
and homelessness, have shifted the nature and intensity of family problems. The advent of formal kinship foster care has also changed the dynamics of relationships among caregiver, parent, child, and agency in
ways that could not have been predicted fifteen years ago (Berrick,
Needell, & Barth, in press). And the large influx of infants and young
children into the child welfare services system has raised new issues for
social workers that were heretofore less obvious. The focus groups with
child welfare workers that we conducted throughout California highlighted their dilemmas, the decision making that goes into their work
with individual families, and the importance of their role within the
child welfare system. Whether child welfare workers as a group have
made changes in daily practice to accommodate the developmental
needs of young children is not clear. Some workers appear to take young
children's unique vulnerabilities into consideration at the front end
of the service system, but during placement in foster care, age does
not appear to be a theme that distinguishes workers' approach to
services.

Decision Making for Young Children

Risk Assessment

Analyses of administrative data (presented earlier) suggest that young children are more frequently reported to the child welfare services system and that they are more likely to be placed in foster care than are older children. Turning to child welfare workers to understand this dynamic, we learned that they often consider children's ages a significant factor when assessing the risk of child abuse and neglect. In some instances, age is a determining characteristic in the decision to investigate a case immediately. When they assess children and their families, the workers said they consider children under age five to be at higher risk because of their physical vulnerability and their inability to verbalize their needs. Young children are less likely to have self-protective skills, and they have a limited ability to find help if a situation escalates. For these reasons, workers said that given equal evidence, they are more likely to remove young children for suspected child abuse and neglect than older children. Yet we see from our cases that the threshold for intervention is still high.

Physical injuries to children under age five are viewed with special consideration. Written policies also address the unique risks faced by young children. One county's policy (County of San Diego, 1994) indicates that workers should seriously consider the temporary separation of children from their parents when these conditions are present:

• Children under one year of age with bruises, burns, breaks, a preliminary diagnosis of Shaken Baby Syndrome or suspicious injuries.

• Children under three years of age with burns, breaks or bruising to the head, face or torso. (p. 20)

In the following cases, reunification services may be eliminated for young children:

• Bruising in infants; bruising to the head, face or torso in children three years of age or younger and multiple and/or healing fractures.

• Any of the following situations where the minor is under five years old: physical trauma if untreated would cause permanent physical disfigurement, permanent physical disability, or death; any act of sexual abuse which causes significant bleeding, deep bruising, or significant external or internal swelling; repeated acts of physical abuse which cause bleeding, deep bruising, significant external or internal swelling, bone fracture, or unconsciousness. (p. 43)

In addition to children's ages, the child welfare workers noted other factors they consider in making an assessment of risk. These elements include (1) whether the child is disabled, (2) if the family is isolated from a support network, (3) if another parent is involved, (4) the degree of the child's fragility and the severity of his or her medical needs, and (5) the history of the child's caregiver. Other issues, such as the type of abuse the child has sustained, the intensity of the abuse, and the family situation, are also important determinants. The combination of factors related to the child, the family, and the environment are all important in the decision to place a child in foster care. When working with older children, they often use the children's comments about the situation to guide their practice—an important factor often missing with young children.

The child welfare workers stated that they are frequently challenged by cases of child neglect since the extent to which neglect exists and its potential harmful effects are often difficult to discern. Some workers said they are more likely to assign "family care workers" or "family/case aides" to neglect cases in an effort to provide in-home services and to continue the assessment process before making a decision regarding removal. They also told us that they often receive multiple reports of neglect on young children yet still have too little evidence to establish a dependency petition.

Once children are placed in foster care, some workers continue to assess risk. Specifically, they take special measures with young children to review their developmental progress. As we discussed in Chapter 1, child abuse and neglect (and perhaps foster care placement) may result in developmental lags for young children. Because of the possibility of developmental lags, workers often play with young children; watch them reach, crawl, and walk; and hold, feed, and change them to observe their growth and catch developmental delays. When given sufficient time, workers can observe parents with their children and can teach parents parenting skills they may lack. With young children, thoughtfulness about child development sometimes complements concern about protecting them.

Sensitivity to issues of child development is, by and large, an approach to practice that is not shared by all workers; our recommendation is that continuous assessment of risk to children's safety and developmental well-being should be incorporated into all child welfare practice.

Time Lines for Permanency Planning

Some states identify a narrow range of family circumstances that may permit workers to forgo conventional permanency planning time frames and move children directly into adoptive placements—bypassing conventional eighteen- or twenty-four-month efforts to reunify families. (In California, these regulations were adopted as part of the Welfare and Institutions Code 361.5, b and e.) Some specific criteria allow workers to petition for such a "reunification bypass." In California the criteria include (1) a parent's severe mental illness, confirmed by two practicing psychologists; (2) the death of a younger child at the hands of the birth parent, although the death of an older child has no apparent bearing on the risk to a younger child; or (3) abandonment of at least six months' duration. Proceeding with a bypass takes substantial administrative approval, is time consuming and is administratively cumbersome.

Most child welfare workers in California are unfamiliar with the bypass mechanism and have not used it. Their views about shortening the time frame for permanency planning are widely divergent and reflect individual philosophies more than county policies. For example, some workers believe that more young children should qualify for the bypass on the basis of a parent's history of parenting other children. One worker summed up her feelings by stating, "If a parent has had six prior removals, maybe her new baby should be placed on 'fast track.' " Other workers invoke the age of the child as an important factor to consider in shortening the time frame. Some told us that family reunification services should be offered for a maximum of twelve months when young children are involved, so the children might be rapidly placed in adoptive homes. "A six-month period is half a lifetime for a one-year-old child," one worker said.

Other child welfare workers are satisfied that a number of barriers restrict the use of the bypass. They are especially sensitive to the seriousness of terminating parental rights and the importance of giving parents extended opportunities to rear their children. One worker stated, "Even if a mother has had other [drug-exposed] children, we should give her the benefit of the doubt with this child. Sometimes the mother can succeed, especially if she has good social worker support."

Parents' drug abuse complicates the discussions of shorter time lines for permanency planning. "The drug problem has really affected us," said one worker. "Eighteen months really doesn't work with these families. You have to work on services [and] we need to acknowledge [drug addiction] as an illness."

The notion of changing the time frame of permanency planning for young children might be more palatable if families were offered parallel (or concurrent) planning services. Many child welfare workers support this approach because it would ensure greater stability for young children without denying parents the right to regain custody.

Fost-Adopt Programs and Parallel Planning

Fost-adopt programs are used in some, but not all, California counties. In one county with a well-developed fost-adopt program, referrals to fost-adopt are made on the basis of the chronicity and severity of parental problems and the workers' assessment of the likelihood of reunification; medically fragile infants and infants who are placed because of extensive parental drug abuse are especially likely to be placed in fost-adopt. Cases are referred to the fost-adopt program within six months of initial placement. To ensure that reunification services proceed for the biological parents, parallel planning is incorporated into the children's service plans. In parallel planning, one child welfare worker is assigned to assist the biological parent or parents to work toward reunification at the same time that a separate fost-adopt staff member works with the child and foster parents to achieve an alternative permanency goal.

The child welfare staff in one county indicated that biological parents occasionally become more motivated when they understand that their young children have been placed in fost-adopt homes. They reported that the fost-adopt program gives young children, in particular, a better opportunity for permanence either through reunification with their biological parents or through eventual adoption by other caregivers.

Intensity of Services

To provide truly "reasonable efforts," many child welfare workers noted that they frequently make a more intensive attempt to reunite infants who were removed at birth with their biological parents. They told us that they spend additional time arranging and supervising visits between parents and infants to help establish a close relationship. Generally, however, workers are reluctant to suggest that a child's age is a dominant factor in the amount or duration of services they provide to families. Each family presents individual characteristics and needs, some requiring more time and attention than others.

Substance Abuse

After a brief period in the 1980s, when drug-exposed infants were regularly (and sometimes automatically) placed in foster care at birth, a 1990 California law (Senate Bill 2669, Chapter 1603) mandated that each county develop specific protocols for assessing drug-related cases before removing children from their homes. We have shown that young children's entries to foster care leveled in the early 1990s, and it is likely that this law contributed to these changes. In recent years, hospital staff usually notify child welfare officials when drug-exposed infants are born. Child welfare workers then conduct assessments of all drug-involved families to review their special needs. If the only indicator of a problem is a positive toxicology screen, but other factors in the home and the child's environment appear to be relatively stable (that is, the mother and child are developing a relationship, the mother recognizes her drug addiction, and this is the mothers' first baby), then removal is generally not recommended. Factors that may lead to the removal of a child include the mother's extensive history of severe drug abuse, little or no prenatal care, the mother's lack of interest in the newborn, little or no family support, little or no participation in a drug-treatment program, and the mother's involvement with the criminal justice system (when the mother is incarcerated, the child is usually taken into custody).

Drug-exposed infants are often placed first in specialized foster homes. Foster parents in these settings usually receive special training and a specialized care rate to handle the unique needs of these infants. Whether these caregivers are selected to provide adoptive homes to many of these infants who will not be going home is less clear.

Kinship Care

Kinship foster care has grown considerably in recent years, and its impact on the entire service delivery system for children and families has been significant. Child welfare staff generally embrace the shifting focus toward the use of kin because of their belief in the importance of children having strong ties to their families. As we described elsewhere in this volume, however, the permanent placement of young children who live with kin poses unique problems.

The child welfare workers indicated that legal guardianship and adoption are sometimes explored with kin, but that kin are generally reluctant to consider these options. The workers suggested that kin are often convinced that the children's parents will "get better" or tire of using drugs and hence, offer a window of opportunity for later reunification. Other kin are more comfortable with the temporary nature of foster care; they think that the termination of parental rights is too drastic and painful for the family. Still other workers expressed concern that the Adoption Assistance Payment subsidy is significantly lower than the foster care rate; presumably they share these concerns with kinship caregivers even though the rates are usually similar. Some child welfare staff harbor concerns about kin adopting children. Because of kin caregivers' relationship to the children and the length of the placements, such adoptions are often automatically approved, even if the quality of the kinship homes is such that these kin would not normally be approved under conventional standards of care. Adoption workers are therefore somewhat more comfortable with the use of guardianship, rather than adoption, for relatives, although problems associated with payment (there is none for relatives in most counties in California) often militate against the use of this alternative.

Legal Guardianship

The child welfare workers were not enthusiastic about legal guardianship as a permanency outcome for young children, yet this is not an uncommon outcome. The workers often expressed their concern that guardianship placements may be disrupted during adolescence. As one worker described the problem, "Guardians who take care of young children do not want them when they grow up."

As we noted in our earlier analyses, legal guardianship is more frequently granted to kin than to nonrelatives. Legal guardianship for kin, according to the child welfare workers, is a close alternative to a long-standing legal relationship without the psychological and emotional associations of terminating parental rights.

Multiple Placements

Our work on the dynamics of foster care, reported earlier in this book and elsewhere (Needell, Webster, Barth, & Armijo, 1996), has shown that many young children experience multiple placements. The child welfare workers shared our concern about the potential effects of multiple placements on young children and considered the problem regrettable for children and one that reflects poorly on the agencies. Workers often feel frustrated by foster parents' low threshold of tolerance for children's behavioral problems and discouraged by their own limitations, suggesting that if they had more time to commit to troubled placements, many changes in placements might be avoided. "It's always wrong to move a kid," said one worker. "Especially between six months and three years [old]. . . . That's when we treat them like suitcases." Another noted, "I think we're just beginning to realize that moving babies has an effect. Some kids are really damaged by being moved."

Some of the factors contributing to multiple placements include (1) insufficient time to make complete assessments of children so appropriate matches can be made between children's needs and the characteristics of foster homes; (2) inadequate time after children are placed to provide supportive services to foster parents; (3) problems with biological parents, usually centering on disagreements about visiting their children; and (4) the short administrative time limits on emergency foster care placements. In some counties, child welfare workers are supported in their efforts to conduct preplacement planning, including time to prepare young children for their new relationships (including frequent visits to foster homes before placements are formalized), work with foster parents to inform them fully about the children's needs, and lengthy conversations with biological parents to ensure that they are comfortable with their children's placements. In other counties, workers are especially pressed for time and indicate that preplacement planning is sufficient for the children, foster parents, and biological parents.

Although some workers said they try to offer services to maintain stable placements, many others indicated that services are difficult to locate and gain access to. Some workers also suggested that higher monthly board rates might play a role in stabilizing placements. Higher payments might guarantee better-quality foster placements. In general, the workers stated that they face significant obstacles to locating foster parents who will care for sibling groups or special-needs children, and virtually all expressed the need for greater recruitment efforts to expand the pool of homes available to all children. The quality of care provided in foster homes varies, and the workers usually did not describe these homes in glowing terms, characterizing them only as from "decent" to "good."

As we discussed earlier, some of the changes in placements for young children are the result of flaws in the design of the system that child welfare workers cannot avoid. When infants and young children remain in the hospital, are then placed in emergency foster homes, and then are moved to regular foster homes before they return home or are being placed fost-adopt homes, they experience multiple placements within a matter of a few months or a year. The review of one such case, Alfredo, illustrates the kinds of circumstances and decision making that contribute to multiple placements for babies.

Alfredo

When Alfredo was born at Mid-Town Hospital in 1991, he had symptoms associated with prenatal exposure to drugs and syphilis. Trembling and irritable, he had difficulty sleeping and had a severe case of diarrhea. Alfredo was kept in the hospital for a month while medical personnel treated him for his fragile condition. The local child welfare agency was notified about the baby, and a social worker was assigned to the case. In addition to Alfredo's medical condition, the hospital staff were also concerned about his mother Susanna's ability to care for him. At the hospital, she was observed forgetting when she had just fed the baby and talking to herself, and she seemed confused about where she was and who was caring for her. The hospital staff indicated that she was likely suffering from brain damage or significant mental illness, and a police hold was placed on Alfredo while a more thorough evaluation was made.

Susanna, aged twenty-seven, was unemployed at the time of Alfredo's birth and had a history of substance abuse, including amphetamines, cocaine, heroine, and marijuana. She also had been arrested eight times (but not convicted) for the possession of drugs, theft, prostitution, and failure to appear in court. She appeared to have mental health problems, and her case file indicated that previous social workers had requested psychological evaluations of her but that she had never been "sober enough" to complete an evaluation and had never fully engaged in treatment. Alfredo's older siblings Anthony and Anna, both born of different fathers, had been removed from Susanna's custody; Anthony was placed permanently with his paternal grandmother, and Anna was placed in an adoptive home.

Alfredo's father, Salvador, was married to Susanna at the time of the baby's birth, but the two adults were separated. Salvador was employed full time as a construction worker, but also had a history of arrests for drunk and disorderly conduct, vehicle-code violations, grand theft, armed robbery, petty theft, and illegal entry. According to the case record, Salvador did not have substance abuse or mental health problems.

After a month's stay in the hospital, Alfredo was placed in an emergency foster home, where the foster mother had special training to work with medically fragile infants. He remained in this placement while his health stabilized and his social worker determined whether he could return home. Three months later, he was moved from the emergency foster home to a foster family home. Alfredo remained in this home for the following seven months.

During Alfredo's stay in care, Susanna had to submit to a number of requirements in her case plan. She was asked to acquire stable housing, to visit with her baby, to meet with the social worker regularly, to enroll in substance abuse treatment, to submit to regular drug testing, to develop a legal source of income, and to agree to a psychological evaluation. Salvador was also required to visit with Alfredo, to acquire stable housing, and to meet with the social worker. Susanna did not comply with any of these requirements. However, Salvador made great efforts to do so; although he was initially embarrassed to visit Alfredo in the emergency foster home, he began to visit regularly once Alfredo was placed in regular foster care. After he requested that the child be returned to his home, Salvador was required to identify a plan for protecting Alfredo in case Susanna decided to visit her son and to establish child care arrangements while he was at work. Salvador moved in with his mother and arranged for her to care for his son during his working hours, and Alfredo was returned to his home. Following reunification, in-home services were provided for an additional six months.

Alfredo was sent home with his father after being in care for 340 days. During that time, he experienced three placements. First, Alfredo was cared for in the hospital while he was treated for his medical condition. Then he was transferred to an emergency foster home for three months, and finally to a traditional foster home for the remaining seven months. Because of his fragile medical condition, Alfredo required specialized care immediately after he was released from the hospital. Whether he needed to be placed in a setting that was temporary by design, however, is less clear. Could Alfredo's worker have placed him in a specialized foster home where he could have stayed for the next ten months? Such a decision would have been more costly, but would have ensured greater stability for the child. Given Susanna's history with the child welfare agency, it was unlikely that she would reunify with her son quickly—if at all. Instead, Alfredo was moved when he was four months old and again seven months later. One of these placements could have been avoided if the social worker and her agency had determined that Alfredo's developmental needs were as important as their fiscal considerations.

Discussion

How can some of the challenges of serving young children be addressed within the child welfare system? According to child welfare workers, the quality of services could be improved considerably if resources were expanded to allow them time to do their jobs well. When limited resources result in caseloads of thirty to forty children, mediocrity is the highest attainable standard. Smaller caseloads would give workers more time to understand families' and children's needs; conduct better preplacement assessments; assess the appropriateness and suitability of all foster homes, including kinship foster homes; and provide aftercare (postadoption or postreunification) services for families in need. Expanded resources would allow workers to do parallel planning for all young children in foster care (discussed in more detail in Chapter 9). Under the current system, many young children must wait years until their parents have "failed"; such a system reduces children's opportunities for developing lifetime, permanent relationships with alternative caregivers.

Although child welfare workers have an obvious commitment to the children and families they serve, it is also apparent that many lack an overarching philosophy of practice to guide their decision making. Close attention to the unique needs and circumstances of young children, in particular, is often absent from their considerations. Frequently, child welfare workers appear to be serving families without a clear or uniform notion about which value they are trying to optimize. That is, when faced with choices to maximize the protection of children or the preservation of families or to foster children's cultural continuity or to promote permanence, they often proceed as if the weight given to each consideration should be determined on a case-by-case, worker-by-worker basis. Relying on individual workers to determine how they will optimize one value over another results in inequitable services for children and families. Instead, uniform standards of practice should be implemented so that child welfare workers have principles that will guide them in making thoughtful decisions on behalf of young children. In the next chapter, we lay out such a value-based framework.

Summary of Key Findings and Recommendations Regarding Public Child Welfare Practice

Finding	*Recommendation*
8.1. Age is a significant factor in workers' assessments of risk.	8.1. Age-sensitive practice in determining risk of harm is appropriate for young children, and we applaud workers who understand the unique vulnerabilities of young children.

Finding	*Recommendation*
8.2. Staff are frequently challenged by cases of child neglect among young children. These are the hardest cases to confirm and the ones that are the most likely to reemerge in the child welfare system.	8.2. Many workers suggested that case aides should be assigned to families who are reported for child neglect and for whom workers have concerns, but whose difficulties are not so severe that they can verify the maltreatment.

Finding	*Recommendation*
8.3. Occasionally, workers continue to assess the developmental risks for children after they have been placed.	8.3. We strongly recommend that all staff who work with young children have up-to-date knowledge of the developmental milestones of young children, so that they can feel confident in their assessments of children's progress in care. Children who fall behind these milestones should be offered special services to address these lags; caregivers may also need special services and attention to ensure that they are not posing developmental risks to young children.

Finding	*Recommendation*
8.4. Many workers recognize that some families have a poor prognosis for reunification. These families typically include those whose older children were removed and not reunified and those whose young children are reentering care for a second or third spell.	8.4. Workers should have strategies at their disposal to expedite the establishment of permanent placements for certain groups of young children. This process would include conducting a special administrative review, in addition to a court review, and rapidly placing cases that fall within certain guidelines in fost-adopt settings.

Finding	*Recommendation*
8.5. The child welfare workers indicated that the ages of young children do not dictate the amount of time or effort they expend in ensuring reunification services for them. However, they are more likely to be concerned about providing more intensive services to infants who are placed at birth.	8.5. For infants who are placed at birth, special efforts should be made to ensure that parents who seriously attempt to reunify with their babies have extra time to visit them to develop a relationship during the early months of life.

Finding	*Recommendation*
8.6. Parents' substance abuse poses significant challenges to child welfare workers. According to the workers, it is implicated in the placement of a large percentage of young children.	8.6. Child welfare workers may not be able to address problems associated with substance abuse directly, but may need to develop partnerships with public health, law enforcement, and substance abuse recovery programs to serve many substance-abusing families.

Finding	*Recommendation*
8.7. The counties in California had different perspectives on the usefulness of fost-adopt programs. Our review of the data for counties with effective fost-adopt programs showed the strong, positive results associated with fost-adopt, especially for young children.	8.7. We recommend that all states implement parallel planning programs by assessing all children for adoption early in their placement and simultaneously pursuing reunification and adoption. Increased federal funding through Title IV-B (of the Social Security Act) should support such programs to ensure that the positive outcomes outlined in the statute are financially encouraged.

Finding	*Recommendation*
8.8. Child care workers are discouraged about multiple placements but describe a series of systemic barriers to achieving greater stability of placements for young children.	8.8. The size of caseloads must be reduced to allow workers to make appropriate matches between children and foster parents and to strengthen foster care placements. Promoting beneficial experiences while in care and achieving positive outcomes from care cannot occur when caseloads are especially large.

9

Reconceptualizing the Child Welfare System for Very Young Children

The most important goal of the child welfare system is to protect children from harm by their parents or other caregivers. When the family does not guarantee protection to its most vulnerable members, the state has a legitimate interest in the welfare of its citizens that overrides the family's right to privacy (Otto & Melton, 1990). Although some contend that the value placed on family privacy undermines the state's ability to protect children from abuse and neglect, others argue that family privacy is not afforded sufficient regard in cases of alleged abuse. Given the potential risks to a child otherwise ignored by the state, a balanced approach would include coercive intervention only when it is clear that substantial harm would result from inaction.

In addition to children's need for basic protection from harm, it is widely believed that children have the right to be cared for by their biological parents and that parents have the right to have custody of and control over their children (Mason, 1994). The family is considered the fundamental social unit in the United States, and one of the secondary responsibilities of the child welfare system is to promote family members' moral obligations to take care of one another to the best of their ability.

At the point of entry to the foster care system, the next duty of the child welfare system is to give all children the opportunity to develop lifetime, legal relationships with adult caregivers who are concerned about their development and well-being. Because family life is so central to the organization of our society, the ensurance of a permanent family connection must be the centerpiece of a well-developed child welfare services system.

Basic Goals of Child Welfare

Protecting children from harm, supporting families, and promoting permanence then, are the three basic tenets on which child welfare policy should be based and are characterized in Figure 9.1. But these principles are easily lost or confused in the tumult of daily practice and are afforded no special importance when young children are involved. To increase attention to the unique circumstances of children in their tender years requires a further review of the relationship between the primary and secondary goals of the child welfare system.

Primary Goal

Child protection must be given the greatest weight in child welfare decision making. Of course, child welfare service providers must endeavor to find new approaches that help to achieve all basic child welfare goals, but if a choice must be made, protecting children from harm is clearly the most critical.

Protection from harm. Children who are physically hurt; sexually molested; or left without adequate food, clothing, shelter, or supervision must be protected from the harm that may result from these actions. But protection from harm has a broader meaning when young children are involved. Conventional child welfare practice too rarely takes into consideration the developmental harm that may befall a child in state custody. During this time of unparalleled growth, the protection of young children's developmental progress should be afforded special importance.

Examples of actions that compromise children's healthy development include placements in settings that are so deteriorated that they pose hazards to a child's physical development or basic cognitive stimulation. Multiple changes in placements endanger children's healthy affective development because they may preclude the formation of trusting relation-

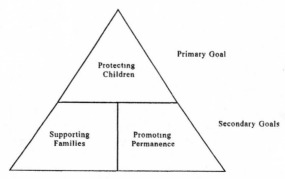

Figure 9.1 The fundamental goals of the child welfare system

ships. Furthermore, although placement in a group care setting may promote a fragile child's physical well-being, the absence of a single, consistent caregiver with whom he or she can form a lasting relationship may do developmental harm.

The goal of protection from developmental harm must become a guiding principle in child welfare practice with young children. Because of the lack of training, funding, and a clearly articulated mission, child welfare practitioners may do all they can to protect children from unsafe circumstances but do little to protect children's developmental futures. Without sufficient concern for the great damage that may result if children's developmental growth is compromised, the child welfare system fails to achieve one of its fundamental goals.

Secondary Goals

Without compromising a child's safety, child welfare service providers should pursue the goals of keeping children with their families and, failing that, ensuring that they achieve a legally permanent family for life.

Supporting families. Child welfare agencies have a mandate to make reasonable efforts to support families, including children's families of origin and, in some states, extended families. The way that this important goal is operationalized when young children are involved requires proactive planning and action. Many of the agencies, services, and supports that help families care for older children are not available for young children. Schools, recreational and arts programs, clubs, camps, and other activities are all offered, in part, to support school-aged children's healthy growth and development outside their families. These services also establish a circle of concern around older children to offer protection (at least in the form of child abuse reports) for children who are not adequately cared for by their parents.

Young children do not universally participate in any public programs in the United States. Such programs, if available, might be able to offer supplemental support to families who are facing difficult times. Child welfare agencies indeed attend more closely to the activities associated with supporting families with young children, yet still more care is needed; as was shown earlier, case openings for infants who are reported for child abuse drop abruptly after the age of one month. Fostering healthy families during the early years may provide some relief to child welfare agencies later on.

Promoting permanence. Of the permanency planning options available to children in foster care, reunification is and should remain the most highly valued goal. As we discussed earlier, about 45 percent of the young children who are placed with nonkin are reunified with their parents within two years. Efforts to reduce the reasons for placement or to reunify young children with their parents when placement is needed should be brief and intensive; children who can go home should do so rapidly and should be given ongoing support, and those who cannot be reunited with their biological parents should be placed for adoption as quickly as possible.

For young children who cannot return to their parents, other permanency-planning options are severely constrained. For children under age six who are placed with nonkin, long-term foster care should not be a permanent plan, for young children should not face a childhood of foster care. Similarly, legal guardianship does not offer a lifetime, legal relationship and is easily reversed; it should be pursued *only* for older children who have affective or historical ties to their biological parents that they do not want to sever. Adoption is the most permanent long-term alternative for young children who cannot go home. It can provide a new or an additional family for children—with blood and fictive kin—when children cannot remain safely with their biological parents. Yet structural barriers in many social service agencies reduce the opportunities for children to acquire new legal parents. The odds of adoption fall precipitously for children who enter foster care after age one (Barth, 1997); efforts to raise the age boundary are essential if young children's opportunities for permanence are to be increased.

For children in kinship care, opportunities for permanence are especially narrow. Some kin are discouraged from assuming legal guardianship of their relatives' children, since they typically lose their foster care payments when they gain legal authority. Adoption may also be a problem for some kin because of cultural concerns or emotional and personal apprehension about severing the parental rights of the biological parents. Some kin do not want to adopt their relatives' children because they hope that the biological parents will be able to assume their roles as primary caregivers some day (Thornton, 1991).

Parallel planning, reduced time frames for expediting permanence, reduced opportunities for continuances; subsidized guardianship for relatives; and a new form of "kinship adoption" that would be reversible upon a mutual agreement by the biological parent, the kinship caregiver, and the agency, are all important components of a child welfare system that truly promotes permanence for young children.

Current child welfare practice provides the same general services and supports to all children, regardless of age. Promoting permanence for young children, however, requires special considerations. The younger the child, the more consequential the opportunities to make permanency decisions that positively affect an entire lifetime.

Tertiary Goals of Child Welfare Services

The general construct behind the primary and secondary goals of child welfare services—protection from harm, supporting families, and promoting permanence—suggests a limited model of government intervention in family life that is designed to reduce the risk of harm to children. Changing the current approach to child welfare services so that all young children could be guaranteed the protections afforded by these goals would be a significant step forward. Our review of the evidence to date indicates that much work is needed before the child welfare system can claim that it has met its fundamental mission. If the states and federal government can do no more, changing current policies and practices to meet these ultimate goals should be the hallmark of their efforts.

If the chief goals of child welfare were met, would that be enough? Seeking sufficiency in the most desirable child welfare services system— as opposed to the necessary conditions in the fundamental framework— requires that the child welfare system move beyond the essential mission of protecting children from harm to the much larger goal of children's well-being. Extending the mission of child welfare services to include children's well-being would require a new set of tertiary goals, a greater funding base, and public consensus to support the goals. The additional elements consider a broader role for the government and an expanded view of family and community. Figure 9.2 outlines this multilayered approach to child welfare for young children. We embrace the inclusion of this third tier of child welfare priorities, and we underscore the preeminence of child protection, family support, and lifetime permanence in making decisions in child welfare.

Enhancing developmental value. We have raised a series of developmental issues that are relevant to the services that young children receive, but having a developmental perspective requires some understand-

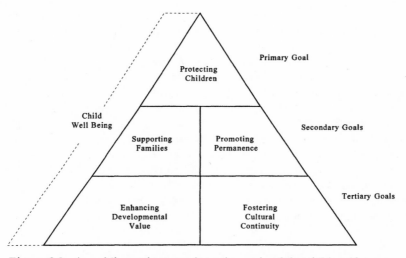

Figure 9.2 A multilayered approach to the goals of the child welfare system for young children

ing of what will not only reduce developmental harm but, ultimately, will add developmental value to a child's life. For children whose custody has been transferred to the state, some recognition of the importance of supporting their developmental progress may be appropriate. Therefore, the child welfare system's efforts to raise the developmental outcomes for children should be guided by the tertiary concept of *added value.* Given a child's developmental level when entering the child welfare system, the true test of the performance of those services is that they have added value to the child's overall well-being.

The current approach to child welfare services considers whether a child is in imminent danger as a result of child abuse and neglect. Once that anticipated danger has been avoided, the child welfare system does not have a clear direction to follow toward enhancing the child's development. There is little agreement that this is even an important goal. Child welfare workers commonly refer to such standards as "minimum sufficient level of care" or the "least detrimental alternative" in describing their guiding practice principles. These terms certainly cannot guide them in making decisions about rehabilitative interventions. Yet child welfare workers may have numerous opportunities to foster young children's developmental growth: by linking caregivers to early intervention services, enrolling young children in enriched early childhood programs, offering saturated and ongoing training models for caregivers that include extensive information about child development and enhancement activities for young children, or selecting permanent caregivers who will be able to help promote children's developmental gains. These opportunities should be grasped, when possible, as long as they do not interfere with the foremost goals of child welfare just described.

Fostering cultural continuity. As we stated earlier, because families have the primary responsibility of raising children, the government has an obligation to promote family care for children. In recent years, as child welfare has moved beyond the notion of saving children to that of preserving families, families have loomed large in child welfare practice. Today, the concept of family is liberal and includes a wide range of individuals related to a child by blood, marriage, and sometimes affinity (Child Welfare League of America, 1994). Broadening the notion of family has led to an inclusiveness that has few boundaries. Popular culture has transformed conventional views of child rearing to a new notion of community responsibility. If it "takes a village" to raise a child, then does child welfare have the responsibility to ensure that children have ties to neighbors and their communities? It may, as long as the responsibility to achieve high-order goals is met.

Children's cultural identity may be an important component of their full identity development (Phinney, Lochner, & Murphy, 1990) and for this reason, promotion of cultural identity is considered good practice for all parents, including foster parents (Spaulding for Children, 1995). As a tertiary goal of child welfare services, the promotion of cultural continuing, cultural identity, and community should also be embraced.

We view the promotion of cultural continuity as a tertiary value in child welfare services for two important reasons. First, all families are embedded in a cultural context, but culture is not synonymous with family. In recent years, some have confused the primary responsibility of government to support families as an equal responsibility to support culture. Recognizing the distinctions, albeit vague in some instances, between family and culture is important. Family, a broad notion in itself, has boundaries that are biologically and socially determined (Skolnick, in press). The boundaries of culture, however, are even broader and much more difficult to define. Individuals may view themselves as belonging to multiple cultures; in these instances, the promotion of culture by child welfare workers can become a task of boundless proportions.

The promotion of cultural continuity falls within the third tier of child welfare priorities not only because of its scope beyond the realm of family, but because culture, although important to the development of children, is not the sum total of children's development (McRoy, Zurcher, Lauderdale, & Anderson, 1982). Of course, when the primary and secondary child welfare goals can be realized, then cultural considerations should be given substantial weight. (We recognize that for children who are under the jurisdiction of the Indian Child Welfare Act, maintaining tribal continuity has a higher standing.)

Current practice for young children does not always achieve the fundamental goals of protecting, providing reasonable family support, and establishing legal permanence. To endeavor to do more—to add developmental value to children served by the child welfare system and to foster cultural continuity—is beyond the basic reductive model we have presented. Such goals, however, are not outside the bounds of child welfare authority and should guide practice when children have first been protected from harm, assured services to support their families, and provided with legal permanence.

Balancing Competing Priorities

All the goals just discussed are complementary and can be infused into child welfare practice with many children. But how do social workers make important decisions affecting the lives of young children when faced with individual circumstances that pit the fundamental goals against each other? Child welfare practice is not formulaic. Few child welfare cases arise in which workers can predetermine the children's needs or the families' outcomes several months later. The work is individualistic and demands a high degree of sensitivity and discretion by child welfare workers. Saying that, however, does not mean that child welfare workers should not be guided by a set group of practice principles with an agreed-upon value base.

Child welfare workers must frequently balance the competing priorities of protecting children and supporting families. They must value family while protecting children's development. And they must provide permanence, even when doing so conflicts with values about family. Child welfare workers may respond to these competing circumstances in myriad ways—sometimes optimizing permanence, at other times optimizing cultural or community continuity, and at still other times weighing considerations of the family more heavily. A multilayered approach to child welfare services, as we have outlined here, is a fundamental framework for decision making. In the following sections, we offer several examples of critical "tiebreakers" that may help guide practice when social workers are faced with difficult decisions on behalf of young children.

Supporting Family versus Protecting Children from Harm

Child welfare practice is not simply concerned with supporting young children's biological families; rather, it is concerned with supporting the group of individuals whom children recognize as family by blood and marriage. In recent years, the United States has shifted its child welfare policy toward the greater use of kin as a placement resource (Kusserow, 1992). In some limited circumstances, placement with kin has taken precedence over children's basic right to protection from harm (Berrick, Needell, & Barth, in press). Kin who cannot reasonably assure that children will be protected from maltreatment (from the biological parents, other individuals, or themselves) or who cannot make reasonable efforts to protect the children from developmental harm should not have their relatives' children placed with them. The child welfare system should not lose sight of its basic mission to protect children in an overly enthusiastic effort to raise children with their families.

When the values of family come into conflict with protection from harm, the vulnerability of the children should weigh heavily in child welfare decisions. Since young children do not have the developmental capacity to protect themselves in marginal environments, social workers should consider the children's capacity to elude possible dangers that may be present in some compromised environments. As we discussed in earlier chapters, protecting children from harm takes on an urgency when young children are involved. Because of their special vulnerability, ensuring their protection must be an active process that guards against a variety of potential dangers. Circumstances that would pose little or no risk to older children or adolescents can be life threatening to young children. Therefore, no matter what their relationship to young children, adults who cannot reasonably ensure the children's protection cannot be considered viable caregivers for them.

Supporting Families versus Enhancing Developmental Value

Because of the significant value placed on family in American society and our reluctance to intrude on family privacy, kinship placements will continue to be a preferred placement resource for children who cannot remain with their biological parents. But what values should a social worker optimize when a kin caregiver is available but unable to promote a young child's developmental growth significantly? The child may not be developmentally harmed in the home of his or her relative, but owing to poverty, low educational attainment, or other reasons, the relative may not be able to enhance the child's development (see Gaudin & Sutphen, 1993, for a discussion of quality of the environments in kin and nonkin homes and Berrick, Barth, & Needell, 1994, for a review of the characteristics of kin caregivers).

Social workers should be guided by the principles of family support but first do no harm in circumstances such as these. Because a secondary goal of the child welfare system is to support families, and promoting children's optimal developmental opportunities is a tertiary goal, kin placements—even those that do not provide enriched developmental opportunities for young children—must remain a priority for placement as long as the children are not harmed in care. Services should be offered to help kin caregivers enhance the developmental opportunities of the children in their care, including enriched infant-toddler and preschool programs, parenting education, and other supports, but the standard for assessing the appropriateness of the kin placement should rest on the assumption of basic protection, rather than the standard of added developmental value.

A more difficult issue arises when a young child who is in kinship care could be placed in another kinship home that has greater access to the social capital (such as exposure to better schools and lower rates of violence in the neighborhood) that may help achieve better social and educational opportunities, when doing so would require moving the child away from the psychological continuity of a beloved kinship caregiver. As always, the wishes of the biological parents and other family members should be given substantial weight. In addition, the child's sense of "family" and each caregiver's ability to provide a supported, permanent home for the child must be given significant consideration. While adults may have a notion of family that is based fundamentally on biologism (Skolnick, in press), including an aunt or an uncle whom the child does not know, the child may perceive such a family member as a stranger. The added developmental value that might be offered in the kinship home with more social capital must be balanced against the support the child may receive in the more familiar kinship home. In essence, the short-term negative effects of disrupting an existing relationship must be weighed against the long-term developmental benefits to the child of placement with a family and community with more resources. If the decision is made to move the child, some of these short-term negative effects could be lessened by a slow and graceful transition from one kinship home to the other.

Supporting Family versus Promoting Permanence

Current child welfare practice often leaves social workers without clear guideposts for making early decisions on behalf of young children. For example, because of the structural design of the current child welfare system, kin may not find satisfaction in conventional permanency planning options (adoption or legal guardianship). Some kin do not want to adopt their relatives' children for the reasons we outlined earlier. Others, of course, do want to adopt for a variety of reasons, one of which is that it gives them legal responsibility and protection from other relatives' claims on the children. The benefits of legal adoption for children, including rights to inheritance, social security, and legal standing, should be described to kin so they can make informed decisions about the nature of their permanent relationship to the children. Forcing kin caregivers into adoption when they are opposed to it but are willing to make a commitment to permanence inappropriately promotes a narrow definition of permanence over supporting family. Kin often claim that they make lifetime commitments to the children in their care (Berrick et al., 1994). When they do, they should be given the legal authority to exercise this commitment outside the bounds of the child welfare system. Therefore, we prefer to seek ways to avoid such conflicts. Rather than place kin caregivers in a position in which such fundamental values must compete, changes should be made in the child welfare system to give kin other avenues for promoting permanence, such as subsidized guardianship and a newly defined "kinship adoption," that will allow both values to be realized for young children.

Legal guardianship with kin is also a problem for some caregivers who need financial assistance to care for their relatives' children. Thrusting legal guardianship on them without regard for the children's financial well-being raises the value of legal permanence over the value of family and should be guarded against when possible. Policy changes that would allow kin to take legal guardianship while collecting subsidies to meet the children's basic needs would ameliorate this dilemma.

Other examples of conflict in child welfare practice arise when young children are offered placement with family members (kinship care) who can provide short-term stability, but long-term uncertainty. That is, a young child may have a long-standing relationship with an aged relative or with a relative whose health is significantly compromised. Such a potential caregiver may be able to raise the child for a few years, but she may not be able to care for the child until adulthood. In such a situation, when the child cannot go home, the child welfare worker must work with the biological parents and other family members to decide whether to disrupt the meaningful early relationship with the relative and place the child with another caregiver who can provide more long-lasting opportunities for family or leave the child in the home of the relative whom he or she now knows.

Child welfare services that are truly family focused endeavor to mirror the choices and actions of healthy families outside the system. When the second-tier goals of supporting family and promoting permanence are in direct conflict with one another, neither is obviously preferred over the other. In such a circumstance, if the family prefers that the child be placed with the older caregiver, the child welfare worker should strive to assist the family to widen the circle of concern around the child, so he or she does not have to rely solely on the elderly caregiver. Efforts to encourage the child to develop close relationships with additional family members should also be made, and the worker should ensure that legal strategies are in place for the child to transfer from one family member to another if it becomes necessary to do so. If arrangements such as these cannot be included in the child's case plan, then a permanent placement in such a home should be avoided and another relative or nonrelative should be sought as a permanent placement.

Finally, critical dilemmas may arise when siblings are placed in care. In general, every effort should be made to place siblings together to support children's family relationships. But what about an infant placed at birth whose siblings are already in foster care? This infant is likely to have a different conception of family than his or her older brothers and sisters and not to have relationships that warrant the same kind of preservation. Therefore, if the older siblings' caregiver is unwilling to provide a permanent placement for the infant, the infant should be placed with a different caregiver who can provide such permanence.

Protection from Harm versus Enhanced Developmental Value

According to child welfare workers, the quality of foster care in many jurisdictions ranges from excellent to abysmal. We have heard social workers indicate that in some instances, the only foster parents available to care for young children are those who cannot guarantee the children's safety and protection. Sometimes social workers have turned to specialized, high-cost treatment-focused foster care to serve these young children. The children in these settings are likely to receive developmentally enhanced services from their well-trained care providers. Such settings are generally less than optimal from a fiscal standpoint, but may be the best alternative for children whose care may otherwise be compromised. Obviously, when young children cannot be assured protection from harm and developmentally enhanced services are the only viable alternative, such placements should indeed be made to promote their well-being.

Promoting Permanence versus Fostering Cultural Continuity

More frequently than they like, child welfare workers are faced with questions pertaining to ethnic matching: Should they demand same-race placements for children? Should they leave children in nonpermanent foster homes while they search for same-race caregivers?

The subject of transracial adoption and same-race placement has been discussed at great length in child welfare, and we do not propose to offer a final and conclusive answer to this sensitive topic. Nevertheless, the analysis of child welfare values that we have laid out must be understood to argue that ensuring children's permanence should be a high priority in child welfare services. Young children should not wait in foster care to get on with the business of having a family. Unfortunately, current opportunities for adoption are fleeting, since children who are placed in foster care after the first year of life have much lower odds of ever being adopted (Barth, 1997), and African American and Hispanic children have, by far, the worst chance. Child welfare agencies must have designated resources available to recruit caregivers of color in much greater numbers. But if no matched families are available and nonracially matched families can be found for young children, these nonmatched families offer lifetime, legal relationships with adult caregivers. It is the child welfare system's higher-order priority to provide permanent families for children promptly.

Fostering Cultural Continuity versus Enhancing Developmental Value

We have laid out a series of predicaments that child welfare workers regularly face in their challenging practice. Solutions to these dilemmas are rarely easy, but having a theoretical and value-based framework to consider may facilitate the resolution to many of them. In general, we suggested that when the chief value of protecting children from harm (including developmental harm) comes into conflict with secondary values, such as supporting families or promoting permanence, or when these principles conflict with tertiary values like enhancing developmental value or fostering cultural continuity, fundamental principles must guide practice. But what if social workers encounter circumstances in which the tertiary values conflict?

Take the example of a young child who cannot be returned to her birth parents and who has no available kin to care for her. The social worker has two nonkin homes available for placement, both fully prepared to protect the child from harm and both promising permanence. In one home, the child will receive adequate care while remaining in a familiar cultural environment; in the other, the child will not have the same opportunities for cultural continuity, but will be in an enhanced developmental environment that her birth or alternative foster home may not have provided.

How to decide in such an instance? Given the child's young age and her chance for developmental growth, it would be reasonable to choose the home that provides enhanced developmental value. All else being equal, the evidence in favor of factors that enhance children's long-term beneficial development (see Chapter 1) would suggest that the child welfare agency would have the unique chance to go beyond the conventional standard of providing adequate care to children and, instead, could optimize the child's lifetime opportunities. If such a home could be further supported to ensure that it could foster cultural continuity, current evidence would weigh heavily in favor of such a placement.

It would also be reasonable to select the alternative home that offered cultural continuity on the premise that the promotion of cultural identity is, in itself, a meaningful developmental value (although evidence to support the importance of cultural continuity for children is not as clear as evidence of the impact of enhanced environments). In this home, the provision of supports and services to the caregiver and the child to enrich the child's development would be another possible strategy for resolving this conflict.

Ultimately, we are not in a position to arbitrate between these opposing views—in our typology of fundamental child welfare goals, enhancing developmental value and fostering cultural continuity are in the third tier of priorities. Social workers who are faced with these unique circumstances will make such decisions on an individual basis, depending on the circumstances presented.

Redesigning Child Welfare Services for Young Children

The foregoing considerations regarding placements, ongoing assessments, and permanence for young children fall within the realm of social workers' discretion and thoughtful child welfare practice. Policy at the state or local level is not necessarily required for workers to infuse their practice with special considerations for young children. But changes in social workers' perspectives on child development will go only so far in ensuring better outcomes for young children. Statutory, regulatory, and judicial changes are needed to improve services equitably to all young children who are touched by the child welfare services system.

To promote these structural changes, policy makers first have to recognize that young children face unique considerations when they are abused, neglected, or placed in foster care. Second, they must have a legal and historical context from which to justify legislative changes. And third, specific research-based recommendations must be forwarded so that changes in the delivery of services follow a rationally based plan.

Perspectives on Placement Through the Eyes of a Child

Today's child welfare system was standardized by federal law in 1980. One of the goals of this law—the Adoption Assistance and Child Welfare Act (P.L. 96-272)—was to ensure that families received equal treatment under the law when their children were removed from their homes. But the guidelines for 6-, 12-, 18-, and 24-month reviews were based on several assumptions that may be less salient for young children. An example of a placement experience that is similar in circumstance except for the child's age may help to illustrate the inequities for children that current practice promotes.

A boy is placed in foster care at age ten and remains in care for twelve months. At the point of reunification, we assume he has the developmental capacity to understand his experience—he can understand why he was placed, with whom he was placed, and why he was returned to his mother—at least intellectually, if not emotionally. Separation from his family lasted for about one-tenth of his lifetime; he had ten years to develop a relationship with his mother before he was placed and during placement, he could draw on his memories and experiences to conceive of a future after he returned home. During reunification, the child welfare worker is confident that if circumstances in his life begin to deteriorate, the boy will have some capacity to protect himself. If times get tough, he will probably be able to find something to eat and put himself to bed. Under more drastic circumstances, of course, he may be able to call out for help, dial 911, or escape his home if dangerous conditions persist.

The infant, toddler, and preschool-age child all stand in stark contrast to the ten year old. These young children are far less able to protect themselves from harm; to call out for help; or, in some circumstances, even to recognize that their care is anything but normative (Smetana, Kelly, & Twentyman, 1984). Once they are placed in foster care, they may not understand the events that have led to changes in the familiar sights and sounds of their environment. These children, particularly those placed at birth, have no maternal relationship that they can draw on for comfort, no memory to attach themselves to, and no sense of a past or a future. Toddlers who remain in foster care for a full twelve months will have little understanding of the process and will probably be confused about who, indeed, is their primary caregiver. Returned to their biological mothers at age two, they will have lived fully half their lifetime in substitute care. Upon returning home, they are likely to experience the anxiety of separation—from their foster caregivers, not their mothers. We do not know how young children experience the passage of time, but we know that time has different objective consequences for children of different ages. The significance of children's need for protection; the importance of developing early, stable relationships; and the implications of offering lifetime permanence are indeed momentous for young children.

A Legal and Historical Context for Changing Policy

If the current system is not developmentally sensitive by its structure, is it politically feasible or appropriate to redesign it to account for developmental differences? There are numerous examples of public policies that reflect social considerations about children's age, development, and ability to participate in various public activities; these policies were based on the assumption either that children are vulnerable members of society in need of special protection or that society must be protected from children's developmental limitations. Age-based criteria restrict, for example, children's ability to vote, drive, consume alcoholic beverages, and work.

Throughout much of this century, the "tender years doctrine" was invoked when custody decisions were at issue (Mason, 1994). Assuming that the attachment between mother and child was inviolable, courts regularly granted full custody to mothers of young children. The law has, albeit slowly, continued to carve out a number of specific child-based criteria related primarily to health and safety and, to a lesser extent, developmental capacity. Both Congress and the state legislatures have enacted numerous child-based safety measures. Two notable federal laws are the Federal Hazardous Substances Act and the Child Protection Safety Act, which attempt to protect consumers by encouraging manufactures to make products safe (Nazario, 1988). Additional laws that are specifically targeted to children include those that require certain children's garments to be fire retardant, special caps on medicines to protect children from poisoning, and warning labels on certain toys to protect children from injuries. Recent years have seen the advent of laws requiring car seats, seat belts, and other devices to protect children in vehicles.

At the federal level, some provisions in health and safety benefits specifically target young children. The federal Early Periodic Screening, Diagnosis, and Treatment (EPSDT) program established a schedule of age-based health programs for young, poor children. The program mandates a variety of services based on the physiological characteristics of young children and established a rational basis for targeting young children because of their higher sensitivity to health-related problems. Age-based criteria are also integrated into the provisions of the Supplemental Food Program for Women, Infants and Children (WIC). WIC provides food assistance to low-income pregnant women, postpartum women and their infants, and at-risk children up to age five. The eligibility criteria are based on age and physiological need, with different types of food vouchers for children younger than one, between one and three, and three to five years old. These health and safety regulations reflect special considerations for promoting young children's physical growth and development through proper food and nutrition.

One of the changes in federal law that specifically targeted young children and their cognitive development was the Education of the Handicapped Act amendments of 1986—Part H (P.L. 99-457). The law provides funding to states to serve infants and toddlers with developmental disabilities and those who are at risk of disabilities in early intervention programs. The bill recognizes the importance of promoting the cognitive development of young children who are specially challenged.

Although some programs speak to developmental considerations in young children, overall, the United States has not demonstrated a firm commitment to promoting policies or programs for children younger than six (Kamerman & Kahn, 1995). Furthermore, some of the special provisions available to young children have been developed as a result of court decisions, rather than as proactive policies by federal legislators. For example, in the early 1990s, a U.S. Supreme Court decision significantly expanded the criteria under which children may qualify for Supplemental Security Income (SSI) as a result of mental disabilities or other impairments (*Sullivan v. Zebley* et al., 1990). In response to the Zebley ruling, the federal government established age-based criteria, or Assessment Domains for Childhood Disability for children receiving SSI. The Zebley decision was the catalyst for establishing functional age-specific criteria for assessing disabilities in children younger than one, between one and three, and from three to eighteen years of age. These age-based criteria represented federal sensitivity to differences in cognitive development for young children. However, the Zebley decision was significantly modified by the Personal Responsibility and Work Opportunity Reconciliation Act of 1996, the welfare reform act, which significantly narrowed the opportunities for young children to receive SSI. Therefore, federal leadership in designing age-sensitive policies suffered a significant setback.

States' efforts and developmentally sensitive child welfare policy. Despite growing evidence confirming the unique needs of young children, few states have used social science research to implement developmentally based child welfare policy. No state has implemented changes so sweeping as to be considered revolutionary, but subtle advances toward the recognition of younger children's unique vulnerabilities and definable needs seem apparent.

Some states have adopted age-based criteria for placing children in group homes. Both Wisconsin and Michigan provide that no child under age twelve (in some counties in Michigan, under age 10) can be placed in group care unless there is no reasonable alternative. As was noted earlier, California also adopted somewhat restrictive laws on placing young children in group homes, although implementation of the regulations has been slow. And in Ohio, special crisis nurseries provide temporary shelter and other care for drug-exposed and HIV-infected children under age six.

Iowa enacted age-based criteria for shortening permanency planning time lines for young children. In that state, parental rights may be terminated if a child is four years old or younger and has spent twelve of the past eighteen months in out-of-home care. The provisions are even more severe for children under age three; in this case, if a child has been in out-of-home care for either six of the past twelve months or the past six consecutive months, parental rights may be terminated (Iowa, Juvenile Justice, 1992). This law is important for two reasons: (1) it clearly defines for parents the time line in which substantial changes in family life must be achieved and sustained and (2) it considers the importance of rapidly developing legal, long-term alternative parents for children when they are unable to live with their biological parents.

In 1996, the California state legislature passed Assembly Bill 1524, (AB 1524 Chapter 1083, Statutes of 1996) which requires revised time lines for children who are placed in foster care before age three. Rather than mandating the provision of court-ordered reunification services to families for a full twelve months, the new law specifies that for children under age three, "court-ordered services shall not exceed a period of six months" (p. 4). Substantial latitude remains, however, for extending services if some progress is being made on a case plan, thereby weakening the intent of the bill considerably. The maximum time for reunification for children of all ages may not exceed the conventional limits of child welfare services—eighteen months.

Colorado is one of the few states that has initiated broad child welfare reform designed to address the special needs of young children in out-of-home care. The original catalyst for the statute was the state foster parent association, whose members were concerned about the length of time children spent in out-of-home placement and frustrated by what they perceived as a bias toward biological parents. Specifically, advocates for the law were concerned that the rights of children to a permanent plan were being sacrificed to give biological parents extended opportunities to achieve family reunification. They focused on the needs of children under age six and highlighted these children's special vulnerabilities in their appeal to the state legislature.

Colorado House Bill 94-1178, Concerning the Placement of Young Children (Colorado Revised Statute, 1994), or expedited permanency planning (Zschoche & Suprenand, 1996), established a new framework for considering child development within the context of child welfare services. The law allows for an expedited placement procedure to ensure that children under age six who are removed from their homes are returned home or placed in permanent homes as promptly as possible. To reconfigure services, the legislation provides for permanency planning hearings no later than three months after the dispositional hearing. At the hearing, the court reviews the progress of the case and may order the county to show cause why it should not file a motion to terminate parental rights. Except in special circumstances, young children must be placed in permanent homes no later than twelve months after their original placement. The law also narrowly restricts the conditions under which delays and continuances may be granted.

The Colorado law addresses issues pertaining to the termination of parental rights and provides a series of age-based indicators, reflecting the significance of the children's ages and levels of development on the long-term prospects for achieving permanence. For example, in the case of a parent's long-term confinement (in prison), when a child is younger than six at the time of adjudicated dependence and the duration of the parent's confinement exceeds thirty-six months (before eligibility for parole), termination of parental rights may proceed.

Evidence of the program's success in expediting permanence may be emerging. According to child welfare staff in Colorado, after one year in placement, 57 percent of the children were reunified with their parents, 16 percent were permanently placed with kin, and 19 percent were in adoptive or fost-adopt homes. Only 8 percent of the children under six were in nonpermanent homes (Zschoche & Suprenand, 1996). To achieve these outcomes, significant changes were required in practice at the level of licensing and child welfare services. All caregivers (kin and nonkin) receive full home studies before children are placed to ensure that they are acceptable as adoptive placements from the start. The approach requires smaller caseloads, diligent efforts to ensure that reasonable efforts are indeed provided, and the use of family meetings (sometimes referred to as the family unity model) to place responsibility for child protection on all members of the family. Others who have followed the development of this model are less sanguine about its effectiveness (J. Fluke, American Humane Association, personal communication, February 25, 1997). Although the changes initiated in Colorado are significant, there is also a growing recognition that the process for changing child welfare and the courts requires substantial time to take effect. We view this new approach in law as an encouraging step toward the greater recognition of the role that child development can play in child welfare practice.

Consideration of Developmentally Sensitive Federal Policies

The Independent Living Skills program, codified in P.L. 99-272, clearly reflects age and developmental considerations for adolescents in the foster care system. Might the federal government, therefore, cultivate a developmentally sensitive approach to child welfare services for young children? Or could other states adopt policies and practices that guarantee real reform for children? The research presented in earlier chapters suggests that young children face a number of unique vulnerabilities in the child welfare system. Developmentally oriented policies and practices are clearly warranted to attain better outcomes for young children than they experience under the current system of supports and services. In the following sections, we present a series of policy and practice decisions that should be considered, in part or in whole, to protect children, support families, and promote permanence for young children.

Reducing Reports of Maltreatment for Young Children

Young children are reported to the child welfare system more often than any other age group. The large majority of reports for young children are for neglect or the absence/incapacity of caregivers—indicators of maltreatment that are closely tied to parents' substance abuse.

• The child welfare services system should develop collaborative relationships with substance abuse treatment services, public health professionals, and other allied service providers to serve families who are substance abusers. It is not the duty or responsibility of the child welfare system to prevent substance abuse in communities. The creation of fiscal or administrative structures that give child welfare agencies direct control over drug treatment services may be necessary.

• When infants and young children are reported to child welfare agencies because of their parents' drug abuse, these cases should be taken seriously and should be uniformly assessed for risk of harm.

Early Intervention for Young Children

In addition to being reported for child neglect more than any other form of abuse, young children are also more likely to be rereported for neglect and other forms of maltreatment. Social workers may have insufficient evidence to place children in these circumstances, but nonetheless may harbor concerns about the children's well-being. We suggest that a standardized approach be adopted to managing the volume of child maltreatment reports on young children that are received each year. The outline of this approach for infants and other young children is presented in Table 9.1.

• Structured decision making protocols and appropriate definitions of neglect should be developed to provide equitable services to young children. Neglect is a concept that is partially socially constructed and partially determined by specific threats to children's health and safety. Definitions of neglect must therefore be decided with a wide spectrum of participants in each state.

• In-home services should be mandatory for all families with young children whose cases are opened for services but whose children are not placed in care. Services should be offered for a minimum of six months and a maximum of three years with full federal financial participation. Families who need other supportive services should be transferred to community programs, such as enriched child care. These actions may reduce the likelihood of further serious maltreatment and would provide a modicum of support to families with young children.

Ensuring Permanence for Young Children

Although about half the young children who are placed with nonkin reunify with their parents within four years of placement, another quarter remain in long-term foster care. Adoption rates are relatively high for infants who are initially placed in nonkin settings, but for children placed with nonkin after age one, adoption rates plummet.

Table 9.1 Early Intervention for Children under Age Six

Age	Child Maltreatment Report	Investigation	Services	
			Mandatory	Voluntary
Under 1 year	All reports should proceed to investigation.	Investigation includes 1. Face-to-face contact with parent. 2. Home visit 3. Collateral contacts with others associated with the family	Cases opened for services should be mandated to receive in-home family maintenance services (unless placed in care) for a minimum of six months and a maximum of three years with full federal financial participation.	Cases investigated but not opened should be offered voluntary in-home services for one year (provided either by social workers or case aides).
1–5 years	Standardized screening protocols should be developed and used to assess the need for an investigation.	Screened cases should be investigated using a standardized protocol for risk assessment—particularly sensitive to statewide standards concerning assessment of neglect.	Cases opened for services should be mandated to receive in-home family maintenance services (unless placed in care) for a minimum of six months and a maximum of two years (or until they can be transitioned to other non-child welfare services) with full federal financial participation.	Cases investigated but not opened should be offered voluntary in-home services for six months (provided either by social workers or case aides).

The child welfare system must make strenuous efforts to reunify young children with their biological parents, but children who cannot go home must be allowed to establish permanent relationships with other adults early in placement. To ensure that young children have real opportunities for permanence, we recommend a revised time frame for achieving these lifetime goals in Figure 9.3.

For all young children, regardless of type of placement:

• In addition to the current court review process that occurs every six months, administrative reviews should be made at three-month intervals for all cases involving young children. The first review should take place ninety days after the jurisdictional hearing to ensure that permanence is actively considered from the first days of care.

• No later than the six-month court review, young children should be placed in a permanent setting either with kin or in a fost-adopt home. Barring extreme circumstances, they should exit from foster care and achieve permanence within twelve months of the first day of placement (calendar time, not court time).

• Long-term foster care is an unacceptable permanent plan for almost every young child. The cases of children under age six who are recommended to long-term foster care should be reviewed by a special administrative team, and all but extraordinary cases should be denied.

• Continuances and delays should be minimized for all young children in foster care. A child's rights to safety and permanence should remain the centerpiece of the court process, and attorneys should honor and support a parent's wish for voluntary relinquishment of parental rights or cooperate with the agency plan for an alternative permanent placement.

• Young children whose parents have such chronic legal, mental health, or drug abuse problems that their other children are already in care or have been placed in other permanent homes should receive increased consideration for the assignment of a parallel adoption worker at intake and to a permanent plan at three months.

• For young children who cannot go home, adoption should always be examined as a potential permanent arrangement. Adoption is frequently the best solution for children because it cannot be overturned by a judge without the adoptive parent's consent, is binding in all states and countries, and includes legal inheritance rights.

For young children who are placed with nonkin:

• If a child who is placed with nonkin does not go home, an adoption worker should be assigned to the case at the three-month review to begin working in parallel to the family reunification worker to prepare the family for adoption.

	Placement	3 Months	6 Months	9 Months	12 Months
Kin placements	Kinship home assessed and family reunification worker assigned	Administrative review** and family meeting*** to plan for permanency.	Permanency planning hearing	Administrative review and family meeting to confirm permanency options.	Exit from care: Reunification, "kinship adoption," or legal guardianship.
Nonkin placements	Family reunification worker assigned	Administrative review. Adoption worker assigned for parallel planning	Permanency planning hearing	Administrative review	Exit from care: Reunification or adoption, including termination of parental rights

At reunification (which can occur at any time at or before 12 months):

Voluntary in-home supportive services offered for six months. One year of mandatory in-home services provided to families at the greatest risk of reentry ↑

At adoption, "kinship adoption," or legal guardianship (which can occur anytime at or before 12 months): ↑

Referral to community supports

*Child may be reunified at any point throughout the time frames listed.

**Administrative review does not involve the courts. During the administrative review, the assigned child welfare worker, the supervisor, and the infant or young-child specialist reviews the progress of the case plan and options for permanence.

***Family meeting includes all relatives and fictive kin who are or will play a major role in planning for the child's permanence.

Figure 9.3 A revised permanency planning time frame for children under age six*

• Exit options for young children who are placed with nonkin include reunification or adoption. Legal guardianship should be strongly discouraged for any child under age six who is placed in nonkin care. Legal guardianship is easily abandoned and does not offer legal permanence for young children.

For young children who are placed with kin:

• When possible, child welfare practice should include opportunities for families to make decisions about the well-being of their children. Therefore, shortly after a child is placed in care with kin, a family meeting should be organized. The family meeting is a tool designed to build on family members' strengths in making decisions to expedite a young child's permanent placement. The meeting brings family, friends, and other significant adults together to develop a plan of action that addresses the concerns, needs, and problems of the family that resulted in the juvenile court's interventions.

• For children who are placed with kin, exit opportunities include reunification, "kinship adoption," and legal guardianship. The benefits of adoption should be thoroughly explored with kin. Many kin make a lifetime commitment to the young children in their care; more may be willing to make their commitment legally binding if they had faith that the adoption could be reversed if the children's mothers or fathers were able to resume parenting one day. Changing adoption laws to make these allowances for kin may expand exit opportunities for young children—what we refer to in this book as "kinship adoption" (although other terms that may be more culturally appropriate should also be considered). For kin who remain opposed to adoption but are willing to include young children in their families, new alternatives should be explored to release children from the child welfare system and return them to their care.

• Assuming that greater exit opportunities are developed for kin through reversible adoptions and subsidized legal guardianship, long-term foster care for children in kinship care should be strongly discouraged.

Reducing Instability for Young Children

Young children often experience a high degree of placement instability in foster care. Among the roughly one-quarter of all young children who remain in foster care four years after placement, about one-fifth of those in kinship care and over one-third of those in nonkin care have three or more placements.

Although infants who are moved from home to home cannot tell us how they feel, we can observe the signs of distress. "You can just see their little lights go out," remarked one child welfare worker, regarding the effect of multiple placements. Multiple placements for young children are often the product of the system's design, rather than of child-specific problems. Although emergency shelter homes are intended to be short term, young children routinely remain in them for several months. After several months in care, the scarcity of emergency homes needed for other incoming children, along with the increased cost of these homes, creates pressure to move young children. Such changes in placement may occur at the least opportune time, particularly from the standpoint of infants' development.

Multiple changes in placements, whether from one foster home to another or from a foster home to the birth home and back to foster care, can be especially difficult for young children. Almost one-quarter of young children who return to their biological parents return to the foster care system within three years.

• Foster parents should be prepared to make an unconditional commitment to the children in their homes to minimize the possibility of further changes in placements.

• Children six years and younger who are recommended to a third placement in care should have their cases reviewed by a special administrative team to understand how future placements can be minimized and how systemic contributors to multiple placements can be reduced.

• To ensure the successful reunification of young children with their biological parents, intensive aftercare services should be provided for one year to targeted families whose circumstances put them at the greatest risk of the failure of reunification. If these families' children still reenter care despite such services, it is appropriate to consider the children's total time in placement in determining how many additional months of reunification services should apply.

Reconsidering Placement Settings for Young Children

About half the young children in out-of-home care reside with kin, a third live with nonkin, and the remainder are placed in other settings. When abused or neglected young children must be taken from their parents, foster care can either provide the nurturance they have lacked or continue the damaging insensitivity that appears to have long-lasting consequences. It can either be a protective factor in a vulnerable child's life or yet another stressor. Thus child welfare services should address young children's reactions to being separated from their families, not only the situation (the maltreatment) that led to their placement (Eagle, 1993; Molin, 1988). Children should not be further damaged or compromised by a system whose primary goal should be to protect them from harm—including developmental harm—but that sometimes permits adults to lose sight of the children's needs and capacities (Goldson, 1987).

• The current preference for placing young children with kin should be maintained. Family members are a critical resource for children who are experiencing trauma and should be supported in exercising their obligation to their relatives' children. Efforts to ensure that the quality of all kin foster homes meet appropriate standards to foster the healthy affective, cognitive, and physical development of young children should become a routine component of child welfare practice.

• Young children should not be placed in group care settings. Even the "best" group home, with the most competent staff, cannot provide the stable, round-the-clock nurturing that young children require. Alternative placement resources, including the development of specialized foster care, should be promoted for specially challenged young children.

• Caregivers in all placement settings should be given initial and ongoing training about the special needs that children bring to foster care. Strategies to enhance young children's developmental progress should be taught to all caregivers and child welfare workers so that young children can continue to make physical, affective, and cognitive gains while in care.

Special Issues for Infants Who Are Placed at Birth

For better or worse, the child welfare system has many young babies in its care. In California, more than one-sixth of the infants who entered care in 1988–89 were still there six years later. These children have never known parents as other children have; thus, they demand a high standard of service from a government that is acting as their only known substitute caregiver.

Unfortunately, child welfare workers make decisions about infants' care that may ultimately compromise their successful adulthood. Included among these decisions, more often than is acceptable, is the choice to send infants home to parents who are so unprepared for them that they return to foster care within a matter of months.

• Reunification services for infants who have never known their parents demand special consideration from child welfare workers. Efforts to enhance the duration and frequency of parents' visits with their children will be vital as they develop their new relationship with one another.

• Time lines for terminating parental rights should be strictly enforced for infants who are placed at birth in nonkin homes so that opportunities for adoption are not overlooked.

• The cases of infants placed at birth whose older siblings have previously been in care and whose legal relationship has been severed with their parents should be reviewed critically by a special administrative review to determine whether parallel reunification and adoption planning at the point of entry to care should proceed.

• Efforts to minimize changes in placements for infants are essential. If an initial change in placement is necessary, it should be made within the first month of placement. Further changes should be avoided.

• Agencies should redesign services and retrain workers to pay greater attention to the developmental needs of infants. Some agencies have centralized this expertise in a specialized infants' unit. Having a group of specialists on infants whose expertise is distributed across units may be a preferable long-term arrangement.

Child Welfare Services, Culture, and Young Children

In comparison to older children, young children experience a unique life course when they come in contact with the child welfare system. More pronounced than the findings for young children, however, are the consistently poor outcomes for African American children in the child welfare services process. African American children are more likely to be reported for child abuse and neglect and are far more likely to be placed in foster care. Once they are in care, African American children are less likely to be reunified or adopted and are more likely to remain in long-term foster care.

Clearly, using knowledge of child development to improve the quality of child welfare services is complicated by the fact that case managers, service providers, and foster parents often serve children and families from different backgrounds than their own. If service providers and clients do not have a shared reality or theoretical perspectives are used to imply a worldview that is foreign to the clients' (Turner, 1991), interventions for these families are unlikely to be successful.

Although child welfare services cannot be assessed independently of the society in which they exist, rigorous evaluations of policies and programs are needed to determine the role of ethnicity in the efficacy of services (Courtney et al., 1996); at a minimum, child welfare workers should strive to understand the larger social forces that contribute to denying children of color safe and secure family lives.

• Child welfare workers and foster care providers should be culturally competent; they should understand and respect the cultural contexts in which families from all backgrounds raise their young children.

Conclusion

The early years of life offer an unparalleled opportunity for growth and development. The evidence we reviewed in earlier chapters suggests that young children's maturation occurs in multiple domains, including the affective, cognitive, and physical. Although child welfare agencies often follow a mission to protect children, the meaning of child protection takes on special significance when young children are involved. Protecting young children from physical harm is not enough. Young children must also be protected from developmental harm. Their vulnerability, healthy growth and development, and opportunities to form lifetime relationships are usually not considered sufficiently in child welfare services. Young children should be protected from the physical harms that result from maltreatment, malnourishment, ill health, accident, and injury. They must also be protected from environments that acutely stifle their cognitive growth or sabotage their healthy affective development.

Infants and young children are the largest group of children who are reported for maltreatment and enter foster care; African American infants, in particular, have frequent and long contact with child welfare agencies. Popular conceptions of the child welfare system largely as a rescue mechanism for physically and sexually abused children are misguided because neglected children are the ones who most often receive services. The child welfare system provides society's safety net for families whose personal circumstances of substance abuse, criminal activity, mental illness, and poverty are so chaotic and dysfunctional that they cannot care for their children. Parent education and therapy may not be enough for these parents, and basic care and supervision of their children will be insufficient. For these young children, special attention to the unique vulnerabilities of early childhood must be infused into child welfare policy and practice.

The decisions made on behalf of these young children often have lifetime consequences. Therefore, efforts to refocus and crystallize the philosophical constructs that undergird practice with these youngsters are critical. Society's stakes are always high in child welfare services. When young children are involved, a well-considered response to their situation, as opposed to an inappropriate one, can make the difference between successful and disastrous outcomes for them and, perhaps, for generations to follow.

Child welfare agencies have a challenging task of embracing a mission to provide multitiered, complex, and sometimes contradictory services. Children must be protected from harm, but families must be supported in an environment that seeks to promote lifetime permanence. When young children are involved, the task can be especially daunting. The early months of service may add up to a lifetime for young children as the choices child welfare workers and the courts make in supporting or neglecting them play out meaningfully in the life course of families. From a child's perspective, every moment counts.

Appendix

Methods

Overview

The new findings presented in this book are based largely on data from the California Children's Services Archive. This significant policy-based research enterprise draws on a partnership between the School of Social Welfare at the University of California at Berkeley and public agencies, including the California Health and Welfare Agency, the California Department of Social Services, the California Youth Authority, and county welfare departments. The archive provides longitudinal descriptions of children, their service careers, and the outcomes associated with these services. It was developed to provide resources for understanding the involvement and outcomes of children who receive social, mental health, educational, and correctional services in California. At the time of this study, the archive contained statewide birth and death records from the Department of Health Services and statewide foster care placement histories from the Department of Social Services, along with data on child maltreatment from Social Services Departments of nine counties. Population data used to compute incidence and prevalence rates are from projections provided by the California Department of Finance.

Case Studies

The case studies used in most chapters are presented to add vividness to the discussion of caseload dynamics. They are descriptive and are designed to capture, in some detail, the circumstances and events surrounding particular topics. Case studies were used as part of this study not to answer questions about causal relationships between variables—indeed, case studies cannot accomplish such a research task—but to provide a context for the information obtained primarily from administrative sources. The cases that we chose to include are not composite cases but actual cases drawn from one county in California. Although identifying features pertaining to these cases were masked to protect the confidentiality and anonymity of the subjects, the circumstances of the cases are real.

The cases were selected to illustrate common characteristics found in typical cases brought before child welfare authorities—not unique or uncharacteristic circumstances. To select each case, we ran descriptive statistics on the variable of interest and carefully reviewed all case files that had such characteristics. Then we chose the case that included the majority of characteristics found among the selected cases.

Chapter 2: Child Abuse and Neglect for Very Young Children

California does not have a statewide uniform data system for collecting information on child abuse and neglect reports. Thus, data for the study were collected from nine of the eleven counties that use a similar administrative data base—the Social Service Reporting System (SSRS). Together, these counties constitute almost 35 percent of the population of children in the state and of the children who are reported for maltreatment in the state.

The data on child maltreatment reports were collected over five years from Alameda, Contra Costa, Orange, San Diego, San Mateo, Santa Clara, Santa Cruz, Sonoma, and Tulare counties, with a total child and adult population in 1995 of 11,077,602. These counties include urban, suburban-urban, and rural areas and contain three of the 40 largest U.S. cities—Oakland, San Diego, and San Jose. The economic standing; child population; ethnicity; and selected risk factors, including infant mortality, high school dropout rates, teenage births, and the likelihood of children being reported for maltreatment are presented in Table A.1. We do not discuss between-county differences in this book, but our other investigations (Barth, in press) ascertained that these differences are often substantial.

Sample

Since the focus of the study was on children younger than age six, the data from each county were first divided into two groups: from birth through age five and from age six through age seventeen. A certain percentage of children's birth dates were missing in each county, so those children were dropped from the age-group analyses, leaving a final sample of 538,086 children (ages 0–17) reported for maltreatment in nine counties across several years in the early 1990s. Owing to differences in coding procedures among the counties, the starting dates ranged from January 1990 to January 1992. Eight of the counties had a uniform end date of December 31, 1995, but the lack of financial support for data entry in 1995 necessitated an end date of December 31, 1994, for Alameda County. General descriptive analyses were conducted on all children reported from 1990–1995 within the available time periods in all counties.

Coding

The SSRS data system contains multiple categories for ethnicity, reasons for report, and sources of reports. Thus, to promote consistency throughout the book,

Table A.1 Sample County Comparison: Risk Factors for Young Children

	Alameda	Contra Costa	Orange	San Diego	San Mateo	Santa Clara	Santa Cruz	Sonoma	Tulare
% Residents under 18 years*	26%	26%	26%	26%	23%	25%	25%	26%	34%
% Young Children Below Poverty Level**	16.4%	11.9%	11.1%	17.2%	7.6%	10.4%	12.1%	9.7%	36.9%
% Urban**	92.6%	98.2%	99.8%	95.2%	98.9%	97.9%	88.3%	72.3%	69%
% African Amer.*	20%	12%	2%	8%	5%	4%	1%	2%	2%
% Caucasian*	40%	59%	51%	51%	43%	45%	61%	75%	40%
% Hispanic*	21%	12%	12%	32%	30%	30%	34%	18%	52%
% Other*	19%	12%	12%	9%	22%	21%	3%	5%	6%
State Rank (higher rank indicated worse outcomes):	--			--		--		--	--
Child abuse reports*	7th	24th	6th	15th	5th	11th	18th	15th	26th
Infant mortality*	19th	13th	3rd	13th	17th	1st	18th	33rd	19th
High school dropouts*	42nd	17th	21st	36th	17th	24th	34th	22nd	36th
Median family income*	7th	7th	2nd	14th	2nd	1st	9th	10th	52nd
Teenage births*	19th	10th	26th	28th	11th	23rd	22nd	14th	45th

*Children Now. (1996). *California: The State of Our Children Report Card '96*
**Hall, R., & Richards, F. (1994). *1994 Report Health Data Summaries for California Counties*

ethnicity was collapsed into four categories—African American, Caucasian, Hispanic, and Other—*reasons for reports* were collapsed into neglect, sexual abuse, physical abuse, and other. In addition, although some counties included in our administrative data detailed over twenty-two different reporting sources, *sources of reports* was collapsed into law enforcement, medical personnel, family, neighbor-community member, school, and other. Throughout Chapter two, (except incidence calculations), *age* is the child's age at the time of the first report. We refer to three age groups throughout the book: *infants* (younger than 1 year), *toddlers* (1 and 2 years old), and *preschoolers* (3–5 years old). Older children (6–17 years old), are included in some analyses for comparative purposes.

Incidence

To correspond to the latest available national statistics, incidence rates were computed for only 1994. The number of children reported during that year was divided by the corresponding population figures obtained from the California Department of Finance. Age was calculated as the age at the time of first report in 1994.

Maltreatment and Poverty Analyses

Maltreatment data from 1992 were included in the analysis because this is the first year for which data were available for all counties. The nine SSRS counties included 448 zip codes. Maltreatment reports were aggregated by zip code using one child per family. As in other research (Drake & Pandey, 1996), zip codes were then selected for analysis based on a density of at least 1,000 families per zip code to ensure that would be a sufficient number of reports in a given area. Zip codes were grouped according to the proportion of families living in poverty and were correlated with rates of maltreatment reports in those groups.

Case Study

In our study of case records, 53 infants (62 percent) were identified as drug exposed at birth, so a case was selected to illustrate the problems associated with *substance abuse*. The cases varied considerably because of the large sample. Some of the characteristics that were common to many of these cases of drug-exposed newborns were as follows: 70 percent had older siblings who were already in foster care, compared to 30 percent of non-drug-exposed children ($\chi^2 = 4.17$, $df = 1$, $p < .05$); the mean number of children in the family was 4.0 versus 2.6 for non-drug-exposed infants; and the mean number of problems at birth was 2.6, compared to 0.7 for the non-drug-exposed infants. Finally, of the children who were prenatally exposed to drugs, about half were returned home to mothers who continued to abuse drugs, and about half were returned to mothers who no longer seemed to be abusing drugs. The case selected to illustrate the challenges associated with substance abuse was characterized by many of these problems.

Chapter 3: From Child Maltreatment to Placement

Information on investigations, case openings, multiple reports, and placement in foster care refer to children who were reported from 1992 through 1994 in nine counties.

Open Cases

Two of the nine counties code every case that is investigated as "open" whether or not the family is eventually served in some way. Generally, the other seven counties consider a case open only when services are provided. To adjust for these differences, only those cases that remained open after ten days were called "open" in our analyses. We did not determine whether the definition we used to identify open cases exactly matched the one used in each county, but the numbers we report here roughly coincide with those reported as moving beyond investigation in other studies (California Department of Social Services, 1993).

Using a 20 percent random sample of young children reported in the nine counties between 1992 and 1994, we developed a logit model to examine the likelihood of having a case opened for services after the first report.

Multiple Reports

A "new" report was defined as one occurring at least five days after a previous report. This length of time was chosen to reflect the passage of a weekend or a typical week of care.

A logit model was constructed to predict the likelihood of a second report. Using the same 20 percent random sample of all young children reported, we restricted cases to all those whose first report occurred before May 1994. This cutoff was chosen because over 95 percent of the second reports on unserved cases occurred within seven months.

Foster Care Placement

Using AutoMatch/AutoStan™ software, we merged administrative data from our SSRS (child abuse) database with the California Foster Care Information System (FCIS) database for all available years, including only children's first placement in care. Over 80 percent of the children who entered care in that period were matched. In other words, of the 37,331 foster care entries across counties in these same years, 30,170 were matched with their maltreatment history. For purposes of analysis, only data from 1992 to 1994 were included.

Case Study

Unlike the definition of multiple reporting (two or more reports) used in Chapter 2, the sample of cases reviewed to illustrate the phenomenon of *multiple reporting* prior to placement was drawn from those cases in which infants had received three or more reports. In our study of case records, this sample included five (4.9 percent) cases. When we reviewed all the cases for common themes, we found that they all included infants who had been reported for neglect or caretakers' absence/incapacity during the first months of life and whose first reports were investigated (or attempted but not completed) and were then closed because of insufficient evidence.

Chapter 4: Foster Care, Reunification, and Adoption

Much of the work in Chapters 4–6 was based on analyses of data drawn from the FCIS, stored as a part of the California Children's Services Archive. FCIS data for each child who enters foster care are prepared by counties, which report them to the state, and have been reconfigured by the archive staff into a longitudinal database, making it possible to follow the individual paths of children through the foster care system over time. The foster care database contains data on over 280,000 children who were in care in 1988 or who entered care at any time between 1988 and the end of 1995 and were followed from the date of their first placement until the end of 1995. A period in foster care is referred to as a spell, which may contain one or more placements. A child may exit one spell in care and then reenter care for a subsequent spell at a later date. Although the archive includes records of each placement for each child who was under the supervision of the juvenile court, this book does not cover children who were under the supervision of probation or other agencies. It includes all children supervised by the child welfare agencies, regardless of whether they received federal foster care funds (Title IV-E), state funds, or services only. Information on fewer than 4,000 children (less than 1.5 percent) was deleted prior to the analyses owing to invalid birth dates or placement histories.

The types of placements were collapsed into five categories: *kinship home* (including relative guardian and relative nonguardian), *foster home* (nonrelative nonguardian and nonrelative guardian), *SFC home* (specialized foster care, under the supervision of a foster family agency), *group home* (regardless of capacity, and including residential treatment), and *other* (special small family homes, county shelters or receiving homes, medical facilities, and specialized pilot-project homes). Since kinship foster care is qualitatively different from other types of foster care, we stratified most analyses into *kin* and *nonkin* sections. Because a child may have several placements during a spell in foster care and may move from one type of placement to another, the placement type we use in this book usually refers to the primary placement, or where the child spent most of her or his days during the first spell in care.

Eligibility for federal foster care funds is an important variable for children in kinship homes. One of the main criteria for eligibility is that the child has to come from a home that was eligible for Aid to Families with Dependent Children (AFDC, now Temporary Assistance to Needy Families—TANF) at the time of removal. However, eligibility for these federal funds has different implications for children in kin care than it does for those in nonkin care. Kin caregivers for noneligible children do not receive foster care funds, but may be paid at the lower, incremental AFDC rate. Noneligible children in nonkin care, however, can receive funding from the state, equal to the amount paid for federally eligible children.

Reasons for children's removal from foster care were grouped into four categories: *neglect* (general neglect, severe neglect, or caretaker's incapacity), *physical abuse, sexual abuse,* and *other* (emotional abuse, exploitation, child's disability or handicap, relinquishment, disrupted adoptive placement, or voluntary placement). Exits from foster care were grouped into *reunification* (returned home, returned home on a trial visit, and placement with a relative outside the foster care system), *adoption, guardianship,* and *other* reasons (including death, commitment to a psychiatric or medical facility, abduction, and termination of AFDC funds). Nonrelatives who assume guardianship may receive guardianship subsidies, and the children they care for may remain on the foster care caseload.

Exits from Foster Care

The 29,562 young children who entered care in 1988 and 1989 were used to examine exits after two, four, and six years in care by age. The 26,927 young children who entered in 1990 and 1991 were the basis of the consideration of exits at four years by ethnicity, reason for removal, eligibility for federal funds, and type of placement.

Length of Stay

The estimates of median length of stay were Kaplan-Meier estimates for children entering foster care between 1989 and 1995 (78,601 kin and 70,086 nonkin). The multivariate model used Cox's (1972) proportional hazards method. The model was restricted to children who entered foster care before age six; one child per family was randomly selected ($n = 58,057$). The method assumes that the hazard rates for reunification (including exits to guardianship), adoption, and other exits for individuals with different characteristics, are proportional over time. Variables for ethnic group membership, age groups, and reason for removal satisfied this assumption, but a comparison of kin and nonkin types of placements did not. As was mentioned in Chapter 4, children who are placed with nonkin go home at a much faster rate in the early months of placement than do those who are placed with kin, after which the rates tend to even out. Therefore, type of placement (further divided for children in kinship care by eligibility for federal funds) was allowed to vary over time. The numbers corresponding to African American, Hispanic, and Other ethnic groups signify how the hazard rates compared to the Caucasian group; toddlers and preschoolers are compared to infants, and physical, sexual, and other abuse are compared to neglect. A categorical variable was created that indicates whether children were under agency jurisdiction in Los Angeles, one of thirty-seven relatively large California counties (Alameda, Butte, Contra Costa, El Dorado, Fresno, Humboldt, Imperial, Kern, Kings, Madera, Marin, Mendocino, Merced, Monterey, Napa, Orange, Placer, Riverside, Sacramento, San Bernardino, San Diego, San Francisco, San Joaquin, San Luis Obispo, San Mateo, Santa Barbara, Santa Clara, Santa Cruz, Shasta, Solano, Sonoma, Stanislaus, Sutter, Tulare, Ventura, Yolo, Yuba), or one of the twenty smaller counties (Alpine, Amador, Calaveras, Colusa, Del Norte, Glenn, Inyo, Lake, Lassen, Mariposa, Modoc, Mono, Nevada, Plumas, San Benito, Sierra, Siskiyou, Tehama, Trinity, Tuolumne). A preliminary analysis of exits to adoption indicated that data from Los Angeles county were incomplete in this regard, so the findings should be interpreted with caution.

Reentry

The cumulative probability of reentry was estimated using the lifetable method for the 112,087 children who exited to reunification between 1989 and 1995. A proportional hazards model was used to estimate the hazard ratios of reentry for the 37,455 children who went home before age six. One child per family was randomly selected.

Stability of Placements

Preliminary analyses of changes of placements indicated that the data from Los Angeles County were incomplete in this regard. Therefore, the analyses included young children who entered care in 1988 or 1989 in the fifty-seven other California counties and who remained in care for at least two, four, or six years (n = 3,392 kin and 4,421 nonkin at two years, 1,838 kin and 2,273 nonkin at four years, and 1,318 kin and 1,493 nonkin at six years).

Case Study

Because *kinship placements* loom large in current child welfare practice, one case was selected to illustrate some of their features. For example, as earlier chapters of this book indicated, children who are in kinship care are more likely to experience more-stable placements in care and are less likely to reunify with their biological parents quickly, although they are just as likely ultimately to reunify as are children in foster family care. In addition, these children are less likely to be adopted, and their caretakers are more likely to be granted guardianship. Evidence from other studies has pointed to some characteristics of kinship caregivers, including the fact that the majority are grandparents to the children in care, are older than foster family caregivers, are in more fragile health, have fewer financial and educational resources, and are more likely to work outside the home (Berrick, Barth, & Needell, 1994).

In addition to these characteristics the 41 (40.6 percent) cases reviewed in our county sample where kinship placements were made suggested that other relatives play a role in supporting the primary kinship caregiver and that the caregiver who is selected for care is a known relative who is close to the biological mother. Some of these characteristics of kinship cases are featured in the case identified for study.

Chapter 5: Group Care

To study the dynamics of placement for young children in group care, we used data from the FCIS, described earlier. We defined children's placements as *foster care* (excluding kin) or *group care*, depending on where the children spent the majority of their time during their first spell (their primary placement while in care).

Stability of Placements

We examined an entry cohort of young children (from birth to age 5) who were placed between 1988 and 1991 and were still in care four years later. As in Chapter 4, we excluded children placed in Los Angeles County. Children who were primarily in group care (n = 179) and a cohort of their peers who were primarily in foster homes (n = 3,204) were included in these analyses. Kinship care was not examined because previous chapters showed the greater stability afforded by kinship foster care than by foster family care.

Length of Stay

The sample used to analyze children's length of stay in care included all young children who entered care between January 1, 1988, and December 31, 1994 (n = 52,613). The sample was divided into two groups on the basis of children's primary placement—group care or foster care. Survival curves were constructed for length of stay.

Permanency

The data are for all young children who entered care for the first time from 1988 to 1990 ($n = 23{,}791$). Four years after their initial placement, we examined the number and proportions of children who were reunified with their parents, adopted, had other outcomes (including legal guardianship), or were still in care. The *reunification rate* includes all children who were returned to their biological parents following a stay in out-of-home care. The *adjusted reunification rate* is the proportion of cases that were in their birth homes from the time of reunification to the end of the four-year period, excluding those who had reentered foster care.

Case Study

This chapter focuses largely on *group care*, yet the county in which we conducted our case-record reviews does not use group care placements for infants and toddlers. However, we asked the county to draw a sample of cases in which children under age six were residing in group care. Of the 3,635 placements countywide, 13 children under age six were in group care during 1995. Half these case files ($n = 7$) were reviewed to determine whether common themes characterized these placements. Of the seven randomly selected cases, the majority involved five and six year olds, and two involved three year olds. All cases were of African American boys. The three year olds in group care had short stays in care during 1995, and the placements were used on an emergency basis. The five and six year olds had more lengthy stays in their group homes.

All the cases we reviewed were of children whose behavior was extremely difficult. The decision to place them in group homes did not appear to be well considered in any of the cases. Instead, child welfare workers conducted what appeared to be a cursory review of available foster homes and specialized foster homes. Or, the immediate needs for a new placement subverted the time that might have been allowed to make a more carefully considered decision.

Chapter 6: Focus on Infants

We direct the reader to the methods section for Chapters 2 and 3 for an overview of the data on maltreatment and to Chapter 4 for an overview of the data on foster care.

Analyses in this chapter were drawn from the archive's data on 43,066 children who entered foster care before their first birthday between 1988 and 1994. For this chapter, we excluded infants who were voluntarily placed in care or were initially placed with legal guardians and who were not deemed to be abused or neglected (that is, they were removed for reasons other than abuse, neglect, or exploitation).

Figures 6.4 and 6.5 compared children with poor and nonpoor mothers, respectively, who entered foster care within ninety days of birth for reasons of neglect from 1989 to 1994 with a random sample of all births in California. The sample of all births was drawn from vital statistics data supplied by the Department of Health Services; these records were matched to children in the foster care database (approximately 80 percent of the newborns in foster care were successfully matched with their birth records). Poor mothers were those for whom payments for the births were expected from Medi-Cal (Medicaid) or who were medically indigent, according to birth records, and the nonpoor mothers were those for whom payments for births were expected from other sources.

Placement Constellations for Infants

The duration and type of placement a child experienced within four years during the first spell of foster care were explored for infants who entered care between 1988 and 1990. In this chapter, we present findings for the 2,262 children who were still in care four years after their entry into care in the fifty-seven California counties excluding Los Angeles. Because the distributions for duration are quite skewed, the median was chosen as the measure of central tendency for this analysis. Unlike means, medians are not additive, so the overall median duration of a spell that included multiple placements is not always equal to the sum of the medians of each placement. In many cases, the sum of the durations was less than the forty-eight months considered and never exceeded forty-eight months. Therefore, the durations of placements should be considered conservative estimates.

Permanence

Logit regression models were developed to consider the likelihood of reunification and adoption compared to being in care at four years for infants who entered foster care in 1990 in the fifty-seven California counties excluding Los Angeles. One infant per family was randomly selected ($n = 3,048$). Infants who were removed for reasons other than abuse or neglect and those who had exits other than reunification or adoption were excluded from the analyses. Odds ratios and 95 percent confidence intervals are reported.

Case Study

Several kinds of *exits from care* are described in this book, including reunification, adoption, and legal guardianship. We chose to highlight reunification because it is the first goal of permanence for children and is achieved for well over half the children who are placed in care. In spite of the fact that a large proportion of children are returned to their biological parents, the case files we reviewed for this study did not inspire great confidence that children were regularly returned to safe and stable environments. Instead, our staff who reviewed the case files were regularly left with the impression that a large proportion of children are returned to homes where housing is unstable (27 percent of the cases), parents are still actively using drugs (33 percent of the cases), and parenting capacity is compromised (54 pecent of the mothers had mental health problems and 23 percent had engaged in recent criminal activity). The case selected to illustrate children's exits to reunification combined several of the features just listed and is illustrative of the challenges associated with reunification.

Chapter 7: Understanding Children and Families Served by the Child Welfare System

Reviews of Case Records

A random sample of 120 cases was generated from the archive that included infants (aged one day to twelve months) who were placed in care in one urban California county. All the infants entered care between January 1, 1990, and December 31, 1992 and had subsequently reunified with their biological parents.

The case records were located by the agency staff and were made available to four research assistants trained at the University of California at Berkeley. The research assistants read each case file and extracted information from each case into a standardized case-extraction form. Only 101 cases examined were included in the study. Of the remaining cases, 5 could not be included because they had not yet reunified with their parents (they were misidentified) and therefore did not fit our criteria, 3 did not include sufficient information on the infants, and 11 could not be located by the agency staff.

A data-extraction form was developed for reviewing case records in conjunction with the agency staff. The data collection instrument was designed to capture information about (1) the child and his or her birth outcomes; (2) the biological mother; (3) the biological father, alleged father, or putative father; (4) the household; (5) the services received while the family was under court jurisdiction; and (6) the reporting and placement histories for the child. The instrument was pilot tested on three sample cases to ensure that it included all relevant and available variables. The four research assistants met after the pilot test to resolve outstanding coding questions. Interrater reliability in coding each case record was fairly high at 87.5 percent. Each review lasted 1½ to 2 hours.

Focus Groups

Three focus groups were held over the course of one week with a total of nineteen mothers whose infants had been removed from their care in the early 1990s. These mothers had subsequently reunified with their children, and the children had not returned to foster care. The focus groups were designed to elicit parents' views about the factors in their own lives and the characteristics of their workers or the services they received that contributed to their positive outcomes.

Case Study

Thirty percent of the case files reviewed included children who reentered foster care—a proportion similar to the overall reentry rate for California. The characteristics found in a large proportion of the reentry cases included the following: Reentry cases had large families (a mean of 4.9 children), the mother was likely to be abusing crack cocaine (97 percent), the mother had a criminal record (89 percent), the child had siblings in foster care, the child was not placed in kinship care, and the mother did not visit the child regularly. Several of these characteristics are captured in the case presented in the chapter.

Chapter 8: Public Child Welfare Practice

Data for this chapter were obtained from focus groups with child welfare workers in four California counties. The focus groups were conducted with as few as 4 workers to as many as 12, with the typical group size being 8 to 10 workers. Interviews were conducted with staff from five Emergency Response (Intake and Initial Services) units, eight Family Maintenance/Family Reunification units, and four Adoption or Fost-Adopt units to understand more about the ways in which the issues of children's ages and vulnerability come into play in daily decision making.

Focus groups were conducted with 117 child welfare workers over the course of sixteen sessions. We interviewed 36 workers from Emergency Response, Intake, or Court Intervention units, asking a series of questions that specifically arise during the early days and weeks after a child abuse report is received. We also interviewed 48 workers from Continuing Services, Family Maintenance, and Family Reunification units. Finally, we interviewed 33 Adoptions or Fost-Adopt staff from across the four counties. The child welfare workers had worked in the child welfare field for about nine years, on average, $3\frac{1}{2}$ of those years have been spent working in their current units. Seventy-three percent of the workers had previously worked in other units, which gave them some perspective on the challenges of serving families from various vantage points in the system. More than 80 percent of the workers were women, 15 percent were African American, 68 percent were Caucasian, and the remaining were other staff of color. The average age of the workers was 43, and the majority had graduate degrees (70 percent had an MA, MS, or MSW).

Case Study

The mean number of days in the initial spell in care for the county sample was 255. Given that length of stay, 14 cases (13.86 percent) were identified in which children had experienced three or more foster care placements. These cases were examined to select a case that would be representative of *multiple placements.*

Each of the 14 cases was carefully reviewed to determine whether common themes were evident. The majority of the infants had lengthy stays in the hospital and were made dependents of the court during their hospital stays. The majority were also placed from the hospital into emergency foster homes that were temporary by design. The case that was selected for inclusion had characteristics that matched those of the majority of the cases reviewed in which multiple placements were a factor.

References

Aber, J. L., Allen, J. P., Carlson, V., & Cicchetti, D. (1989). The effects of maltreatment on development during early childhood: Recent studies and their theoretical, clinical, and policy implications. In D. Cicchetti & V. Carlson (Eds.), *Child maltreatment: Theory and research on the causes and consequences of child abuse and neglect* (pp. 579–619). New York: Cambridge University Press.

Aber, J. L., & Zigler, E. (1981). Developmental considerations in the definition of child maltreatment. In R. Rizley & D. Cicchetti (Eds.), *Developmental perspectives on child maltreatment* (pp. 1–29). San Francisco: Jossey-Bass.

Abbott, G. (1938). *The child and the state, Vol. II.* Chicago: University of Chicago Press.

AFCARS. (1996). *Adoption and foster care analysis and reporting system—Report # 1* (Log No. ACYF-IM-96-CB-16). Washington, DC: U.S. Department of Health and Human Services.

Ainsworth, M. S., Blehar, M. C., Waters, E., & Wall, S. (1978). *Patterns of attachment: A psychological study of the strange situation.* Hillsdale, NJ: Lawrence Erlbaum

Albert, V., & Barth, R. (1996). Predicting growth in child abuse and neglect reports in urban, suburban and rural counties. *Social Service Review, 70*(1), 58–82.

Alter-Reid, K., Gibbs, M., Lachenmeyer, J., Sigal, J. & Massoth, N. (1986). Sexual abuse of children: A review of the empirical findings. *Clinical Psychology Review, 6,* 249–266.

American Public Welfare Association/Voluntary Cooperative Information System. (1985). *Characteristics of children in substitute and adoptive care: A statistical summary of the VCIS National Child Welfare Data Base.* Washington, DC: American Public Welfare Association.

Anderson, C., Nagle, R., Roberts, W., & Smith, J. (1981). Attachment to substitute caregivers as a function of center quality and caregiver involvement.
Child Development, 52, 53–61.

Anthony, E. J. (1987). Children at risk for psychosis growing up successfully.
In E. J. Anthony & B. Cohler (Eds.), *The invulnerable child* (pp. 147–184).
New York: Guilford Press.

Apsler, R., & Bassuk, E. (1983). Differences among clinicians in the decision
to admit. *Archives of General Psychiatry, 40,* 1133–1137.

Ards, S. (1989). Estimating local child abuse. *Evaluation Review, 13,* 484–515.

Ards, S. (1992). Understanding patterns of child maltreatment. *Contemporary
Policy Issues, 10*(4), 39–50.

Ards, S., & Harrell, A. (1993). Reporting of child maltreatment: A secondary
analysis of the national incidence surveys. *Child Abuse and Neglect, 17,*
337–344.

Ashby, L. (1984). *Saving the waifs: Reformers and dependent children,
1890–1917.* Philadelphia: Temple University Press.

Barahal, R. M., Waterman, J., & Martin, H. P. (1981). The social cognitive
development of abused children. *Journal of Consulting and Clinical
Psychology, 49,* 508–516.

Barone, N., Adams, W., & Tooman, P. (1981). The screening unit: An experimental approach to child protective service. *Child Welfare, 60,* 198–204.

Barth, R. P. (1990). On their own: The experiences of youth after foster care.
Child and Adolescent Social Work Journal, 7, 419–440.

Barth, R. P. (1994). Shared family care: Child protection and family preservation. *Social Work, 39,* 515–524.

Barth, R. P. (1997). Effects of age and race on the odds of adoption vs. remaining in long-term out-of-home care. *Child Welfare, 76*(2) 285–308.

Barth, R. P. (in press). Permanent placements for young children placed in foster care: A proposal for a child welfare services performance standard.
Children and Youth Services Review.

Barth, R. B., Berry, M., Carson, M. L., Goodfield, R., & Feinberg, B. (1986).
Contributors to disruption and dissolution of older child adoptions. *Child
Welfare, 65,* 359–371.

Barth, R. P., & Blackwell, D. L. (1996). *Death rates among California's foster
care and former foster care populations.* Unpublished report, Child Welfare
Research Center, University of California at Berkeley.

Barth, R. P., Courtney, M., Berrick, J. D., & Albert, V. (1994). *From child
abuse to permanency planning: Child welfare services pathways and placements.*
New York: Aldine deGruyter.

Bays, J. (1990). Substance abuse and child abuse: Impact of addiction on the
child. *Pediatric Clinics of North America, 37,* 881–904.

Beckwith, L. (1990). Adaptive and maladaptive parenting: Implications for intervention. In S. J. Meisels & J. P. Shonkoff (Eds.), *Handbook of early childhood intervention* (pp. 53–77). New York: Cambridge University Press.

Belsky, J. (1988). The "effects" of infant day care reconsidered. *Early
Childhood Research Quarterly, 3,* 235–272.

Benedict, M. I., & White, R. B. (1991). Factors associated with foster care
length of stay. *Child Welfare, 70,* 45–57.

Berrick, J. D., & Barth, R. P. (Eds.). (1994). Kinship care [special issue].
Children and Youth Services Review, 16(1–2).

Berrick, J. D., Barth, R. P., & Needell, B. (1994). A comparison of kinship foster homes and foster family homes: Implications for kinship foster care as family preservation. *Children and Youth Services Review, 16*(1–2), 33–64.

Berrick, J. D., & Duerr, M. (1997). Preventing child neglect: A study of an in-home program for children and families. In J. D. Berrick, R. P. Barth, & N. Gilbert (Eds.), *Child Welfare Research Review, Vol. II.* New York: Columbia University Press, pp. 63–83.

Berrick, J. D., & Needell, B. (in press). Recent trends in kinship care: Public policy, payments, and outcomes for children. In P. A. Curtis & G. Dale (Eds.), *The foster care crisis: Translating research into practice and policy.* Lincoln: University of Nebraska Press.

Berrick, J. D., Needell, B., & Barth, R. P. (in press). Kin as a family and child welfare resource: the child welfare worker's perspective. In R. L. Hegar & M. Scannapicco (Eds), *Kinship foster care: Practice, policy, and research.* New York: Oxford University Press.

Berrick, J. D., Needell, B., & Barth, R. P. (1995). *Kinship care in California: An empirically-based curriculum,* Unpublished manuscript. Child Welfare Research Center, University of California at Berkeley.

Besharov, D. (1992). Improving child protective services: How to expand and implement the consensus. *Children Today, 21*(2), 14–22.

Bowlby, J. (1969). *Attachment and loss: Vol. 1. Attachment.* New York: Basic Books.

Bremner, R. H. (1971). *Children and youth in America: A documentary history, 1866–1932* (Vol. 2). Cambridge, MA: Harvard University Press.

Bronfenbrenner, U. (1979). *The ecology of human development.* Cambridge, MA: Harvard University Press.

Brooks-Gunn, J., & Duncan, G. J. (1996). It's poverty that skews children's IQs. *Institute for Policy Research, 18*(1), 4–5.

Brooks-Gunn J., Klebanov P. K., & Duncan, G. J. (1996). Ethnic differences in children's intelligence test scores: Role of economic deprivation, home environment, and maternal characteristics. *Child Development, 67,* 396–408.

Brooks-Gunn J., Klebanov P. K., & Liaw, F. (1995). The learning, physical, and emotional environment of the home in the context of poverty: The Infant Health and Development Program. *Children and Youth Services Review, 17*(1–2), 251–276.

Brown, J. L., & Pollitt, E. (1996). Malnutrition, poverty and intellectual development. *Scientific American, 274*(2), 38–43.

Burgess, R. L., & Conger, R. D. (1977). Family interaction patterns related to child abuse and neglect: Some preliminary findings. *Child Abuse and Neglect, 1,* 269–277.

California Department of Social Services. (1993). *Preplacement preventative services characteristics survey.* Sacramento, CA: Author.

Cappelleri, J. C., Eckenrode, J., & Powers, J. L. (1993). The epidemiology of child abuse: Findings from the second national incidence and prevalence study of child abuse and neglect. *American Journal of Public Health, 83*(11), 1622–1624.

Capron, C., & Duyme, M. (1989). Assessment of effects of socioeconomic status on IQ in a full cross-fostering study. *Nature, 340,* 552–554.

Carlson, V., Cicchetti, D., Barnett, D., & Braunwald, K. (1989). Disorganized/disoriented attachment relationships in maltreated infants. *Developmental Psychology, 25,* 525–531.

Centers for Disease Control. (1989). First 100,000 cases of acquired immun-odeficiency syndrome—United States. *Journal of the American Medical Association, 262,* 1453, 1456.

Centers for Disease Control. (1993). Preschool children at high risk for measles: Opportunities to vaccinate. *American Journal of Public Health, 83,* 662–667.

Centers for Disease Control. (1995). *Facts about women and HIV/AIDS.* Rockville, MD: Author.

Chaffin, M., Kelleher, K., & Hollenberg, J. (1996). Onset of physical abuse and neglect: Psychiatric, substance abuse and social risk factors from prospective community data. *Child Abuse and Neglect, 20,* 191–203.

Chamberlain, P., & Reid, J. B. (1991). Using a specialized foster care community treatment model for children and adolescents leaving the state mental hospital. *Journal of Community Psychology, 19,* 266–276.

Chasnoff, I. (1988). *A first: National hospital incidence study.* Unpublished report, National Association for Perinatal Addiction Research and Education, Chicago.

Child Welfare League of America. (1994). *Kinship care: A natural bridge.* Washington, DC: Author.

Children's Defense Fund. (1978). *Children without homes: An examination of public responsibility to children in out-of-home care.* Washington, DC: Author.

Cicchetti, D. (1989). How research on child maltreatment has informed the study of child development: Perspectives from developmental psychopathology. In D. Cicchetti & V. Carlson (Eds.), *Child maltreatment: Theory and research on the causes and consequences of child abuse and neglect* (pp. 377–431). New York: Cambridge University Press.

Cicchetti, D., & Lynch, M. (1993). Toward an ecological/transactional model of community violence and child maltreatment: Consequences for children's development. *Psychiatry, 56,* 96–118.

Cicchetti, D., & Rizley, R. (1981). Developmental perspectives on the etiology, intergenerational transmission, and sequelae of child maltreatment. In R. Rizley & D. Cicchetti (Eds.), *Developmental perspectives on child maltreatment: New directions for child development* (pp. 31–56). San Francisco: Jossey-Bass.

Cicchetti, D. & Toth, S. (1996). A developmental psychopathology perspective on child abuse and neglect. *Journal of the American Academy of Child and Adolescent Psychiatry, 34,* 541–565.

Clarke-Stewart, A. (1988). The "effects" of infant care reconsidered. *Early Childhood Research Quarterly, 3,* 293–318.

Cohen, N. (1986). Quality of care for youths in group homes. *Child Welfare, 65,* 481–494.

Colorado Revised Statute. (1994), §19-1-102, et seq.

Colton, M. (1990). Specialist foster family and residential child care practices. *Community Alternatives: International Journal of Family Care, 2*(2) 1–20.

Columbo, D. (1993). *Infant cognition: Predicting later intellectual functioning.* Thousand Oaks, CA: Sage.

Conway, E. S. (1957). *The institutional care of children: A case history.* Unpublished doctoral dissertation, London.

Cook, R. J. (1994). Are we helping foster care youth prepare for their future? *Children and Youth Services Review, 16*(3–4), 213–229.

Costello, J. (1995). *Notes on issues concerning alternatives to family care.*

Unpublished manuscript, Chapin Hall Center for Children, University of Chicago.

Coulton, C. J., Korbin, J. E., Su, M., & Chow, J. (1995). Community level factors and child maltreatment rates. *Child Development, 66,* 1262–1276.

Coulton, C., & Pandey, S. (1992). Geographic concentration of poverty and risk to children in urban neighborhoods. *American Behavioral Scientist, 35,* 238–257.

County of San Diego Department of Social Services. (1994, June). *Practice manual for Children's Services Bureau.* San Diego, CA: Author.

Courtney, M. E. (1994). Factors associated with the reunification of foster children with their families. *Social Service Review, 68,* 1, 82–108.

Courtney, M. E. (1995). Reentry to foster care of children returned to their families. *Social Service Review, 69,* 226–241.

Courtney, M. E. & Needell, B. (1997). Kinship care: Lessons learned from California. in R. P. Barth, J. Duerr Berrick, & N. Gilbert (Eds.), *Child welfare research review, Vol. 2* (pp. 130–147). New York: Columbia University Press.

Courtney, M. E. & Piliavin, I. (1996). Analysis of incentive and selection effects on foster care case outcomes: The impact of kinship foster care. Paper presented at the 1996 Annual Workshop of the National Association for Welfare Research and Statistics. Madison: School of Social Work and Institute for Research on Poverty, University of Wisconsin.

Courtney, M. E., Piliavin, I., & Grogan-Kaylor, A. (1996). *The Wisconsin study of youth aging out of out-of-home care: A portrait of children about to leave care* [on-line]. Available: http://polyglot.lss.wisc.edu/socwork/foster/fcreport.

Courtney, M. E. (1993). Standardized evaluation of child welfare services out-of-home care: Problems and possibilities. *Children and Youth Services Review, 15,* 349–369.

Courtney, M. E., Barth, R, P., Berrick, J. D., Brooks, D., Needell, B., & Park, L. (1996). Race and child welfare services: Past research and future directions. *Child Welfare, 75,* 99–137.

Courtney, M. E., & Wong, Y. L. I. (1996). Comparing the timing of exits from substitute care. *Children and Youth Services Review, 18*(4–5), 307–334.

Cox, D. R. (1972). Regression models and life tables. *Journal of the Royal Statistical Society* (Series B 34), 187–202.

Curtis, P. A., Boyd, J. D., Liepold, M., & Petit, M. (1995). *Child abuse and neglect: A look at the states: The CWLA Stat book.* Washington, DC: Child Welfare League of America.

Department of Children and Family Services, Illinois. (1995). Child fatality study: Fiscal years 1866–1993. Springfield, IL: Author.

DePanfilis, D. (1995). *The epidemiology of child maltreatment recurrences.* Unpublished doctoral dissertation, University of Maryland School of Social Work.

Drake, B., & Pandey, S. (1996). Understanding the relationship between neighborhood poverty and specific types of child maltreatment. *Child Abuse and Neglect, 20,* 1003–1018.

Dumaret, A. (1985). IQ, scholastic performance, and behavior of siblings raised in contrasting environments. *Child Psychology, 26,* 553–580.

Duncan, G. J., Brooks-Gunn, J., & Klebanov, P. K. (1994). Economic deprivation and early childhood development. *Child Development, 65,* 296–318.

Eagle, R. (1993). "Airplanes crash, spaceships stay in orbit": The separation experience of a child "in care." *Journal of Psychotherapy Practice and Research*, 2, 318–334.

Eamon, M. (1994). Poverty and placement outcomes of intensive family preservation services. *Child and Adolescent Social Work Journal*, 11, 349–361.

Eckenrode, J., Laird, M., & Doris, J. (1993). School performance and disciplinary problems among abused and neglected children. *Developmental Psychology*, 29(1), 53–62.

Edlin, B., Irwin, K., Faruque, S., McCoy, C., Word, C., Serrano, Y., Inciardi, J., Bowser, B., Schilling, R., & Holmberg, S. (1994). Intersecting epidemics: Crack cocaine use and HIV infection among inner-city young adults. *New England Journal of Medicine*, 331(21), 1422–1427.

Egeland, B., & Sroufe, L. A. (1981). Attachment and early maltreatment. *Child Development*, 52, 44–52.

Egeland, B., Sroufe, A., & Erickson, M. (1983). The developmental consequences of different patterns of maltreatment. *Child Abuse and Neglect*, 7, 459–469.

Ekstein, R. (Ed.). (1983). *Children of time and space, of action and impulse*. New York: Appleton-Century-Crofts.

Emlen, A., Lahti, J., Downs, G., McKay, A., & Downs, S. (1978). *Overcoming barriers to planning for children in foster care*. Portland, OR: Regional Research Institute for Human Services, Portland State University.

Erickson, M. F., & Egeland, B. (1987). Psychologically unavailable care giving. In M. Brassard, B. Germain, & S. Hart (Eds.), *Psychological maltreatment of children and youth* (pp. 156–168). New York: Pergamon Press.

Erickson, M. F., Egeland, B., & Pianta, R. (1989). The effects of maltreatment on the development of young children. In D. Cicchetti & V. Carlson (Eds.), *Child maltreatment: Theory and research on the causes and consequences of child abuse and neglect* (pp. 647–684). New York: Cambridge University Press.

Eyer, D. E. (1992). *Mother-infant bonding: A scientific fiction*. New Haven, CT: Yale University Press.

Famularo, R., Kinscherff, R., & Fenton, T. (1992). Parental substance abuse and the nature of child maltreatment. *Child Abuse and Neglect*, 16, 475–483.

Fanshel, D., Finch, S. J., & Grundy, J. F. (1990). *Foster children in a life course perspective*. New York: Columbia University Press.

Fanshel, D., & Shinn, E. (1978). *Children in foster care: A longitudinal investigation*. New York: Columbia University Press.

Farber, E. A., & Egeland, B. (1987). Invulnerability among abused and neglected children. In E. J. Anthony & B. Cohler (Eds.), *The invulnerable child* (pp. 253–288). New York: Guilford Press.

Ferguson, T. (1966). *Children in care—and after*. London: Oxford University Press.

Festinger, T. (1983). *No one ever asked us: A postscript to foster care*. New York: Columbia University Press.

Festinger, T. (1994). *Returning to care: Discharge and re-entry in foster care*. Washington, DC: Child Welfare League of America.

Finkelhor, D. (1995). The victimization of children: A developmental perspective. *American Journal of Orthopsychiatry*, 65, 177–193.

Folks, H. (1902). *The care of destitute, neglected, and delinquent children*. New York: Macmillan.

Freeman, J., Levine, M., & Doueck, H. (1996). Child age and caseworker attention in child protective services investigations. *Child Abuse and Neglect, 20,* 907–920.

Frost, S., & Zurich, A. P. (1983). *Follow-up study of children residing in The Villages.* Topeka, KS: The Villages.

Fryer, G., & Miyoshi, T. (1994). A survival analysis of the revictimization of children: The case of Colorado. *Child Abuse and Neglect, 18,* 1063–1072.

Gaensbauer, T. J. (1982). Regulation of emotional expression in infants from two contrasting caretaking environments. *Journal of the American Academy of Child Psychiatry, 21,* 163–171.

Gallagher, S., Finison, K., Guyer, B., & Goodenough, S. (1984). The incidence of injuries among 87,000 Massachusetts children and adolescents: Results of the 1980–1981 Statewide Childhood Injury Prevention Program Surveillance System. *American Journal of Public Health, 74,* 1340–1347.

Garbarino, J. (1982). *Children and families in the social environment.* Hawthorne, NY: Aldine.

Garbarino, J. (1990). The human ecology of early risk. In S. J. Meisels, & J. P. Shonkoff (Eds.), *Handbook of early childhood intervention* (pp. 78–96). New York: Cambridge University Press.

Garbarino, J. (1995). *Raising children in a socially toxic environment.* San Francisco: Jossey-Bass.

Garbarino, J., & Ebata, A. (1983, November). The significance of ethnic and cultural differences in child maltreatment. *Journal of Marriage and the Family,* pp. 773–783.

Garrett, P., Ng'andu, N., & Ferron, J. (1994). Poverty experiences of young children and the quality of their home environments. *Child Development, 65,* 331–345.

Gaudin, J. M., & Dubowitz, H. (1997). Family functioning in neglectful families: Recent research. In J. D. Berrick, R. P. Barth, & N. Gilbert (Eds.), *Child Welfare Research Review, Vol. II* (pp. 28–62). New York: Columbia University Press.

Gaudin, J. M., & Sutphen, R. (1993). Foster care vs. extended family care for children of incarcerated mothers. *Journal of Offender Rehabilitation, 19*(3–4), 129–147.

Gelles, R. J. (1992). Poverty and violence toward children. *American Behavioral Scientist, 35,* 258–274.

General Accounting Office. (1994). *Foster care: Parental drug abuse has alarming impact on young children.* Washington, DC: Author.

George, C., & Main, M. (1979). Social interactions of young abused children: Approach, avoidance, and aggression. *Child Development, 50,* 306–318.

George, E. (1993). *Needling the system: Welfare agency approaches to preschool immunization.* Washington, DC: Center for Law and Social Policy.

Gilbert, N., Karski, R., & Frame, L. (1996). *The emergency response system: Screening and assessment of child abuse reports.* Unpublished report. Center for Social Services Research, School of Social Welfare, University of California at Berkeley.

Giovannoni, J. (1995). Reports of child maltreatment from mandated and non-mandated reporters. *Children and Youth Services Review, 17,* 487–501.

Goerge, R. M. (1990). The reunification process in substitute care. *Social Service Review, 64*(3), 422–457.

Goerge, R. M., & Harden, A. (1993). *The impact of substance affected infants on child protection services and substitute care caseloads (1985–1992): A report to the Illinois Department of Children and Family Services.* Chicago: Chapin Hall Center for Children, University of Chicago.

Goerge, R., VanVoorhis, J., Sanfilippo, L., & Harden, A. (1996). *Core data set project: Child Welfare Services Histories. Final report to the Office of the Assistant Secretary for Planning and Evaluation* (Report No. HHS 100-93-0024). Chicago: Chapin Hall Center for Children.

Goerge, R. M., Wulczyn, F. H., & Harden, A. W. (1994). *A report from the multistate data archive: Foster care dynamics 1983–1992.* Chicago: Chapin Hall Center for Children, University of Chicago.

Goerge, R. M., Wulczyn, F. H., & Harden, A. W. (1995). *An update from the multistate foster care data archive.* Chicago: Chapin Hall Center for Children, University of Chicago.

Goldson, E. (1987). Child development and the response to maltreatment. In D. C. Bross & L. F. Michaels (Eds.), *Foundations of child advocacy.* Longmont, CO: Bookmakers Guild.

Goldstein, J., Freud, A., & Solnit, A. J. (1973). *Beyond the best interests of the child.* New York: Free Press.

Goldstein, J., Freud, A., & Solnit, A. J. (1979). *Beyond the best interests of the child: New edition with epilogue.* New York: Free Press.

Gomby, D., & Shiono, P. (1991). Estimating the number of substance-exposed infants. *Future of Children, 1*(1), 17–25.

Greenberg, M. T., Speltz, M. L., & DeKlyen, M. (1993). The role of attachment in the early development of disruptive behavior problems. *Development and Psychopathology, 5,* 191–213.

Groze, V., Haines-Simeon, M., and Barth, R. (Feb. 1994). Barriers in permanency planning for medically fragile children: Drug affected children and HIV infected children. *Child and Adolescent Social Work Journal, 11*(1), 63–85.

Hampton, R. L., & Newberger, E. H. (1985). Child abuse incidence and reporting by hospitals: Significance of severity, class and race. *American Journal of Public Health, 75*(1), 56–60.

Harris, T., Brown, G. W., & Bifulco, A. T. (1986). Loss of a parent in childhood and adult psychiatric disorder: The role of adequate parental care. *Psychological Medicine, 16*(3), 641–659.

Hartley, R. (Fall, 1989). A program blueprint for neglectful families. *Protecting Children, 6*(3), 3–7.

Haveman, R., & Wolfe, B. (1993). *Children's prospects and children's policy* (Discussion paper 1010-93). Madison, WI: Institute for Research on Poverty.

Haveman, R., & Wolfe, B. (1995). *Succeeding generations.* New York: Russell Sage Foundation.

Hegar, R. L., & Yungman, J. J. (1989). Toward a causal typology of child neglect. *Children and Youth Services Review, 11,* 203–220.

Herrenkohl, R. C., & Herrenkohl, E. C. (1981). Some antecedents and developmental consequences of child maltreatment. In R. Rizley & D. Cicchetti (Eds.), *Developmental perspectives on child maltreatment.* San Francisco: Jossey-Bass.

Hochstadt, N. J. Jaudes, P. K., Zimo, D. A. & Schacter, J. (1987). The medical and psychosocial needs of children entering foster care. *Child Abuse and Neglect, 11,* 53–62.

Hodges, J., & Tizard, B. (1989). IQ and behavioral adjustment of ex-institutional adolescents, Social and family relationships of ex-institutional adolescents. *Journal of Child Psychology & Psychiatry & Allied Disciplines, 30,* 53–75, 77–97.

Hoffman-Plotkin, D., & Twentyman, C. T. (1984). A multimodal assessment of behavioral and cognitive deficits in abused and neglected preschoolers. *Child Development, 55,* 794–802.

Howard, B. (1994, November–December). Can "broken" child protection system be fixed? *Youth Today,* pp. 20–21, 24.

Howes, C. (1988). Relations between child care and schooling. *Developmental Psychology, 24,* 53–57.

Howes, C. (1989). Infant child care. *Young Children, 44*(6), 24–28.

Howes, C., Rodning, C., Galluzzo, D. C., & Myers, L. (1988). Attachment and child care: Relationships with mother and caregiver. *Early Childhood Research Quarterly, 3,* 403–416.

Howes, C., & Stewart, P. (1987). Child's play with adults, toys, and peers: An examination of family and child care influences. *Developmental Psychology, 23,* 423–430.

Howing, P. T., Wodarski, J. S., Kurtz, P. D., & Gaudin, J. M. (1993). *Maltreatment and the school-age child: Developmental outcomes and system issues.* Binghamton, NY: The Haworth Press.

Hubbell, R. (1981). *Foster care and families: Conflicting values and policies.* Philadelphia: Temple University Press.

Huston, A. C. (Ed.). (1991). *Children in poverty: Child development and public policy.* New York: Cambridge University Press.

Iowa, Juvenile Justice (1992), §232.116.

James Bell & Associates. (1993). *Report to Congress: National estimates on the number of boarder babies, the cost of their care, and the number of abandoned infants.* Washington, D.C.: U.S. Department of Health and Human Services, Children's Bureau.

Jaudes, P. K., Ekwo, E., & VanVoorhis, J. (1995). Association of drug abuse and child abuse. *Child Abuse and Neglect, 19,* 1065–1075.

Jenkins, S. (1967). Duration of foster care: Some relevant antecedent variables. *Child Welfare, 46,* 450–455.

Johnson, D., & Fein, E. (1991). The concept of attachment: Applications to adoption. *Children and Youth Services Review, 13,* (5–6), 397–412.

Johnson, P. R., Yoken, C., & Voss, R. (1995). Family foster care placement: The child's perspective. *Child Welfare, 74,* 959–974.

Johnson, W., & L'Esperance, J. (1984). Predicting the recurrence of child abuse. *Social Work Research & Abstracts, 20*(2), 21–26.

Jones, E., & McCurdy, K. (1992). The links between types of maltreatment and demographic characteristics of children. *Child Abuse and Neglect, 16,* 201–215.

Jones, M. A., & Moses, B. (1984). *West Virginia's former foster children: Their experiences in care and their lives as young adults.* New York: Child Welfare League of America.

Kadushin, A., & Martin, J. A. (1988). *Child welfare services* (4th ed.). New York: Macmillan.

Kaiser Commission on the Future of Medicaid (1995, May). *Medicaid facts.* Unpublished report, author, Washington, DC.

Kamerman, S. B., & Kahn, A. J. (1995). *Starting right: How America neglects its youngest children and what we can do about it.* New York: Oxford University Press.

Kates, W. G., Johnson, R. C., Rader, M. N., & Strieder, F. H. (1991). Whose child is this? Assessment and treatment of children in foster care. *American Journal of Orthopsychiatry, 61,* 584–591.

Kempe, C. H., Silverman, F. N., Steele, B. F., Droegemeuller, W., & Silver, H. K. (1962). The battered child syndrome. *Journal of the American Medical Association, 181,* 17–24.

Klerman, L. V., & Parker, M. (1990). *Alive and well? A review of health policies and programs for young children.* New York: National Center for Children in Poverty.

Knitzer, J., & Allen, M. J. (1978). *Children without homes.* Washington, DC: Children's Defense Fund.

Korenman, S., Miller, J. E., & Sjaastad, J. D. (1995). Long-term poverty and child development in the United States: Results from the NLSY. *Children and Youth Services Review, 17*(1–2), 127–155.

Korner, A. F., Zlanak, C. H., Linden, J., Berkowitz, R. I., Kraemer, H. C., & Agras, W. S. (1985). The relation between neonatal and later activity and temperament. *Child Development, 56,* 38–42.

Kotch, J., Browne, D., Ringwalt, C., Stewart, P., Ruina, E., Holt, K., Lowman, B., & Jung, J. (1995). Risk of child abuse or neglect in a cohort of low-income children. *Child Abuse and Neglect, 19,* 1115–1130.

Kramer, R. A., Allen, L., & Gergen, P. J. (1995). Health and social characteristics and children's cognitive functioning: Results from a national cohort. *American Journal of Public Health, 85,* 312–318.

Kruttschnitt, C., McLeod, J., & Dornfield, M. (1994). The economic environment of child abuse. *Social Problems, 41,* 299–315.

Kusserow, R. (1992). *Using relatives for foster care.* Washington, DC: U.S. Department of Health and Human Services, Office of the Inspector General.

Lahti, J., Green, K., Emlen, A., Zadny, J., Clarkson, Q. D., Kuehnel, M., & Casciato, J. (1978). *A follow-up study of the Oregon Project.* Portland, OR: Portland State University, Regional Institute for Human Services.

Lamb, M. E., Gaensbauer, T. J., Malkin, C. M., & Schultz, L. A. (1985). The effects of child maltreatment on security of infant-adult attachment. *Infant Behavior and Development, 8,* 35–45.

Lamb, M. E., & Hwang, C. (1982). Maternal attachment and mother-neonate bonding: A critical review. In M. E. Lamb & A. L. Brown (Eds.), *Advances in developmental psychology, Vol 2,* (pp. 1–39), Hillsdale, NJ: Lawrence Erlbaum.

Lawder, E. A., Poulin, J. E., & Andrews, R. G. (1986). A study of 185 foster children five years after placement. *Child Welfare, 65,* 241–251.

Leitenberg, H., Burchard, J. D., Healy, D., & Fuller, E. J. (1981). Nondelinquent children in state custody: Does type of placement matter? *American Journal of Community Psychology, 9,* 347–360.

Lerman, P. (1982). *Deinstitutionalization and the welfare state.* New Brunswick, NJ: Rutgers University Press.

Levy, H., Markovic, J., Chaudhry, U., Ahart, S., & Torres, H. (1995). Reabuse rates in a sample of children followed for 5 years after discharge from a child abuse inpatient assessment program. *Child Abuse and Neglect, 19,* 1363–1377.

Liaw, F., & Brooks-Gunn, J. (1994). Cumulative family development and low-birthweight children's cognitive and behavioral development. *Journal of Clinical Child Psychology, 23*, 360–372.

Lindsey, D. (1994). *The welfare of children*. Oxford, England: Oxford University Press.

Maas, H. S., & Engler, R. E. (1959). *Children in need of parents*. (New York: Columbia University Press.

Main, M., & Hesse, P. (1990). Parents' unresolved traumatic experiences are related to infant disorganized attachment status—Is frightened and/or frightening parental behavior the linking mechanism? In M. Greenberg, D. Cicchetti, & M. Cummings, (Eds.), *Attachment in the preschool years* (pp. 161–182). Chicago: University of Chicago Press.

Maluccio, A. N., Fein, E., & Olmstead, K. A. (1986). *Permanency planning for children: Concepts and methods*. London: Routledge, Chapman, & Hall.

Maluccio, A. N., & Marlow, W. (1972). Residential treatment of emotionally disturbed children: A review of the literature. *Social Service Review, 46*, 230–250.

Marcus, R. F. (1991). The attachments of children in foster care. *Genetic, Social, and General Psychology Monographs, 117*, 365–394.

Mare, R. D. (1982). Socioeconomic effects on child mortality in the United States. *American Journal of Public Health, 72*, 539–547.

Marsden, G., McDermott, J. F., & Minor, D. (1977). Selection of children for residential treatment. *Journal of the American Academy of Child Psychiatry, 16*, 427–438.

Mason, M. A. (1994). *From father's property to children's rights*. New York: Columbia University Press.

Massey, D., & Denton, N. (1993). *American apartheid: Segregation and the making of the underclass*. Cambridge, MA: Harvard University Press.

Masten, A. S., & Garmezy, N. (1985). Risk, vulnerability, and protective factors in developmental psychology. In B. B. Lahey & A. E. Kazdin (Eds.), *Advances in clinical child psychology, Vol. 8* (pp. 1–52). New York: Plenum Press.

Matas, L., Arend, R. A., & Sroufe, L. A. (1978). Continuity of adaptation in the second year: The relationship between quality of attachment and later competence. *Child Development, 49*, 547–556.

Maza, P. L. (1996). *Children in care: 1977 vs. 1994*. Unpublished report, U.S. Children's Bureau, Washington, DC.

McCall, R. B., & Carriger, M. S. (1993). A meta-analysis of infant habituation and recognition memory performance as predictors of later IQ. *Child Development, 64*, 57–79.

McDonald, T., Allen, R., Westerfelt, A., & Piliavin, I. (1993, February). *Assessing the long-term effects of foster care: A research synthesis* (Report No. 57-93). Madison, WI: Institute for Research on Poverty.

McIntyre, A., & Keesler, T. Y. (1986). Psychological disorders among foster children. *Journal of Clinical Child Psychiatry, 15*, 297–303.

McLoyd, V. C., & Wilson, L. (1991). The strain of living poor: Parenting, social support, and child mental health. In A. C. Huston (Ed.), *Children in poverty* (pp. 105–135). New York: Cambridge University Press.

McMillen, J. (1992). Attachment theory and clinical social work. *Clinical Social Work Journal, 20*, 205–218.

McMurty, S. L., & Lie, G. (1992). Differential exit rates of minority children in foster care. *Social Work Research & Abstracts, 28*, 42–48.

McRoy, R. G., Zurcher, L. A., Lauderdale, M. L., & Anderson, R. N. (1982). Self-esteem and racial identity in transracial and inracial adoptees. *Social Work, 27*, 522–526.

Meier, E. G. (1965). Current circumstances of former foster children. *Child Welfare, 44*, 196–206.

Melton, G., & Barry, F. (Eds.). (1994). *Protecting children from abuse and neglect: Foundations for a new national strategy.* New York: Guilford Press.

Miller v Youakim (1979). 440 U.S. 125.

Milton, J. (1996). Suffer the little children? The death of a child opens a window on a fatally confused bureaucratic system. *National Review, 48*(3), 50–54.

Minty, B., & Patterson, G. (1994). The nature of child neglect. *British Journal of Social Work, 24*, 733–747.

Molin, R. (1988). Treatment of children in foster care: Issues of collaboration. *Child Abuse and Neglect, 12*, 241–250.

Moore, T. (1996, December 5). New group home standards. *San Francisco Chronicle*, pp. A1, A24.

Murphy, J., Jellinek, M., Quinn, D., Smith, G., Poitrast, F., & Goshkorn, M. (1992). Substance abuse and serious child mistreatment: Prevalence, risk and outcome in a court sample. *Child Abuse and Neglect, 15*, 197–211.

National Association of Psychiatric Treatment Centers for Children. (1990). *The emerging role of psychiatric treatment centers for children.* Unpublished manuscript, author.

National Center for Children in Poverty. (1990). *Five million children: A statistical profile of our poorest young children.* New York: Author.

National Center for Children in Poverty (1995). *News and issues, 5*(3), 1.

National Center for Health Statistics. (1994). *Monthly vital statistics report,* 42(13).

National Center on Child Abuse and Neglect. (1996). *Child maltreatment 1994: Reports from the states to the National Center on Child Abuse and Neglect.* Washington, D.C.: Author.

National Committee to Prevent Child Abuse. (1995). *Current trends in child abuse reporting and fatalities: The results of the 1994 annual fifty state survey.* Unpublished report, author, Chicago.

National Institute on Drug Abuse. (1994). Women and drug abuse. *NIDA Capsules.* Rockville, MD: Author.

National Research Council (1993). *Understanding child abuse and neglect.* Washington, D.C.: National Academy press.

Nazario, T. A. (1988). *In defense of children.* New York: Charles Scribner's Sons.

Needell, B., Webster, D., Barth, R. P., & Armijo, M. (1996). *Performance indicators for child welfare services in California: 1995.* Unpublished report, Child Welfare Research Center, University of California at Berkeley.

Needleman, H. L., Schell, A., Bellinger, D., Leviton, A., & Allred, E. N. (1990). The long-term effects of exposure to low doses of lead in childhood. *New England Journal of Medicine, 322*, 83–88.

Nelson, K., Saunders, E., & Landsman, M. (1993). Chronic child neglect in perspective. *Social Work, 38*, 661–671.

Ney, P., Fung, T., & Wickett, A. (1994). The worst combinations of child abuse and neglect. *Child Abuse and Neglect, 18*, 705–714.

Neuspiel, D. R., Zingman, T. M., Templeton, V. H., DiStable, P., & Drucker, E. (1993). Custody of cocaine-exposed newborns: Determinants of discharge decisions. *American Journal of Public Health, 83*, 1726–1729.

Nunes-Dinis, M. (1993). Drug and alcohol misuse: Treatment outcomes and services for women. In R. P. Barth, J. Pietrzak, & M. Ramler (Eds.), *Families living with drugs and HIV: Intervention and treatment strategies* (pp. 144–176). New York: Guilford Press.

Osborne, Y., Hinz, L., Rappaport, N., Williams, H., & Tuma, J. (1988). Parent social attractiveness, parent sex, child temperament, and socioeconomic status as predictors of tendency to report child abuse. *Journal of Social and Clinical Psychology, 6*(1), 69–76.

O'Toole, A., O'Toole, R., Webster, S., & Lucal, B. (1993). Nurses' recognition and reporting of child abuse: A factorial survey. *Deviant Behavior: An Interdisciplinary Journal, 14*, 341–363.

Otto, R. K., & Melton, G. B. (1990). Trends in legislation and case law on child abuse and neglect. In R. T. Ammerman & M. Hersen (Eds.), *An evaluation of factors contributing to child abuse and neglect* (pp. 55–83). New York: Plenum.

Palmer, S. E. (1976). *Children in long term care: Their experience and progress.* London, Ontario: Family and Children's Services of London and Middlesex.

Pelton, L. H. (1978). Child abuse and neglect: The myth of classlessness. *American Journal of Orthopsychiatry, 48*, 608–617.

Pelton, L. H. (1989). *For reasons of poverty.* New York: Praeger.

Perry, B. D., Pollard, R. A., Blakley, T. L., Baker, W. L., & Vigilante, D. (1995). Childhood trauma, the neurobiology of adaptation, and "use-dependent" development of the brain: How "states" become "traits." *Infant Mental Health Journal, 16*(4), 271–291.

Phinney, J. S., Lochner, B., & Murphy, R. (1990). Ethnic identity development and psychological adjustment in adolescence. In A. Stiffman & L. Davis (Eds.), *Ethnic issues in adolescent mental health* (pp. 53–72). Newbury Park, CA: Sage.

Polansky, N., Gaudin J., Jr., & Kilpatrick, A. (1992). The Maternal Characteristics Scale: A cross validation. *Child Welfare, 71*, 271–280.

Pollitt, K. (1996). The violence of ordinary life. *The Nation, 262*(1), 1.

Pringle, M. L., & Bossio, V. (1960). Early prolonged separation and emotional adjustment. *Journal of Child Psychology and Psychiatry, 1*, 37–48.

Proch, K., & Taber, M. A. (1985). Placement disruption: A review of research. *Children and Youth Services Review, 7*, 309–320.

Richters, J. E., & Martinez, P. E. (1993). Violent communities, family choices, and children's chances: An algorithm for improving the odds. *Development and Psychopathology, 5*, 609–627.

Riese, M. L. (1987). Longitudinal assessment of temperament from birth to 2 years: A comparison of full-term and pre-term infants. *Infant Behavior and Development, 10*(3), 347–363.

Ringwalt, C., & Caye, J. (1989). The effect of demographic factors on perceptions of child neglect. *Children and Youth Services Review, 11*, 133–144.

Rivera, B., & Widom, C. S. (1990). Childhood victimization and violent offending. *Violence and Victims, 5*(1), 19–34.

Robins, L. N., & Mills, J. L. (1993). Effects of exposure to street drugs. *American Journal of Public Health, 83*(suppl.).

Roy, P. (1983). *Is continuity enough? Substitute care and socialization.* Paper presented at the Spring Scientific Meeting, Child and Adolescent Psychiatry Specialist Section, Royal College of Psychiatrists, London.

Ruff, H. A., Blank, S., & Barnett, H. L. (1990). Early intervention in the context of foster care. *Developmental and Behavioral Pediatrics, 11,* 265–268.

Rutter, M. (1989). Intergenerational continuities and discontinuities in serious parenting difficulties. In D. Cicchetti & V. Carlson (Eds.), *Child maltreatment: Theory and research on the causes and consequences of child abuse and neglect* (pp. 317–348). New York: Cambridge University Press.

Rutter, M. (1990). Psychosocial resilience and protective mechanisms. In J. Rolf, A. S. Masten, D. Cicchetti, K. H. Nuechterlein, & S. Weintraub (Eds.), *Risk and protective factors in the development of psychopathology,* (pp. 181–214). New York: Cambridge University Press.

Rutter, M., & Rutter, M. (1993). *Developing minds: Challenge and continuity across the life span.* New York: Basic Books.

Rzepnicki, T. L. (1987). Recidivism of foster children returned to their own homes: A review and new directions for research. *Social Service Review, 61*(1), 56–70.

Sabotta, E. E., & Davis, R. L. (1992). Fatality after report to a child abuse registry in Washington State, 1973–1986. *Child Abuse and Neglect, 16,* 627–635.

Sagatun-Edwards, I., Saylor, C., & Shifflett, B. (1994). Drug exposed infants in the social welfare system and juvenile courts. *Child Abuse and Neglect, 19*(1), pp. 83–92.

Sameroff, A. J., & Chandler, M. J. (1975). Reproductive risk and the continuum of caretaking casualty. In F. D. Horowitz (Ed.), *Review of child development research* (Vol. 4, pp. 187–244). Chicago: University of Chicago Press.

Sameroff, A. J., Seifer, R., Baldwin, A., & Baldwin, C. (1993). Stability of intelligence from preschool to adolescence: The influence of social and family risk factors. *Child Development, 64,* 80–97.

Scarr, S., & Ricciuti, A. (1991). What effects do parents have on their children? In L. Okagaki & R. J. Sternberg (Eds.), *Directors of development: Influences on the development of children's thinking* (pp. 3–23). Hillsdale, NJ: Lawrence Erlbaum.

Schor, E. L., Chang, A. E., Erickson, C. G., Evans, B. J. M., Hammar, S. L., Keathley, S. A., & Simms, M. D. (1993). Developmental issues in foster care for children. *Pediatrics, 91,* 1007–1009.

Schwartz, I., Ortega, R., Guo, S., & Fishman, G. (1994). Infants in nonpermanent placement. *Social Service Review, 68*(3), 405–416.

Sedlak, A. J., & Broadhurst, D. D. (1996). *Third National Incidence Study of Child Abuse and Neglect.* Washington, DC: U.S. Department of Health and Human Services, National Center on Child Abuse and Neglect.

Sheehy, G. (1987). *Spirit of survival.* New York: Bantam Books.

Shiono, P. H. (1996). Prevalence of drug-exposed infants. *The Future of Children, 6,* 159–163.

Shyne, A. W., & Schroeder, A. G. (1978). *National Study of Social Services to Children and Their Families.* Washington, DC: U.S. Department of Health and Human Services.

Skolnick, A. (in press). Solomon's children: The new biologism, psychological parenthood, attachment theory, and the best interests standard. In M. A. Mason, A. Skolnick, & S. Sugarman (Eds.), *The evolving American family*. New York: Oxford University Press.

Skolnick, A. S. (1986). *The psychology of human development*. San Diego, CA: Harcourt, Brace, Jovanovich.

Small, R., Kennedy, K., & Bender, B. (1991). Critical issues for practice in residential treatment: The view from within. *American Journal of Orthopsychiatry, 61*, 327–335.

Smetana, J. G., Kelly, M., & Twentyman, C. T. (1984). Abused, neglected, and nonmaltreated children's conceptions of moral and conventional transgressions. *Child Development, 55*, 277–287.

Sorenson, S., & Peterson, J. (1994). Traumatic child death and documented maltreatment history, Los Angeles. *American Journal of Public Health, 84*, 623–627.

Spaulding for Children. (1995). *Cultural competence in child welfare*. Southfield, MI: Author.

Spearly, J., & Lauderdale, M. (1983). Community characteristics and ethnicity in the prediction of child maltreatment rates. *Child Abuse and Neglect, 7*, 91–105.

Starr, R. H., MacLean, D. J., & Keating, D. P. (1991). Life-span developmental outcomes of child maltreatment. In R. H. Starr, Jr., & D. A. Wolfe (Eds.), *The effects of child abuse and neglect* (pp. 1–32). London: Guilford.

Steinberg, L. D., Catalano, R., & Dooley, D. (1981). Economic antecedents of child abuse and neglect. *Child Development, 52*, 975–985.

Straus, M., & Gelles, R. (1992). *Physical violence in American families*. New Brunswick, NJ: Transaction Publishers.

Sullivan v. Zebley, et al. 493 U.S. 521, 110 S.Ct. 885 (1990).

Swire, M. R., & Kavaler, F. (1978). The health status of foster children. In S. Chess & A. Thomas (Eds.), *Annual progress in child psychiatry and child development* (pp. 626–642). New York: Brunner/Mazel.

Teichert, N. (1996). Drive to preserve families puts many kids at risk, experts say. *Sacramento Bee*, pp. A1, A20.

Thornton, J. L. (1991). Permanency planning for children in kinship foster homes. *Child Welfare, 70*, 593–601.

Tizard, B., & Hodges, J. (1978). The effect of early institutional rearing on the development of eight-year-old children. *Journal of Child Psychology and Psychiatry, 19*, 99–118.

Trasler, G. (1957). The effect of institutional care on emotional development. *Case Conference, 4*(2), 35–40.

Triseliotis, J., & Russell, J. (1984). *Hard to place: The outcome of adoption and residential care*. London: Heinemann.

Turner, R. J. (1991). Affirming consciousness: The Africentric perspective. In J. E. Everett, S. S. Chipungu, & B. R. Leashore (Eds.), *Child welfare: An Africentric perspective*, (pp. 36–57). New Brunswick, NJ: Rutgers University Press.

U.S. Department of Health and Human Services. (1991). *National household survey on drug abuse: Population estimates* (Publication No. ADM 92-1887). Washington DC: U.S. Government Printing Office.

U.S. Department of Health and Human Services. (1996). *Trends in the well-being of America's children and youth: 1996.* Washington, DC: Author.

U.S. House of Representatives, Committee on Ways and Means. (1994). *Overview of entitlement programs: 1994 green book.* Washington, DC: U.S. Government Printing Office.

Vega, W., Kolody, B., Hwang, J., & Noble, A. (1993). Prevalence and magnitude of perinatal substance exposures in California. *New England Journal of Medicine, 329,* 850–854.

Wald, M. (1975). *Child development and public policy: Juvenile justice.* Transcription of speech presented to the Society for Research in Child Development Panel Symposium: Denver, CO.

Wald, M. (1976). State intervention on behalf of "neglected" children: Standards for removal of children from their homes, monitoring the status of children in foster care, and termination of parental rights. *Stanford Law Review, 28,* 623–707.

Wald, M., Carlsmith, C. M., & Liederman, P. H. (1988). *Protecting abused and neglected children.* Palo Alto, CA: Stanford University Press.

Walker, C., Zangrillo, P., & Smith, J. (1991). *Parental drug abuse and African American children in foster care: Issues and study findings* (Publication No. SA-90-2233-1) Washington, DC: U.S. Department of Health and Human Services, Office of the Assistant Secretary for Planning and Evaluation, Division of Children and Youth Policy.

Wells, K. (1991). Placement of emotionally disturbed children in residential treatment: A review of placement criteria. *American Journal of Orthopsychiatry, 61,* 339–347.

Wells, K. (1993). Residential treatment as long-term treatment: An examination of some issues. *Children and Youth Services Review, 15,* 165–171.

Wells, S., Fluke, J., & Brown, C. (1995). The decision to investigate: Child protection practice and 12 local agencies. *Children and Youth Services Review, 17,* 523–546.

Werner, E. E. (1990). Protective factors and individual resilience. In S. J. Meisels, & J. P. Shonkoff (Eds.), *Handbook of early child intervention,* (pp. 97–116). New York: Cambridge University Press.

Werner, E. E., & Smith, R. S. (1982). *Vulnerable but invincible: A longitudinal study of resilient children and youth.* New York: McGraw-Hill.

Whitebook, M., Howes, C., & Phillips, D. (1989). *Who cares? Child care teachers and the quality of care in America. National Child Care Staffing Study.* Oakland, CA: Child Care Employee Project.

Whittaker, J. K., Overstreet, E. J., Grasso, A., Tripodi, T., & Boylan, F. (1988). Multiple indicators of success in residential youth care and treatment. *American Journal of Orthopsychiatry, 58,* 143–147.

Wiese, D., & Daro, D. (1995). Current trends in child abuse reporting and fatalities: The results of the 1994 Annual Fifty State Survey. Unpublished report, National Committee for the Prevention of Child Abuse, Chicago.

Wilson, D. B., & Chipungu, S. S. (1996). *Child Welfare, 75*(5) [Special issue: Kinship Care], 387–395.

Wojtkiewicz, R. A. (1993). Simplicity and complexity in the effects of parental structure on high school graduation. *Demography, 30,* 701–717.

Wolfe, D. A., Jaffe, P., Wilson, S. K., & Zak, L. (1985). Children of battered women: The relation of child behavior to family violence and maternal stress. *Journal of Consulting and Clinical Psychology, 53,* 657–665.

Wolfe, D., & McGee, R. (1994). Dimensions of child maltreatment and their relationship to adolescent adjustment. *Development and Psychopathology, 6,* 165–181.

Wolins, M., & Piliavin, I. (1969). Group care, friend or foe? *Social Work, 14,* 35–53.

Wolkind, S., & Rutter, M. (1985). Separation, loss and family relationships. In M. Rutter & L. Hersov (Eds.), *Child and adolescent psychiatry.* Cambridge, MA: Blackwell Scientific Publications.

Wolock, I., & Horowitz, B. (1979). Child maltreatment and material deprivation among AFDC-recipients families. *Social Service Review, 53,* 175–194.

Wolock, I., & Magura, S. (1996). Parental substance abuse as a predictor of child maltreatment re-reports. *Child Abuse and Neglect, 20,* 1183–1193.

Wulczyn, F. (1994). Status at birth and infant foster care placement in New York City. In R. Barth, J. D. Berrick, & N. Gilbert (Eds.), *Child Welfare Research Review, Vol. 1* (pp. 146–184). New York: Columbia University Press.

Wulczyn, F. H. (1991). Caseload dynamics and foster care reentry. *Social Service Review, 65,* 133–156.

Yarrow, L. J. (1979). Historical perspectives and future directions in infant development. In J. D. Osofsky (Ed.), *Handbook of infant development* (pp. 897–917). New York: John Wiley & Sons.

Zeitz, D. (1969). *Child welfare: Services and perspectives.* New York: John Wiley & Sons.

Zelizer, V. A. (1985). *Pricing the priceless child: The changing social value of children.* New York: Basic Books.

Zellman, G. (1992). The impact of case characteristics on child abuse reporting decisions. *Child Abuse and Neglect, 16,* 57–74.

Zigler, E., & Hall, N. W. (1989). Physical child abuse in America: Past, present, and future. In D. Cicchetti & V. Carlson (Eds.), *Child maltreatment: Theory and research on the causes and consequences of child abuse and neglect* (pp. 38–75). New York: Cambridge University Press.

Zimmerman, R. B. (1982). *Foster care in retrospect. Tulane Studies in Social Welfare* (Vol. 14). New Orleans: Tulane University Press.

Zingraff, M., Leiter, J., Myers, K., & Johnsen, M. (1993). Child maltreatment and youthful problem behavior. *Criminology, 31,* 173–202.

Zschoche, L., & Suprenand, M. (1996, September 20). *Expedited permanency planning.* Paper presented at the 11th National Conference on Child Abuse and Neglect, Washington, DC.

Zuravin, S. J. (1991). Unplanned childbearing and family size: Their relationship to child neglect and abuse. *Family Planning Perspectives, 23,* 155–161.

Zuravin, S., & DePanfilis, D. (1995). *Factors affecting foster care placement of children receiving child protective services: Literature review and presentation of data.* Paper presented at the Third National Colloquium of the American Professional Society on the Abuse of Children, Tucson, AZ.

Zuravin, S., & Greif, G. L. (1989). Normative and child-maltreating AFDC mothers. *Social Casework: The Journal of Contemporary Social Work, 70*(2), 76–84.

Author Index

Subject Index

Printed in the United States
48389LVS00004B/82-99